PRA...
SHE TOOK A TURN

"In the delicate dance of hope and fear, this book stands as a profound testament to the power of vulnerability. The narrative moves with the rhythm of a life lived in earnest search for truth, courage, and understanding. And this is not just a recount of personal evolution, but an invitation to all of us to ponder our place and our voice within the chorus of humanity. In a world that often pressures us to conform, Smith's generous, authentic, and heartfelt writing encourages and empowers us to cherish our accents—both literal and metaphorical—and to use them to sing our own unique songs of self, community, and change."

—**AMY ELIZA WONG**, author of the critically acclaimed *Living On Purpose: Five Deliberate Choices to Realize Fulfillment and Joy*

"*She Took a Turn* is a riveting memoir that fearlessly explores the journey of self-discovery and transformation. From challenging her conservative roots in Alabama to embracing life as a wife and mother, Kristi Smith's candid narrative resonates with raw honesty and unwavering determination. Reminiscent of Glennon Doyle and Elizabeth Gilbert, Kristi's writing inspires and empowers readers to embark on their own paths toward personal growth and societal change."

—**DR. JENNY MCGLONE**, cofounder and brand director, Mathkind

"On the increasingly crowded shelf of memoirs, Kristi's words constitute a tonic: bracing, honest, unflinching, and curative."

—**REVEREND MOLLY SHIVERS**, director, Conflict Transformation Ministries, North Carolina Conference of the United Methodist Church

A Memoir of Climbing
over Guardrails into Growth

SHE TOOK A
TURN

KRISTI J. SMITH

RIVER GROVE
BOOKS

This book is a memoir reflecting the author's present recollections of experiences over time. Its story and its words are the author's alone. Some names, details, and characteristics may be changed, some events may be compressed, and some dialogue may be recreated.

Published by River Grove Books
Austin, TX
www.rivergrovebooks.com

With gratitude, the following are used with permission from the copyright holders:

Excerpt from "Not Waving but Drowning" by Stevie Smith from *All the Poems* (New Directions) and *The Collected Poems and Drawings of Stevie Smith*, (Faber and Faber Ltd), copyright © 1937, 1938, 1942, 1950, 1957, 1962, 1966, 1971, 1972 by Stevie Smith. Copyright © 2016 by the Estate of James MacGibbon. Copyright © 2015 by Will May. Reprinted by permission of New Directions Publishing Corp. and Faber and Faber Ltd., respectively.

The text originally published by Molly Shivers in a 2014 UUMC Sunday School Parenting Class handout, © 2014 by Molly Shivers.

Distributed by River Grove Books

Design and composition by Greenleaf Book Group and Mimi Bark
Cover design by Greenleaf Book Group and Mimi Bark
Cover image used under license from ©Shutterstock.com/Jozef Micic

Publisher's Cataloging-in-Publication data is available.

Print ISBN: 978-1-63299-827-9

eBook ISBN: 978-1-63299-828-6

First Edition

This is for everyone who would like a turn:
Your story matters.
I hope you have the opportunity to
live it and tell it.

It is also for
my family,
the friends who have become family,
and everyone who has shared their stories with me.

Nobody heard him, the dead man,
But still he lay moaning:
I was much further out than you thought
And not waving but drowning.

—excerpt from "Not Waving but Drowning" by Stevie Smith

CONTENTS

PROLOGUE

I t is 1992. I am sitting cross-legged in a circle of people, meeting my college dormmates for the first time. We have been called here by our new Residential Advisor. Over the course of the next hour, she will introduce us to our new home, to each other, and to what she views as the basics of college life. The air is filled with music from an artist I have never encountered and voices from classmates I have yet to meet. It is also filled with a palpable sense of anticipation. Something is beginning, a new phase.

No one knows me here.

That means I can start over, which is both thrilling and a bit scary. I need something different. I'll take different—whatever it looks like—but it will be hard to see the view if I immediately fall flat on my face.

The group consists of freshmen and sophomores. The sophomores are chatty, eager to catch up with one another after a summer away. As a newbie, I content myself to listen and look around. I am in a diverse group: coed, a variety of skin tones, and a few different accents. None of the voices are exactly like mine, though. I know, in this northern setting, my deep Alabama twang will draw attention as soon as I speak.

Near me, on a window bench seat, is a classmate. We are still getting to know each other, so I am unsure how to comfort her when she makes a critical error during a round of "Introduction Alliteration." In this game, we must all reveal ourselves by selecting an adjective that both describes us and begins with the same sound as our first name. In this manner I meet Jaunty Jim, Powerful Priya, and at least a dozen others. The girl in the window seat panics when it is her turn and introduces herself as "Crusty Cora."

Let us pause to acknowledge the untimely social slump of a coed—and to punctuate that pause as my Southern teenage self would have, with an "amen."

Cora's adjective will be referenced by a dormmate later in the hour, when we are guided through a "How to Practice Safe Sex" activity that involves working in pairs to place a condom on a banana. The girls in our group will be asked to hold the bananas between their knees while the boys unroll the condoms. The stakes are high. Several of us—me included—will be proclaimed "pretend pregnant." Apparently, you're supposed to "pinch the tip" as you unroll the contraceptive, so you don't end up with a balloon of air that tears when ejaculation occurs. We have failed our first informal exam, and several of us are blushing. My own blush deepens when one of the boys whispers that there is more than one reason to wear a condom correctly; you never know when a partner might be *crusty*, he says.

I wince in camaraderie with Cora, who I am guessing would give anything for a do-over. She will not get one. Neither will I, but my problem has less immediate consequences. My issue is that I will not claim the name I wanted to own that evening: Creative Kristi. That piece of me will not find expression in that moment—or really at any point during the next four years of my college career.

I wish I could have been more like Addy, whom I met several years later at a women's shelter. I was a volunteer there—too young to do anything but help pass out papers at the beginning of each session—and I encountered Addy while handing out a page titled "How are you feeling?" The page was covered with cartoon faces bearing a variety of expressions, each labeled as an emotional option. In the shelter's circle, you were not limited by alliteration. Addy could have been feeling "tired," "angry," "relieved," or "shy"—all common answers. She surprised us all when she chose "lovestruck." When the counselor asked if she wanted to share her lovestruck story, she revealed there was no story there. "I didn't choose it because I *am* lovestruck. I chose it because that's what I *want* to be. I mean, are we here to start on a new path or what?"

So, with hopeful, lovestruck Addy–like intentions, I could have faced a new circle and given airtime to who I *wanted* to be—who I thought I *could* be: Creative Kristi. Instead, I said something forgettable that was quickly buried under an avalanche of attention to a more striking thing: my accent.

One of the sophomores whooped immediately upon hearing it.

"Yes!" he shouted. "*Yesssss.* Can we just listen to her talk for the rest of the hour? Where are you from? Alabama! Tell us anything about it . . . everything about it. Is it true there are dirt farms there—where people actually sell *dirt*?"

"Grade A topsoil can fetch top dollar," I tell him.

He whoops again.

"This year," he informs the group, "is off to a *fantastic* start."

I am not certain about that. Neither is Cora. But his grin seems good-natured, and I want to be optimistic. If nothing else, I know the year will be educational. Personally, I have already learned several things. I've learned what a condom looks like, and how to unroll it correctly. I've learned that claiming a new identity is only easy if it's a negative one. Finally, I have learned that I will not be starting over with a clean slate as much as expounding—and expanding—upon my roots.

Deeply
Rooted

ALABAMA, BEFORE

My grandmother's first day of college was a bit different from mine. I have heard the story enough times that I can actually picture her, seventeen-year-old Mary Sue, in a faded flower dress, standing at a train depot in rural Alabama. It was the late 1920s. It was dusty. It was hot. She stood because it was not proper to sit on her trunks while she waited, even though she wanted to.

Those trunks contained items collected over seventeen years of life: a Bible, a blanket, some clothes, a few photographs. And pencils. She would need pencils at "The University." For the uninitiated, I will clarify that this means the University of Alabama, but in my family only *other* institutions are required to produce identifiers. The University only refers to one place, and it is in Tuscaloosa. Amen.

Mary Sue's trunks had been polished to a sheen by her uncle, and her purse contained a sandwich wrapped in cloth by her aunt. This was the couple who raised her from infancy, after her biological parents died of tuberculosis when she was only six months old. Her childhood was spent on their farm, where she was both loved and leaned on. Children were expected to contribute, and her job was to feed the farmhands. She began this task at such an early age that her uncle had to build her a stool so she could reach the stovetop. She remembered her delight in ringing the dinner bell, merging her girlish desire to make it clang with her more adult appreciation for what it symbolized—the short break she received between fixing the meal and cleaning up after the men who ate it.

On the day of her matriculation to college, she was unaccompanied. This was because her family was on the farm. It was not Sunday, after all; work had to be done. And she was not a southern debutante who required an escort. No. She was a farmer's daughter, and she was alone.

But Mary Sue was not alone for long. The boy who loved her—the boy to whom she had already said a final geographic and relational farewell—unexpectedly approached, and he had a ring. On one knee, he asked her to reconsider college. To reconsider him. Wouldn't she stay—in the town, and in the relationship? She touched his wrist, avoiding the ring, told him goodbye again, and then boarded the train.

As the train rumbled, she watched her town—her life—shrink and disappear through the window. The enormity of what she was doing hit her. Women in her town did not go to college, and they certainly did not leave potential fiancés at the depot in order to do it, but on her train rolled.

Until it reached its next stop, and—to her shock—there was her suitor. In a truck borrowed for the day, he had raced the train to this station. He had sprinted to board the locomotive during its pause, and in the aisle, he made one last effort.

Panting with the exertion of his sprint, and aware that he had the attention of everyone on the train including the conductor, he beseeched, "Please get off the train, Mary Sue. Please come with me. Please just come *home*."

No, she thought.

"No," she said.

She was going to The University.

And that was that.

~

I have no idea what my grandmother's life was like once she got to college, and it's too late to ask her. I don't know where she lived, how she paid for it, or what subject she liked best. I have vague memories of hearing about how she met my grandfather, Lloyd, there—perhaps in the movie theater where he worked? Apparently, he was a good-looking guy, athletic, and popular. She liked wearing his varsity letterman sweater—earned on The University's basketball court—while she walked with him around campus. Eventually, she accented his sweater with his engagement ring.

Their engagement was long. My grandfather—the oldest of nine children and the man of the house once his father died—refused to set a wedding date until he had helped put all of his siblings through college. In that era, it was striking that this included all of the girls. My grandmother mentioned often, and with a tone of great contempt, that his youngest sister, Adine, switched her major *seven times* before landing on home economics and earning the diploma that would green-light my grandparents' wedding. Adine and my grandmother were never close after that, and years later my own mother would hurl what was considered to be the greatest family insult in my direction, threatening that if I remained on my rudderless path of isolated exploration I would become "as lonely and selfish as my great-aunt Adine."

I could debate that characterization—of Adine and other unaccompanied explorers—but I want to stay focused on my grandfather, who valued education enough to make sure everyone under his care earned a diploma. He was actually somewhat famous in my hometown of Florence for this insistence. Decades after Adine's degree drama, once I was a teenager and my grandfather was long gone, I had been presented with an athletic achievement certificate by my county's superintendent of education. After the presentation, the official had pulled me aside.

"Your grandfather," he told me, "was quite a man."

Then this gentleman—the superintendent of education—told me the story of a time he had tried to quit school. He had been a student at The University, and it had proven to be too much. He was struggling with academics and loneliness, so one day he called his family, packed his things, and went back to his hometown.

My grandfather, who lived in the same town and knew the boy's parents, was surprised to encounter him walking out of a local eatery mid-semester. Was he home because his family was unwell?

"No," was the answer. He had just come to realize that higher education was not for him.

"Let me give you a ride home," my grandfather told him. The boy accepted, grateful to avoid even a short walk in the Alabama heat. But once he climbed into the car, he realized he would be traveling much farther than anticipated. My grandfather did not stop the car until he had driven his passenger 127 miles back to The University. "Get out," he told him. "Get your education. I'll let your family know."

"Quite a man!" the superintendent told me. "He changed my life for the better, your grandfather." And quite a story, I now realize. Did my grandfather really leave him there with nothing? Did his family drive down with his clothing later?

I have no idea. When you are young, celebrating a victory in the all-county basketball tournament, you don't take the time to ask follow-up questions. In fairness to my teenage self, it was not an unusual exchange for the setting. When you live in the same southern state as your ancestors, it is fairly common to encounter the ghost of your grandfather, so you don't really think to seize moments and note them precisely in your journal. Instead, the stories are constantly poured upon you like layers of glaze on a bun. Any event can be saturated with the sugar or salt of your predecessors. Their presence adds flavor and—usually welcome, but sometimes suffocating—weight.

~

Mary Sue and Lloyd gave birth to my dad, Lloyd Jr., in 1938. This new Lloyd was also athletic and intelligent, but not quite as invested in education as his parents—at least initially. He deviated from the academic track once as a teenager, telling his parents he wanted to adopt the local practice of intentionally failing eighth grade to gain an athletic advantage later in high school. He was promptly—and literally—slapped straight.

After that, he followed much of his father's path. Lloyd Jr. attended The University on a basketball scholarship, just like his father—and he declared his major as business, just like his dad. The summer after his freshman year in college, he even took a job in his father's company, going door-to-door to sell life insurance, walking miles of road in a suit amid the Alabama heat. That is where he veered onto a different path.

"I switched my major to pre-med as soon as I got back to campus," my father later told me. "I needed a job where people came to *me*, needed *me*. Not one where I was dependent on them to agree to a sale."

My dad would eventually become an orthopedic surgeon. It provided him with an identity he loved and a lifestyle he appreciated. It also provided him with enough money to invest in a fraternity brother's real estate ventures.

Those investments would give me a childhood filled with privilege.

I would eventually rebel against it, or fail to appreciate it, depending on your perspective.

~

My maternal grandparents lived a few hours away from us, so I only saw them on occasion. Still, I heard the stories.

I know that my great-great-grandfather was a German immigrant who owned a service station in the early 1910s and that it went out of business when locals refused to buy from "the enemy" during World War I. His sons resurrected the family name when they became wealthy doctors and took their sisters on a European tour. One of those sisters married and birthed my grandmother, Isabel, an only child. Isabel was raised among adults in a northern state and said her internationally minded mother was her biggest influence.

Isabel's future husband, Norman, was raised by another strong-minded woman, though his upbringing looked quite different. Norman was six when his father died. His widow took Norman and his younger brothers (ages four and two) with her to work in a sausage factory every day in order to pay the bills.

My grandparents, Norman and Isabel, married in Illinois after both graduated from college. They soon left for Washington, DC, where my mother, Joan (the first of three daughters), was born. Over the next several years, the family followed Norman's career path to Pittsburgh, then Chicago, before settling permanently in Birmingham, Alabama, when my mother was only seven years old.

You should know that in my home state, "Yankees" are people from the North, "damned Yankees" are the ones who visit, and "goddamned Yankees" are the ones who come south and stay. My grandparents, taught a valuable lesson by the German immigrant ancestor who had failed to acclimate quickly, were determined to blend in and avoid that last label if possible. They spoke southern, dressed southern, and raised their daughters southern.

Spirited southern, I should qualify.

I once went with my friend Laura to see the movie *The Divine Secrets of the Ya-Ya Sisterhood*. She hated it, concluding the film with a rant. "Why is it," she asked me, "that in all these movies the ultimate symbol of a southern woman's strength is to *endure*? Preferably in *silence*? I'm sick of it. Why can't it be strength to buck it all and break free?"

My grandparents did not raise my mother to buck it all. But they also did not raise her to be silent. They respected her mind and allowed her to give it some voice (in a southern accent, after she was called on, and when it wouldn't hurt her long-term prospects).

And my mother's mind was brilliant.

～

In 1958, at the age of fifteen, Joan began studying chitin, the key component in the exoskeleton of insects. When insects grow, they shed their exoskeleton and emerge in a new one. My mother collected the shed exoskeletons and fed them to mice. She weighed and studied the mice to determine the impact of the metabolized chitin. Spoiler alert: Ingesting chitin is a good thing—for mice and for humans.

When Joan was seventeen, she presented her project at local and then state science fairs. When she qualified to compete at a national competition, she shipped her project, boarded a plane, and stayed solo in a Kansas City hotel so she could reveal her thinking on a national stage. Along the way, she picked up college scholarship money from various organizations and tuition offers from several universities. At one point, after a victory at the state-level competition, she also picked up a headline in her hometown paper. It read, in celebration of her accomplishments, "LOCAL BEAUTY WINS SCIENCE FAIR."

The article mentioned nothing about her ambition to be a doctor. Unfortunately, it would not be the last time her good looks would divert focus from her intelligence or her dreams.

Years later, after using a Gorgas scholarship to attend Auburn University—and graduating a year early—she would apply to medical school at the University of Alabama in Birmingham. She was beyond qualified, but as she would learn during her interview, "way too pretty to receive an immediate offer of admission." The explanation was that medical students were not just people; they were investments made within a state that desperately needed doctors. She was a bad investment because she would end up getting married—she was "too pretty not to"—and leaving her practice to raise her children. "Take a year," they told her, "and decide whether you can commit to a lifetime of medicine—forgoing any ideas about a future family." My mother took that year to work in a medical lab out of state.

She came back to Birmingham after making her choice. She abandoned her dream of becoming a physician and took a job working in the hospital lab. Very quickly she became the head of the immunology and parasitology lab and spent a portion of her days teaching medical students.

One day during a trip through the hospital halls, Joan saw a young doctor. Later she would speak to him in the cafeteria, and he'd ask for her phone number. Joan—who lived in a dorm-like building with only one phone at the end of each hall—checked each day to see if she had any messages. It was two months before Lloyd actually called.

She later asked him why it took him so long to reach out. Well, he replied, it had taken him two months of extra shifts at a neighboring hospital to save enough money to take her somewhere he thought might impress her. Their first destination: the symphony. After that there were more dates, including an eventual wedding date at a church.

~

During those early days of their relationship, my parents had almost no money. My mother made $350 per month in the lab. My dad made less, and certainly not enough to buy any extras. The most striking testament to his temporary poverty was a lack of furniture; as a bachelor, he did not even own a mattress.

He'd owned a few things at one point: a bed, table, and two chairs. But his med-school roommate, who had dropped out and left him with extra rent to pay, hired movers who mistakenly loaded everything, including all of my dad's things, into their truck. When the truck was involved in an accident hours later, the furniture was damaged beyond repair.

For the remainder of his residency, Lloyd slept, ate, and lived on a black couch, which is still a prized possession in my family. For so long, it was his only possession. Still, he felt lucky. He had met the woman who would become his wife, and he had begun the career that would eventually reward him in a myriad of ways. Even now, it guaranteed sustenance. As compensation for their long hours and small salaries, medical residents had access to a lounge that held all the peanut butter and bread they could eat.

~

I think you can learn a lot from stories, but I think you learn the most about people by paying attention to which stories they choose to share. Most of the stories my family shared with me were about strong men and women who made sacrifices for this family's future. They were about the value of education: Schooling can be hard to achieve, and it is not something we quit. They were about careers—particularly careers in medicine, which were the dream and the pinnacle. For years I heard about how Joan's father loved my dad because my dad was a doctor—about how he would show up when my dad was on call and hang out in the ER (an attendance permitted back then). These family stories were about generations of people who worked and dreamed and built. They were stories about *us*: how my ancestors found and loved each other, how they put in effort and encountered obstacles as they rose, and how together they poured a foundation on higher ground for my generation.

Together, these stories constitute a history and carry a message. Like my grandmother Isabel—who once saved a single green grape "for later," wrapping it carefully in reusable aluminum foil—I should not take things for granted. And I certainly shouldn't throw them away.

I also believe it is important to note which stories are not told.

My parents lived in Birmingham, Alabama, in the 1960s. They were in the city infamous for Commissioner "Bull" Connor's use of firehoses and attack dogs against nonviolent protesters (including young children). They were not far away when Martin Luther King Jr. wrote his "Letter from a Birmingham Jail."

I had never put that together until I was in college, despite my being fairly obsessive about history from a young age. The moment I realized it, I called my folks and asked what they had been doing during the heart—and heat—of the Civil Rights Movement.

"I was working like a dog," my dad told me, "to get a job that would pay tuition at a top college where you would learn to ask obnoxious questions."

My parents were not actively opposing the Civil Rights Movement; it simply wasn't their focus. They were busy, with lives to build. Lives that would include medical mission trips, charitable donations, four children, and the occasional "obnoxious" inquiry. Lives they would begin to shape in earnest once their wedding was planned.

~

The drama surrounding my parents' wedding spans three generations. It was about religion. Everyone in my family believed in the Christian God, but they worshipped Him in different ways. My mother, Joan, was raised Catholic. My father, Lloyd, was raised Protestant, in a group called the Disciples of Christ.

In order for my parents to marry in Joan's Catholic church, Lloyd needed to sign a document agreeing to raise their children as Catholics. My dad (known for being extraordinarily agreeable, until he isn't) was willing to sign. He was very content to say his nonexistent children would be Catholic. Of course, he told Joan, what became of their actual children would be another matter entirely.

Joan balked. She did not want Lloyd to sign and then disregard a church document. If he was willing to disregard that vow on their wedding day, what other vows would he take lightly? Ultimately, they altered their wedding plans and announced they would marry in a Protestant church.

They stuck to this plan, despite a decree from Joan's Catholic church forbidding its members to go to the Protestant ceremony. This meant Joan's Catholic-school friends and original church family would not attend.

They stuck to this plan even as Joan's Catholic father revealed that neither he nor Joan's Catholic sisters would be at the wedding. This meant Joan would not be walked down the aisle by her dad.

They stuck to this plan even as they realized Joan's mother, Isabel—a Protestant who had signed the exact document they were now refusing (committing to raising Joan and her sisters as Catholics)—would be solo while offering her presence as their household's blessing. This meant Isabel would sit in the pew for the bride's immediate family alone.

Joan and Lloyd were married with her father standing outside on the church lawn, refusing to enter the building, with her younger sisters peering in through stained glass windows hoping to catch a peek, and with a member of her extended family at the altar giving her away.

Joan and Lloyd. My mom and dad. Taking a stand about what their children's faith would look like—a stand that came at great cost.

In later years, when they spoke of their wedding, my dad would speak of a beautiful bride, a fancy exit car, and a hopping reception. My mom would talk about a handsome groom, a bouffant hairdo, and how, on that day, she felt both peace and resentment.

The peace came from knowing they were now free to raise their children as they saw fit—as Christians. Period. Free to explore within (but only within) that umbrella. The resentment came from knowing it was one of the most important moments in Joan's life, and her dad was not there.

Many of Lloyd's friends and family were far less concerned about the religious drama than they were about the fact that a man from The University was marrying someone who graduated from Auburn. A mixed marriage, indeed.

They were relieved to discover—upon intense investigation—that my mother was not particularly passionate about athletics. This group of friends (fully aware of the future-religion-of-the-children drama) stopped just short of suggesting an additional document for consideration. It was whispered that there should be a document for Joan (the Auburn grad) to sign acknowledging that the children would be raised as Alabama sports fans. "Where was that paper?" they teased.

The friends did not stop short of drafting it because it was too much for them—it wasn't. They simply guessed that, given all the religious drama going on, it might be too soon to make the semiserious joke.

Besides, they felt it was obvious; anyone with a choice was going to root for The University. And so we did.

~

Joan and Lloyd moved back to Lloyd's hometown of Florence, Alabama, in 1970. Both attended his family's Protestant church regularly, and Lloyd opened an orthopedic practice in a two-story building next to the hospital. Joan retired her lab coat, bought bell-bottom maternity pants, and ultimately bore four children: Lloyd III, Kristi (that's me), Todd, and Ashley.

Since Lloyd III is my older brother, I only know about his infancy through stories. He was close in age to our cousin, and both had scary medical moments where my mother's lab expertise trumped that of their doctors, whom she begged to listen to her (once even running unauthorized tests on a burp cloth to convince them my brother was vomiting blood). My brother recovered and spent his earliest years in the two-bedroom house my parents rented while building their dream home.

I was born three years after Lloyd. Todd arrived five years after me, and Ashley completed our clan four years later. This spread across years means I remember a bit about Todd's infancy and almost everything about Ashley's.

Todd arrived in early June, and the five-year-old version of me committed two things to memory about the occasion: We celebrated it with a bucket of Kentucky Fried Chicken, and we saw the season's first fireflies that night. I grew up calling them "lightning bugs," and still today I think of Todd whenever I see their first flash of the summer. It has become a family tradition to mark the occasion with an announcement—now done over text—that the fireflies have arrived. Some years I get to make the announcement: "Saw a lightning bug that made me think of you, Todd!" Other years Lloyd or Ashley will beat me to the punch.

Ashley's arrival was marked with a different type of announcement, one made over the loudspeaker in my fourth-grade classroom. My mother's labor had been induced that morning, and she had promised that if I went to school, she would get word to me as soon as the baby arrived. I already had two brothers, and I was desperate to know if my new sibling would be a girl. I waited all morning for a knock at the door, expecting someone to deliver a note from the office. Instead, the speaker crackled: "Pardon the interruption, please. We need to let Kristi Johnson know she has a new little sister."

I don't know if my dad received the cigars and pats on the back that some used to mark such occasions back then, but I received lots of hugs and hollers from the girls in my class. I also received Ashley, a green-eyed gal with dark ringlets who would eventually become my best friend, despite the nine-year age gap.

~

Of course, I only know of my own birth through stories. I arrived on May 9, 1974. My mother spent the bulk of her labor trying to track down my father. She refused to go to the hospital without him because my dad had so many friends and colleagues who worked there, and she knew they would tease him relentlessly if she showed up to give birth while his where-abouts were unknown.

Back in those days, she could not call her husband on a cell phone. She tried all of his landlines, but he never picked up. He was not at home, not in his office, and his physician answering service was not able to reach him on his pager, which seemed to be out of range. Well, my mother had a good guess about what that meant, so she drove out to a property Lloyd Jr. had been keeping his eye on. There she spotted him, walking with his fraternity real estate buddy, inspecting land that would eventually prove to be a phenomenal investment.

But when they saw my mother, waving them over as she braced for another contraction, it was clear the sale was not happening that day.

Instead, I was happening. And at 9:20 p.m., I entered their world.

~

When I say that I entered their world, I am choosing my words precisely. My family crafted that world carefully, and my parents monitored it assid-uously. There were plans.

Some of their plans for me were conscious—my religious training was well thought-out, for example. Other plans were held as unspoken assumptions, only consciously considered, articulated, and asserted when I did something that surprised my family. Still more of their plans for me existed as reflections; my parents assumed that whatever career or lifestyle or location made them happy would make me happy. And they wanted me to be happy; there is no question that every plan was formulated, or subconsciously structured, for a daughter they loved.

Still, regardless of why or how each expectation found expression along the way, their plans for me were present from my very beginning. From the moment of my birth, it was presumed that, unless something went drastically wrong, I would become a wealthy, conservative, Christian, medical doctor who trained up North, where it was believed that no one would hold my gender against me. If all went fully to plan, my gender might even work in my favor. It would have a polished expression, cultivated and refined through hours of debutante training, thus enabling me to attract a White male of appropriate social and financial standing. This man would father our children while respecting my mind, my desire to return to my southern home, and our shared Christian faith. This last piece would be particularly important, as most of our milestones would be marked in a church.

These were clear expectations, wrapped as a gift. I would have happiness, fulfillment, and eternal salvation. And I would hear the stories and be grateful to everyone who had worked so hard to make it all possible. Amen.

CHILDHOOD

My mother had been a full-time homemaker since moving to Florence, but she was still a scientist at heart and had done her research when it came to child-rearing. That research identified everyone's expectations of me as a viable plan. The prevailing philosophy of the day informed her that, more than anything else, I was the equivalent of wet cement—able to be molded.

Much to her chagrin, I was more like dried cement: able to be altered if you were willing to pull out a jackhammer. Stubborn. Strong-willed. A bullheaded Taurus. Also, desperately independent. As a baby I was known as "the only infant who screams until you put her down."

My aunt is still traumatized by the time she took me swimming when I was a toddler. At the ripe old age of two, I had decided that I would independently climb out of a pool without using steps or a ladder. In toddler speak, "I do it *myself*." This was very close to a physical impossibility. It would require me to use thin arms that were restricted by oddly angled floaties to heft my dripping wet body over a pool ledge that was made of concrete. I would scrape layers of skin off with each attempt. After a half-hour of screaming at the scrapes—yelling *no* to anyone who suggested the steps or ladder—and raging at any offers of help, I managed to heave myself over the side. As I lay there, I was wet, bleeding, and panting. But I was *not* wet cement.

This defiant, independent streak of mine grew along with me. During my preschool years, over a span of just twelve months, I managed to split my head open on three separate occasions. All were the result of forging my own path, and all required stitches. The first was trying to climb into an old, wooden high chair *by myself* after being told to wait. When the chair toppled and its heavy tray came down on my forehead, my father arranged for his friend—our town's only plastic surgeon—to stitch me up. Today, the scar is barely visible.

The second occasion was similar. I was told to wait for assistance before getting out of the car, but I decided to proceed on my own. A tumble resulted in another gash. My father, too embarrassed to call the same plastic surgeon, took me to the emergency room, where I was stitched up by the doctor on call. That scar is slightly more evident, even today.

The third incident saw me following the letter of the law but refusing to embrace its spirit. I was spinning with my arms outstretched while my mother attempted to fix dinner. I was making myself—and everyone around me—dizzy. My mother finally told me to "stop spinning around in the kitchen." Gleefully recognizing a loophole, I began spinning around in the family room, right next to a stone fireplace. After a particularly dizzy stumble, I crashed into the stones, splitting open the center of my forehead. At that point, my parents were concerned a trip to any doctor would trigger a call to Child Protective Services. After a brief debate, my dad took me to his orthopedic office. My mother held me down while my dad sewed the stitches. Eventually, my mom took me for a professional haircut, where I received bangs to cover my most prominent scar.

~

By the time I advanced to kindergarten, my parents desperately hoped I had outgrown an extended period of the "terrible twos."

No such luck.

The power struggle continued, and my mother was determined to make it clear who was in charge. The next battle lines would be drawn at the dinner table.

I was now five years old, and my dinner plate was in front of me. Unfortunately, there was dinner food on it. Sigh. This was a disappointment to me—a hungry girl who had decided she wanted oatmeal.

My mother said no to the oatmeal, but she could not force me to eat anything else. I went to bed without supper.

I was shocked when my dinner plate reappeared at the breakfast table. My mother had decided that this was the time when she must make a point. I would eat what I was given or nothing.

I decided to make a point also. I would eat nothing.

Four hours later, my plate was reheated for lunch. I rejected it. Reheated again for supper. I pushed it away.

The following day, over forty hours after my last bite of food, my mother took me to the pediatrician. He told her to throw the plate away and cook my favorite meal—anything except the oatmeal I was demanding. She made a dish full of my favorites. I rejected it. I would have oatmeal or starve. After forty-eight hours without food, the oatmeal appeared in front of me. Relishing my victory, I proceeded to eat oatmeal—and only oatmeal—as my main dish for the next *year* of my life. I even took packets to kindergarten and used cold water from the water fountain to create my lunch.

Years later, I asked my mother if she ever sprinkled protein powder or any types of vitamins into the cereal to make sure I was receiving necessary nutrients. "No," she told me. "I figured whatever happened as a result of that nightmare, you deserved."

~

My favorite photo from those years was taken in December when I was five years old. I had, yet again, shocked my parents by asking for only one item for Christmas: a football uniform. I specified that I was not asking for a jersey. I wanted a *real uniform*, complete with a helmet and pads.

My parents decided this fell into the category of costume and bought it for me. In the photo I am wearing the uniform, including the helmet. You can see my long hair coming out from underneath it and resting on my shoulder pads. My arms are outstretched, far too wide to have any shot at catching the leather ball that is coming right toward my head. I am clearly about to be knocked flat by a toss from my dad.

"You wanted to play real football, and you were dressed for it," he told me. "So we played."

What is a parent to do when they admire a child's spirit, but regret its expression? One option is to let her have the uniform and everything that comes with it—then see if and where she stands.

These stories are told with a chuckle in my family, but there is heartache there also. Several things broke during those years. My mother felt she had failed. When you believe your children are wet cement, you feel a responsibility to shape them. My mother was a strong, brilliant, perfectionist who had sacrificed a career for her family and was told her effort would be reflected in my presentation. Then I looked nothing like what she envisioned.

This would have been hard for anyone, but it was particularly hard for my mother, since her perfectionism had very deep roots. Even as a child, part of what drove her to achieve was a determination to impress an alcoholic father who, in her words, "only ever praised me after a few drinks." I only have one memory of my grandfather Norman, who died the same year I received my football uniform. In my memory, he is sitting in an orange chair. But there are other snapshots provided through my mother's stories.

Once, she presented herself to him on the way to a school dance, with her hair styled to perfection, only to have him place his hand on the coiffure and ruffle it—a gesture of affection coupled with complete disregard. Several times, she arrived at her college classes to find him sitting in the lecture hall, having driven four hours round trip to remind her that "he would know if she ever did skip a class."

As the oldest child and daughter, she was determined to please and eager to be found beyond reproach. Still, it was clear she would be mussed or doubted, no matter what she did. Her idea that achieving perfection would win her father's approval was never realized, but also never abandoned. She wanted to hear him say she was enough.

He died without conveying that message, and her feeling of inadequacy was enhanced by what was happening in her new arena. She had not achieved perfection as a daughter, and now she was struggling with it as a mother. If her child was wet cement, why wasn't she able to make that little girl—me—fit her mold?

~

My mother will tell you it was during my early years that she truly found religion. I was the most contrary of her four children, and she jokes that raising me would have forced anyone to turn to a higher power. For years I received the message that I broke her, and God put her back together; that her frustration with me was the turning point in her faith.

This message was underscored recently when, at the age of seventy-six, she gifted devotional books to my children. She included a note:

> Though I had been raised in a Christian home, been baptized, and attended regular church services, I did not understand until I was a frustrated young mom of 33 that being a Christian was not about being good enough but about accepting Jesus's atoning sacrifice . . . You see, to have a relationship with a Holy God, we have to be perfect which was impossible for me. God Himself made a relationship possible when He paid in full my sin debt on the cross.

This is a woman who is still attempting to be perfect for a father and has finally discovered a route to accomplishing it. Her new mantra is that none of us will achieve perfection on our own, but if we accept Jesus, His death will pay our sin debt. We will become perfect through our faith in Him.

This religious awakening renewed my mother's spirit when I was a toddler. She knew that she would not be perfect in this life, and that I would not either. But she would get each of us as close to perfection as possible, within both secular and spiritual realms.

~

When my older brother and I were young, my parents visited every school near our hometown to find the right fit. Unfortunately, in rural Alabama, the pickings proved somewhat slim.

Undeterred, my parents forged a solution. They tapped into their connections and resources and—in an astounding act of parental investment—created a school.

In the basement of my father's orthopedic office, they opened my hometown's first Montessori academy for pre-K and kindergarten. They hired a teacher from Sri Lanka to lead the educational component and created a board to take care of the administration. My mom was the dominant voice on that board.

The school opened the year my big brother, Lloyd, was of age to enroll and my parents' affiliation with it ended fifteen years later, when their youngest child, my little sister, Ashley, graduated. Right after Ashley's graduation, my parents sold thousands of dollars' worth of classroom supplies to the teacher for $1 and let her continue on her own.

My siblings and I eventually inherited the building. When we sold it, years later, I kept the wooden plank that housed thirteen hooks for tiny preschooler jackets. My parents had bought that plank, built that school, and given us as close to a perfect educational start as they could manage. I am awestruck by everything that must have gone into that.

~

I was privileged, obviously. The word my family uses is "blessed." And since those of us who are blessed are supposed to be charitable, when I was a child, my mother modeled this by delivering meals to struggling families while I was at school.

One day, the year I was in kindergarten, a new family was added to her route. They were a different race, lived in a different section of town, and had very little money. During that first delivery, my mother discovered they had a daughter who was a bit younger than me and needed a warm winter coat.

"Easily fixed," my mother reasoned. The child could have my old one; she would love it. It was pink with white trim around the hood. But there was a problem, I told my mother in a young child's voice register: It was *my* coat, and I didn't care if it was too little. Yes, I'm sure that other girl would love it, but I loved it, too.

Me, wearing the pink coat, circa 1978

My mother had learned that forcing me into things wouldn't work, so she tried a different tactic. She rearranged the next meal delivery for a time when I could go with her—right after school. As my mom unloaded food for the family, I was told to go out and play with their small, coatless daughter. As we stood in their tiny yard, surrounded by a chain-link fence and chilly breezes, she shivered. Maybe chilly isn't the right word. Maybe it's *cold*.

Shame washed over me. This very young child was cold, and I, not much older, had denied her a coat. In that moment, my universe shifted, and I was profoundly altered.

I wanted to give her my pink coat. Also, the coat I was currently wearing. Whatever she wanted. I was serious when I suggested we give her *everything*. What else did we have for her? What else could we get?

I felt ill—like all my possessions had formed an awful mass inside me that churned before settling deep in my stomach. This child—this small, shivering girl—was suffering.

I could see it.

I could see my part in it.

And in that moment, I wanted to give her everything, because then she would have what she needed. As a bonus, if she took the mass, it could not lodge in my gut.

~

That pink coat moment had an immediate and ongoing impact, altering my worldview. Its effects linger, even into my adulthood, but the earliest aftershocks came in elementary school.

It was in elementary school, a few years after the pink coat incident, that I began receiving an allowance. My parents gave me $1 per week, as both a gift and as a financial instructional tool. In addition, my father offered me a job—one that I could do but did not fully understand until I was much older. Each day, I was supposed to take a special page out of the newspaper and trace my finger along an assigned column to a certain row. On that row, I looked for specific letters. Next to those letters, I always found numbers. My job was to copy those numbers into a small spiral notebook—and then place that notebook on my father's desk.

I now realize I was helping my dad track the stock market. In addition to my $1 per week allowance, I earned $1 for each newspaper, Monday through Friday. That means, as an elementary school student, I was pocketing a total of $6 per week.

It was my money, but I did not want to keep any of it. The money, like that pink coat, seemed to lodge in my gut. I could not possess it without feeling ashamed. There were girls without coats out there. And during my oatmeal phase, I had heard quite a bit about the starving children in Africa. Other kids needed this money. I didn't.

My father soon realized that every dollar he handed me was going into an envelope, and that every week the entire envelope went into the collection plate at our church. This concerned him. He was extraordinarily generous, sometimes unbelievably so, but also careful with money. His daughter had learned how to give, but she must also learn how to save.

He doubled my salary and forbade me to give away the extra. I could spend some of it, but I should save a portion. And we wouldn't be saving it in a piggy bank; I wouldn't get any interest. Besides, I'd had an account at the bank—in my name—since the week I was born.

That's right. The week I was born, my parents opened the account and placed a few dollars in it. The very first dollar was a gift from my older brother. He was three, and my parents had explained to him how we take care of family, starting with "sharing one of your dollars with your new little sister." Since then, every time anyone gave me a few dollars (tucked in a birthday or Christmas card), my parents had put it into my savings. As they told me about the account, they produced a tiny blue ledger book where I saw how those relatively small deposits were growing. I still had my $6 a week to put in the collection plate, but now I had another $6 to spend or put in this savings account. I decided that every penny of that extra $6 would go to that savings. I couldn't give it, but I didn't want to see it. It could just sit there.

It did sit there, earning 2 percent interest. Eventually, all those seemingly small deposits would become a fairly large amount.

~

This money was an advantage, shared and managed by a loving family who worked hard for it. Technically, I worked for some of it too, tracking those stocks for my dad. The end result was that, at an extraordinarily young age,

I learned the value of a job, the value of a dollar, and the value of saving. And I learned it all in my everyday environment: a desk polished by hired help at our riverfront property, not too far from the bank that held my childhood account.

But this privilege was unspoken. Unrecognized, really. What I heard about was the importance of education, effort, and work.

The end result of this was a fascinating juxtaposition that would take me over two decades to unpack and dismantle: *My family gave me every advantage, while insisting that we lived in a meritocracy.*

This was a big deal. I had an edge in almost every arena—a head start in almost every race—but was raised to believe that I earned my wins. By extension, this means others deserved their losses.

I was taught to be a good winner. Sympathetic. Charitable. As a Christian, I was expected to give time and money to those who struggled. But it is important to note that, while I was asked to give time and money to charitable causes, I was taught not to respect "charity cases." And I was told directly not to vote in ways that might lead to handouts. We believed in hard work.

Looking back, I am stunned at how long it took me to see past this filter. There were moments when it was lifted, and I was shocked to see people struggling through no fault of their own. But those moments were quickly explained away by the adults around me. Evidence of the meritocracy was presented to me in the stories of how my own family overcame discrimination (in the case of my German ancestor and my mother) and poverty (present on every past branch of our family tree).

The advantages I had that were too obvious to ignore were explained as *earned* (through the hard work of a family unit—we were not purely individuals in this southern culture) and *fragile* (easily lost if I chose to be lazy or frivolous).

As for skin color as an advantage? Why was I paying attention to skin color? Racists pay attention to skin color, and we were not racists. In this family, we looked deeper than that, young miss.

Once I reached the age of adulthood, it was assumed my vote would align with my parents'. Always. To the point that my parents eventually—without my knowledge—intercepted my absentee ballot and used it to vote for their candidate. Not because they wanted to commit fraud, but because they genuinely thought I must have been joking. I could not have been serious. The other guy? *Really?*

But that was still over a decade away. At this moment, I was still young, just out of kindergarten. Life lessons had begun, but they were on their first and most simplistic loop through my psyche. We donated our coats. We earned our dollars. We took care of family. We went to school and to church.

⁓

Surrounding these early educational experiences were the ordinary days of my childhood. I realize now that my "ordinary" was pretty wonderful. I spent my time playing on the swing set in our yard and tossing balls for our Irish Setter, Rusty. My mom read me stories each day before nap time, and I dozed in a beautiful, pink-canopied bed. Many days, post-nap, I built small forts on our property, stacking branches to create lean-tos near our home.

Our house was beautiful, built of wood to blend in with the natural setting. My parents built it before I was born, opting for a lot on the river even though, back then, building "in town" was the thing to do. From the front, our property appeared to be level ground, with a long, flat driveway perfect for learning to ride a bike. But anyone who walked the long path around the side of our home knew it was actually constructed on a cliff that offered a spectacular view of the water. The bluff had a steep slope, but the combination of dense trees on the slant and a wide plateau half-way down made it seem less precipitous. The plateau, which we called the "lower level," housed a garden and (once I began playing softball) a batting cage with a real pitching machine. On the edge of this level was another bluff. From it, we could wave to any family members who happened to be out on our boat.

The house itself had many nice features, but my favorite was that from the back, it seemed to simply melt into the landscape. Huge windows made it feel like we were living in the woods, but with every amenity imaginable, including easy access to Florence.

~

When my parents were building our home there was a strict budget, a good plan, and then a hiccup.

The budget couldn't be revised, so the plan had to be. The contractor said the easiest way to free up funds was to eliminate a bathroom. That seemed like a simple solution, because all my parents had to do was share a bathroom and then both the budget and the build would be back on track.

My dad told the contractor he could remove any other part of the house, but if he didn't get a bathroom to himself, we were finding another contractor. My dad got what he wanted.

His bathroom was a 1970s version of a man cave: large, fully carpeted, containing a black toilet and the best radio in the house. It was Dad's room. This fact was so clearly established and accepted that his gun and bullets lay on the top shelf of his closet, unlocked and untouched. Looking back now, I am appalled they were so accessible. But no one ever handled them without my dad's supervision. He taught us to shoot by firing at cans in the yard. To my knowledge, he only took shots himself a few times: killing poisonous snakes on our property and once killing a squirrel who kept dropping nut shards from a tree limb into our pool.

Because the bathroom was the space my dad built specifically for privacy, it naturally became everyone's favorite room in the house. I especially loved it because it was always warm. It had a special heater built into the ceiling. My dad woke up an hour early each morning so he could get ready slowly. And every morning I would wake up, run barefoot through the morning chill, and settle cross-legged on his bathroom floor. Dad would hand me an olive-green towel to use as a shawl and then drape every other olive-green towel in the bathroom over my head and arms before declaring me his "little green mountain." There was usually bluegrass or spiritual music playing, and my dad often sang "Dwelling in Beulah Land" to me in that room. I am likely the only person who pictures her Beulah Land heaven as a heated, bluegrass-filled bathroom, and its mountain as a pile of green towels.

~

Of course, in the fall, our ordinary days also involved cheering for The University's football team. We went to most of the home games, and we listened to away games on the radio. I have vivid memories of raking leaves next to my parents while the voice of the Crimson Tide—announcer Eli Gold—called out the plays.

My dad always said you couldn't trust Eli for real-time information because Eli became overly excited about every inch gained against an opponent. Eli was too much of a Bama fan—if there could be such a thing. He would get so excited about a player "finding a hole! Heading through it! He's moving! Folks! That play has just gained us . . . wait for it! . . . *two yards.*"

"I do love Eli," my dad would say. "Two yards for us *is* something to be celebrated. 'Course, I thought we had a touchdown, the way he was carrying on."

Still, it was a real treat when an away game was *televised.* On those Saturdays, we put the rakes down and went to my aunt and uncle's house to watch the ball game with the whole extended family. I will never forget one Saturday in 1982 when we played Auburn, our rival. It was a close game, and Auburn's Bo Jackson scored a touchdown with two minutes, twenty-one seconds to go. This gave them the lead over our beloved Alabama.

"Maids" was the word we used to refer to these women back then. They were in our home four days a week, from 9 a.m. to 4 p.m. each day. They cleaned rooms, made beds, ironed clothes, washed dishes, vacuumed floors, polished silver, and took out the trash. But what I really remember about them is not what they did, but how they did it: quietly, consistently, and with incredible patience as four children were always underfoot (or riding on top of the vacuum cleaner, if you can imagine). They were the adult presence who never seemed to mind keeping the kids if my mother ran an errand.

My mother tried to shoo me away from Mabel once, worried I was bothering her. Mabel replied, "If it's OK with you, ma'am, she's welcome to walk right along with me. It's nice to have her to talk with during the day." I spent many hours with Mabel, and when I was much older—a college student home on break—I attended the funeral of Mabel's father. There I met Mabel's daughter, and I saw their community embrace them as everyone grieved. When the service started, I was ushered into a pew with the only other White person in attendance—someone I had never met. He leaned over to me and whispered, "They must assume we're connected." I didn't know anything about the man, and I certainly didn't try to learn anything during the funeral. But in my hometown, shared skin color was a connection, and having different skin colors was a barrier. Mabel had been given a place from which to view and assist in my White world for years without really being allowed in it; now it was my turn to view hers. My invitation had been a gift, an acknowledgment that "you always come talk to me when you're home from college." I was honored to be there. I would honor her by accepting my place respectfully, whispering condolences after the service, and leaving her community to grieve. Our worlds were like a huge Venn diagram with only the tiniest sliver of overlap.

Here's what it looked like within that tiny sliver.

They worked. I ran in and out of the rooms they frequented, chatting with them and also making more messes, which they always cleaned. My parents paid them well relative to the going rate and used a different system of compensation than the previous generation. When my dad was young, his parents always had "help" for their home and garden. This help was always Black and used a separate toilet installed just for them in the basement—an in-house amenity that was actually segregation. In our house, we all shared the toilets. That sounds ridiculously hollow, but it made an impression on some back then. The amenity my parents provided was a portable TV the maids were allowed to place in the laundry room whenever they did the ironing. I always knew where Mabel would be between 1 p.m. and 2 p.m., and I didn't disturb her then. That was when she pressed our Sunday best while watching her favorite show.

In terms of compensation, my grandparents paid their gardener for years after he became too old to work, which seemed nice on the surface. I had to rethink this recently when I was talking to a family member who suggested another angle.

"It sounds nice," she told me, "but doesn't it reflect what everyone knew then? His relationship with them was never temporary. Both sides knew it was for life." My own parents rejected this traditional arrangement and opted for a new form of benefit. They wanted to pay through legitimate channels instead of under the table. My mother said some potential employees balked because it was different, and it meant paying taxes. Others took the job and later appreciated the arrangement, as it provided them with a social security check down the road.

But those were all things I came to understand later. The only time I remember the issue of a maid's color being directly discussed when I was a child was when my four-year-old brother pointed at Ida and announced, "You're Black!" Ida was upset and asked my mother to punish him. My mother refused, explaining, "He just learned his colors at school, and he's noticing them everywhere. He is not attaching anything negative to the color or to you."

I asked my mom about that incident recently and she told me, "I wish now that instead of explaining my perspective, I had asked why it upset her. You know, she was only with us a few years, and I never told you kids what happened. Her husband shot her in a murder-suicide. Such an awful, incredible shame."

Her section of our Venn diagram had actually disappeared—exploded—and I had not the slightest inkling. I just knew that one day she wasn't there because she had "moved on."

I moved on also, growing up in a house cleaned by her successor. My eyes opened a bit over the years, and I remember, as a teenager, asking my mother why all of our maids had been Black. She matter-of-factly explained that while *she* did not want to see color, because she believed in looking deeper than that, she knew that *our neighbors* would see it. She explained that "having a White maid could look awkward." If people saw Dad at home with a White woman who wasn't his wife, they might think something illicit was happening. That was never an issue when they saw him with a Black maid.

I had no idea what to say about that at the time, but when I got older, it would come up again.

~

Not surprisingly, one of my most vivid childhood memories took place on a holiday.

Holidays at our house were pretty magical. We pulled out the fancy china, silver, and crystal. We ate with extended family at a large table in a beautiful dining room that had floor-to-ceiling windows on one side (to maximize our view of the river) and floor-to-ceiling mirrors on the other (to reflect the beauty). This table—which was always set with name cards for special occasions—held candy on Halloween, turkey on Thanksgiving, roast beef on Christmas, and ham every Easter. Other rooms held different holiday items: costumes, themed knickknacks, and piles of presents (under a tree or in an Easter basket, depending). As an adult, I now appreciate everything my parents invested in these displays—particularly the time and attention required of my mother. She will tell you it was nothing, that her extroverted nature and appreciation for proper presentation made having people over for a decked-out holiday even more fun and festive. It leaves me—an introvert who hosts close-knit gatherings where everyone brings a dish to eat amid an eclectic (and beloved) collection of kid-crafted ornaments—in awe.

The holiday that contains this particular memory was Christmas the year I was seven. It was only 10 a.m., but we had opened presents, eaten our traditional "Christmas casserole" for breakfast, and done the annual search through the trash for gifts we may have accidentally thrown out; it did seem that every year a check went missing with the wrapping paper.

The phone rang. Alice, a woman my mother met through the charitable meal program, needed help. Her daughter, Naomi, was on a kidney transplant list, and they had received the call that an organ was available. Could my mother help them get to the hospital in Memphis, three hours away? Alice knew there was a bus, but she needed a ride to the bus station and cash for the fare.

My mother loaded me into the car, along with my new favorite doll— just unwrapped that morning—and we listened to Christmas carols en route to their home. Looking back now, I wonder what my mother was thinking. It is possible that she had a thousand things on her mind: gratitude for her own healthy children; joy for Alice, whose prayers have been answered; pain for the family who lost someone and gave that vital organ. More likely, given my mom's propensity to focus on action, she was calculating how much cash Alice would need, how quickly she must drive to catch that bus, and how the timing of Christmas dinner would need to be adjusted.

We pulled into Alice's driveway, parked, and walked to the door. The contrast between their home and ours was always stark, but was especially so on this Christmas morning. There was no wrapping paper, no hidden check, and the small tree fit on top of their one tiny table. I am sure there was joy—they were receiving the gift of life that day—but as a seven-year-old I didn't see things at that level. What I saw was a child without presents. The favored doll I was holding didn't feel right anymore. It still sat in my grasp, but—like the pink coat—its invisible weight had moved into my stomach. We took them to the bus stop, and as Naomi boarded, I gave her the doll. Now she had a toy to take with her, and I didn't have one lodged in my gut.

That is my last memory of Alice and Naomi. We went back to our Christmas. Naomi received a new kidney. She survived. We helped. But she was not a member of my school, my church, or my social circle, and I never saw her again.

I do remember, as a seven-year-old, wondering what she named the doll.

~

Clearly my mother was a force of nature.

She was in charge of 99 percent of our family life. My dad's word was law, but he was a man of few words and laid laws sparingly, so my mom ran the show. And when I say she ran it, I mean it literally. Her pace was astounding.

She tackled new projects with dauntless energy. When my parents launched my dad's medical practice, it was my mother who researched how to establish the business and then orchestrated its opening. When she saw the need for a preschool, she simply created one, and her involvement in our education continued through elementary school. She was a Girl Scout leader, a Boy Scout leader, the Junior Great Books instructor, and the Room Parent for all of us. She was *not* a natural teacher, becoming loud and frustrated if her explanations did not produce our enlightenment quickly, but that frustration always evidenced someone who truly cared.

Whenever specialists came to our house to fix anything—from the dishwasher to the trash compacter—she paid them extra to teach her how to fix it herself the next time. The dryer stumped her once, and when the professional she hired discovered the problem was a tiny Tasmanian Devil charm from my bracelet lodged in the gears, she said, "Well, I can't be expected to perform exorcisms on top of everything else." So that gives you a sense of where the rare limits were.

Her smarts also made her fairly fearless and a quick study of anything unfamiliar. That fearlessness, combined with her on-the-move energy, meant we were highly mobile. She rented RVs and drove us around the country during some summers. My dad, an orthopedic surgeon in a small town, joined us as much as work allowed. My most vivid memory of him in an actual RV was at Mammoth Cave in Kentucky. We returned from a tour of the caverns to discover that the RV's sewage system had backed up into the shower, where we had stored the suitcases with my parents' clothes. My mom sprang into action, unhooking the sewer line and carrying piles of feces-covered clothing to the coin-operated laundry while my father calmly told her not to bother washing his because he was throwing them all out. Sure enough, we were at a Big and Tall shop making purchases that afternoon.

My mom's independent streak was strangely contrasted by her social nature, which required some degree of conformity. Unwilling to conform her mind or spirit, she conformed her physical and material presentation.

She always knew what was in style and wore it. Every year, she prided herself on getting that sold-out, impossible-to-get toy of the season for all of us for Christmas, even if we hadn't circled its picture in the Sears catalog. While my mother and I were similar in many respects (notably our independence), we also had major differences. She took pride in appearance. I took pride in devaluing it. She showed her love with gifts. I tucked them away, not wanting to add to the pile in my gut. She welcomed crowds, while I often retreated. She moved faster than me in every arena. During my childhood, this meant trying to keep up with her in downtown department stores. As an adult, it means I stall on moments she blows past without thought.

SCHOOL DAYS

After preschool and kindergarten at my parents' Montessori, I attended a very small, private, conservative Church of Christ school from grades one through twelve. According to my mother, she knew they could never choose our friends for us, but they could choose the environment within which we picked them. She told me that "a place full of Christian families who were willing to invest in education seemed like a good pool."

Most days were the same. We sat in long rows of wooden desks, all facing the front. We pledged allegiance to the flag, always at exactly 8:20 a.m. Recess was the only free-for-all, with equipment now banned on most modern playgrounds: a long metal slide that was too hot to touch until mid-September and a merry-go-round that sent kids away dizzy (or as human projectiles) all year. The bulk of my school memories are wonderful, and most of my teachers were extraordinarily kind. Still, this was "spare the rod, spoil the child" country, so corporal punishment was an ever-present possibility. My sixth-grade teacher kept a paddle on display in our classroom at all times. He named it Excalibur and explained how he had drilled holes in it to reduce wind resistance during his swing. My cohort had the misfortune to experience Excalibur at a time when Michael Jackson–style parachute pants (with zippers that ran down the legs and on the behind) were considered the height of fashion. More than one classmate blamed Excalibur for zipper-shaped marks imprinted on their skin. I saw classmates hit frequently, since part of the punishment was the indignity of bending over in front of the class. I was only hit once, across my knees, which were in the aisle instead of under the table. I later learned that my parents (who never spanked us but were part of the my-kid-was-in-trouble-at-school-so-will-now-be-in-trouble-at-home generation) were upset about *how* I was punished. My father—the doctor who helped many senior citizens deal with joint pain and encouraged me to always play basketball in kneepads—confronted the teacher and made sure that no child was ever hit on the knees again.

We did not wear school uniforms, but there was a strict dress code. For years, we were not allowed to wear shorts except during athletic events, when we were permitted to don long versions. The girls' shorts were much longer than the boys'—and always within two inches of the knee. Our top halves were also carefully monitored. As an eight-year-old, I once inadvertently exposed an inch of my midriff while raising my hand in class. I was immediately sent to the office, where my mother was called to bring me a longer shirt. I remember that moment of classroom transformation: from excited about sharing a thought to embarrassed as the teacher asked me to leave.

Once properly outfitted, we could learn. Reading. Writing. Arithmetic. And *Bible*. Holy moly, we studied the Bible. Every word of it. One of my few church party tricks is that I can actually recite the "begats," since I was required to memorize them: "Adam begat Seth who begat Enosh who begat Kenan who begat Mahalalel . . ." and on and on, for a total of sixty names. Not only did we read and memorize them, but after doing so, we had to recite them in front of the class.

Clearly, repetition is one way of creating a memory. But it strikes me that the opposite is also true. While some events stick with us because of their frequency, we remember others because they are unusual. We remember some events because they stand out.

~

One memory from third grade stands out.

Picture me again as an eight-year-old: a White, privileged, naïve girl in a private religious school in rural Alabama. There were no Black students in my class, but I had not noticed this, because—up until this particular day—I had never really noticed skin color. My encounters with Black members of our community had been fairly limited, and it would be another year before my younger brother would point out something I had not paid attention to: the color of our maid.

For now, I was in third grade and my teacher, Ms. Gunderson, was trying to engage the class in our history readers. Alas, we were unfocused. We were studying slavery, and she recognized that our group simply wasn't paying attention. But Ms. Gunderson was determined, and she had a remedy. She arranged a field trip to a nearby farm, where she asked our all-White class to pick cotton. This was not a farm most elementary school students would visit. There were no goats to pet or strawberries to sample or shade tents to shield us. Instead, we exited the bus onto a dusty patch of gravel road and squinted into the sun to see cotton. Endless rows of cotton. Cotton all of us had driven by numerous times, but never really noticed.

But today we were going to notice. We were going to be immersed in it. Ms. Gunderson herded us toward the field and then spread us out, directing each child to stand at the end of a different row. She then handed every student a plastic bag and told us to begin the harvest.

I quickly realized that I needed to be careful. While the actual cotton tufts were soft, the portion of the plant that held them—the calyx—was dry and prickly. Avoiding that part of the plant, I carefully pulled out the tuft and put it in my bag. But then the teacher reminded our class that under different circumstances we would not have had the luxury of time, or any luxury for that matter. We were going to need to do it faster, and faster, and then *faster* as we made our way down our row. As my teacher raised her voice, I began harvesting more quickly. Of course, picking up my pace meant I wasn't picking the cotton as carefully. I was no longer only touching a soft tuft; I was now grabbing the tough calyx with its sharp, prickly edges. By the time I got to the end of the row, my hands were bleeding, and I was in tears.

I was in tears because it hurt. I was only eight, after all. But I was also in tears because for the first time I was paying attention. I was trying to imagine life back then, as someone of a different color, and I recognized that I couldn't.

When we returned to our classroom, I slipped my history reader into my backpack. I had finally absorbed the idea that the characters in this book of stories were actual people. I was desperate to know what happened next to them and within their community. The book came home with me every night until I hit the last page.

Twenty years later, I wrote Ms. Gunderson a letter explaining how that experience shaped me. How it made history *real* to me. How it inspired me to learn and—eventually—to teach.

It was a note of gratitude.

~

I paid attention to race on paper that year, reading about slavery in my third-grade history text. I connected the race of those individuals to someone I knew when my brother pointed out the color of our maid the next year. But it wasn't until sixth grade that I realized there was still something happening.

By then, I had one Black student as a classmate. I was our sixth-grade class president, so when tasked with planning a class celebration, I asked my parents if we could host it at our country club. They told me no, because it wouldn't be fair to Jeremiah; our country club would not want him to attend.

I paused, briefly stunned. Then I pivoted.

We'd plan something better than a party at the stupid country club, I told the sixth-grade committee. We'd rent buses, take a day trip to another town, and go *ice-skating*.

To my eleven-year-old mind, we had found a solution. Apparently, the reality of our community was going to have to hit me a bit harder to truly get in.

~

That third-grade trip to the cotton field sparked an interest in history that would never leave me. But I did not spend that whole year buried in my history reader. Other things were happening, too.

I was still eight years old. It was a Sunday. Of course, that meant I was dressed in my finest and sitting in church. My family occupied the same pew we did the week before, and all the weeks before that. Our pew was near the stained-glass window that bore my grandfather's name, and I had a good view of a rose my grandmother had provided from her garden in honor of a new baby in our congregation. I was small enough that my feet swung, clearing the floor by several inches. Despite the inability to reach the floor in that moment, it was apparent that I was supposed to be rooted here.

I had graduated from the childcare wing, and I was jealous of my younger brother, who still played there every Sunday, engaging in all sorts of fun activities. Today, while I attended grown-up church, a preschool teacher would walk his class down the block to visit the local university's mascot: a lion named Leo (yes, an actual living, breathing lion in an enclosure). I was with my mother as we dropped Todd off in the classroom, and I was wistful as we turned to go.

But there was at least one thing for me in the adult service: a five-minute segment when school-aged children were invited to the front of the sanctuary for a lesson. They called this "Children's Church." My main job during this part of the ceremony was to remember that I was wearing a dress and not sit wide-kneed on the steps leading up to the altar while facing the congregation.

A deacon led the lesson. It was brief and to the point. He handed us

PAYDAY candy bars and told us the day we must pay for our sins was coming. "Hellfire is real," he told us, so we'd "better live right."

I was terrified. And then dismissed.

All of the children were dismissed, back to their families. Some of the kids were munching their treats. Others were trying to figure out if they were allowed to consume their PAYDAYS now or if they should save them for later.

After the service, we went to pick up my younger brother from the nursery. He cried when he saw my mom, and his teacher apologized profusely. The lion, trapped in its small enclosure, had peed through the chain-link cage and all over my brother.

I do not remember anything I heard on the car ride home that day, but I remember the smell of urine and fear.

$\sim$

I lingered in that fear of hellfire for decades, but I am not going to linger on it here. Instead, I am going to take us to the place where I was most fearless: the basketball court. As a third grader, I was finally old enough to join my school's official sports program. I was about to trade in my well-worn football uniform for high-top basketball shoes.

Every Saturday morning, for the duration of basketball season (November through March), my family planted itself at my school's sports complex. It contained two gymnasiums, which, combined, could host four elementary school games at a time. There were concessions, entry fees, bleachers, and classmates. It was noisy, competitive, and *fun*.

The year was 1981, so this was before smaller balls, height-adjustable hoops, and participation trophies. As third-grade girls, we played with a full-sized men's ball on a ten-foot goal. None of us were strong enough to score any type of basket other than a short jumper. Envision tiny people, high rims, and mostly air balls. Now insert me, a young girl determined to make as many short jumpers as possible, on a team coached by her very competitive, basketball-loving dad. We were *into it*. Both of us loved it. And if you were on our team, you were playing to win.

One Saturday, we were thrilled to be winning with one minute left in the game, by a score of 12–10. The other team was about to inbound the ball when my dad called a time-out and told me to foul.

"You want me to foul *on purpose*?" I asked my father.

"Yes," he responded, and then he explained. If our opponents hit a short jumper during this possession, it would tie the game.

But if I fouled someone, that player would have to shoot from the free-throw line, which was set at the regulation distance of fifteen feet from the basket. No one in our league had hit a free throw all season. Kids our age weren't strong enough to even come close. All I had to do was foul and watch my opponent airball a free throw. After that we would get the ball back, hold it as the clock ran out, and then celebrate our win.

I liked it but anticipated a problem. "Dad," I asked, "what if they don't give the ball to the girl I'm guarding?"

"No problem," he told me. "Just foul whoever they do give it to."

Aha! I understood and was determined to follow my father's instructions. It was a brilliant plan, and we were going to win. As soon as the referee handed the ball to a girl on their team, I ran over and hit her. Hoops fans will recognize my error immediately: I had reared back and actually punched the girl who was standing out-of-bounds next to the referee— before she even threw in the ball.

Initially, I was thrilled when the referee blew his whistle and sent her to the line for two free throws, both of which she airballed. But I soon became confused. After her air balls, the referee gave *her* team possession. That was *not* part of the plan.

Determined to correct this wrong, my eight-year-old self spoke to the official. Their player had airballed both shots. Why had he given the ball back to them?

The referee leaned down and said two things.

First, he explained that my foul was *so inappropriate* it was considered a technical foul, which meant the other team received two free throws *and* possession of the ball.

Second, he asked why on earth I had punched someone on the other team—someone I was not even supposed to be standing near—before she had even thrown the ball in.

Well, that was an easy question to answer, so I did it at full volume.

"My dad told me to hit her! He said if I fouled whoever got the ball, we were guaranteed to win!"

All eyes in the gym went to my dad in that moment, while his eyes stayed trained on me. "I know I probably should have been embarrassed," he told me later, "but I wasn't. I was *thrilled*. Some athletes never have that killer instinct, and you can't teach it. But when I saw you sprinting toward that inbounder with your fist clenched, I knew you had it. You're a player who is going to do whatever it takes. Athletes with a killer instinct know more than how to play the game—they have a respect for the game itself, and what it requires of us to win."

~

I had the killer instinct. And I loved the game. So I told my mother—who scheduled all of our extracurriculars—that I wanted to go to basketball camp. She signed me up for a weeklong summer session for kids at the local college. On the first day of camp, my mother and I entered and quickly discovered I was the only girl there. This didn't bother me. I was there to play, and I didn't care who I learned with—or played against. My mother recognized this and appreciated it, but she was still thrilled when she saw another ponytailed player walk in at the last minute. My mom pulled me over to meet the new kid and said, "I'm so glad there's another girl here for Kristi to play with! Maybe y'all could have lunch together during the break!" A stony glare told her she had miscalculated. "I'm not a girl," he said.

"Oops . . . so sorry!" my mom exclaimed, while I cringed.

The session began. I was placed in the lowest-level group and picked last for teams. I ate lunch alone, and it was clear the other ponytail had decided to punish me by spreading the word that I was to be avoided. The other campers watched me eat. But the coaches had watched me play. And things changed during the afternoon session.

The counselors moved me into a higher skill group. Someone from my elementary school was in this group—a classmate who I knew to be both athletic and competitive. He knew the same about me.

He was a clear leader in this pack, and he was assigned the role of captain. This meant he and the other captain would take turns choosing players for their teams. He shocked the group when he said, "Kristi."

"*Her*?" another player inquired.

"I know her," he responded, "and I'm telling you, she can *play*."

That was good enough for this crowd, who was focused on winning.

It was a good week, but at the end of it, there was a demonstration for families. Parents filed into the bleachers, while players spread out on the court. The coaches had decided to open the demonstration with a short skit they thought would be funny. They prepped us, telling all the boys to do the first drill incorrectly on purpose. Then they wanted me to interrupt the drill and show everyone how to do it right. The act earned a big laugh. But I wasn't laughing, and neither were my campmates. None of us were sure what to make of it all.

~

I was sure what to do with the basketball drills I had learned: practice them.

I was so focused on this assignment that it never even occurred to me that my parents might not want me to spray-paint basketball markings all over our driveway. The images I created included court markings (a lane and three-point arc) as well as a series of boxes to help me develop my footwork. My mother was shocked but would ultimately be supportive *if* I agreed to blacktop the driveway and redo them with stencils to create neater lines.

Done.

During my sixth-grade year, I was out there every morning at 6 a.m., shooting, jumping, and running a mile before school.

After school, I practiced with the junior high team. I was not age-eligible to play in the games, but—as I told the coach when a friend and I approached him to ask permission to join in team workouts—I wanted to practice as much as possible now so that when I was old enough, I'd be even more ready.

～

My parents were very supportive of my athletic interests, but my mother recognized an unintended side effect. My on-court demeanor—rough, competitive, tomboyish—was spilling over into real life. Fortunately, there had been a plan to refine me—to teach me how to present myself as a young lady—since the beginning. I would attend a weekly class called "White Gloves and Party Manners."

While there, I literally wore white gloves, pairing them with my black Mary Jane party shoes. I also learned what fork to use, when to unfold my napkin, how to sit properly (and quickly, so the gentlemen in the room do not feel compelled to remain standing) and—believe it or not—how to get in and out of a convertible without "exposing oneself."

I kept my head down, my crotch covered, and my dessert fork at the top of my plate until pie was served. But one day, I took my gloves off. Literally. My fingernails were being inspected. They were declared too short—not ladylike at all.

"Do you chew them?" I was asked.

"No," I told the instructor, forgetting that I was supposed to keep my answer short and ask her a question about herself right after. Here was a space where I could insert the real me. "I clip them so I can do my ballhandling drills—you know, for basketball. I do the drills every morning. Anyway, the fingernails were a problem, especially when I tried to spin the ball on my fingertips." I flashed her a smile.

The instructor—who had never heard this many words come out of me (or possibly any student)—was stunned.

"Basketball isn't a ladylike pursuit," she told me. "Grow out your nails."

~

My parents explained to me that I could find a balance. It was a matter of code-switching. I could be rough and tough on the court, clean up in the locker room, then emerge as a lady. It was a matter of compromise. I could keep my nails short, but file and polish them so they had an attractive shape and color.

It was also a matter of paying attention to elements of my on-court demeanor that seeped into off-court presentation. For example, my mom pointed out, I had developed a "masculine posture and walk." This was clearly unacceptable, so she enrolled me in a modeling class for preteens, where I would learn how to sit, stand, and stroll like a lady.

I resisted. My walk was *fine*. What a huge waste of time. But my pleas fell on deaf ears: My mother insisted it would be good for me, and my father insisted my mother was right. "Onto the court like a tiger," he told me, "and out of the locker room like a gazelle."

I protested enough that when the afternoon of the modeling class arrived and I complained of a stomachache, my mother was unimpressed. "Right," she said. "That's enough excuses. Just get in the car." She was wrangling my siblings, making sure she had her checkbook to pay for the classes, and trying to make sure the oven timer was set so we could eat once back home. It was a quiet trip, despite the siblings and my occasional description of "kind of queasy, you know. I'm not making it up . . ." Her hands were clenched on the steering wheel, and I could tell she was praying for patience.

She dropped me off in a room just large enough to contain a tiny stage and a catwalk. I quickly realized that I was the only one not dressed to the nines. While the focus of the class was literal steps for me, it seemed a few others viewed this as a figurative step toward a career in modeling. My mother had picked her battle and left me—an eleven-year-old in jeans and a T-shirt—sitting quietly with the group.

She returned at the end of the hour to an ugly scene. I was sitting alone in the room, sipping a cup of water. The other students were waiting out in the hall, with an instructor who was apologizing to their families. During my first turn on the catwalk, near the end of the path, I had vomited—first onto the stage and then over its edge.

I am not certain whether my classmates or my teachers were more horrified, but the person who was most shocked and deflated was my mother. I remember her trying to wrangle my siblings, comfort me, apologize to the teacher, and clean up the vomit, while repeating over and over, "I'm so sorry. I'm just so, so sorry. I really didn't think you were sick."

That was my final foray into finishing school settings, and my parents never even asked my younger sister if she wanted to attend.

~

There were ample opportunities to practice ladylike behavior, even with official classes taken off my calendar. We dined out in our community, hung out at the country club, and visited my grandmother Mary Sue quite often. These were all opportunities for practice and correction.

I remember those moments of instruction in all arenas: comportment, religion, school, athletics. There were expectations, and my mother was particularly tough. She had standards: for herself, for me, and for anyone under her supervision. Once, in the capacity of elementary school Girl Scout leader, she marched an entire group of my friends into the bathroom of a McDonald's and made them wash their faces. Her co-leader had allowed all the girls riding with her to borrow and apply makeup en route. "Absolutely *not*," countered my mother. We were there to interview a manager, and we were "going to do it with the faces we wore to school today." My friends complained, especially when they realized they had to use that awful-smelling, pink flower soap that fast-food chains often had in their dispensers. I reminded them that my mom had made me *eat* soap once when I told my brother to shut up and encouraged them to watch their tongues. Then I tried to find a table big enough to crawl under and die.

Still, there were moments of mercy. My mother may have continued to prize perfection, but she also acknowledged the role of grace. Sometimes that grace was extended to me.

Once, when I was in fourth grade, I had forgotten to study for a Bible test. When the teacher announced the exam would begin in a few moments, I panicked. I lied, telling her I felt sick and needed to go see the nurse, and then telling the nurse I felt sick and needed to go home. The nurse, concerned about the stomach symptoms I described, called my mother. Forty-five minutes later, I was in our family station wagon.

After two minutes in the car, my mother knew I was fine and asked me for the real story. I thought when I confessed my charade my mother would march me back into the classroom to admit my wrongdoing and accept my punishment. Instead, she softened and said, "I bet you did feel sick to your stomach when you realized there was a test you weren't ready for." She let me run errands with her, then had me study at home.

~

My parents loved me and provided a wonderful childhood. They drove me to a variety of activities so I could pursue my extracurricular interests. We took wonderful vacations to Disneyworld or in the RV. Saturdays, they would drop me off at the sports complex with a few dollars so I could buy myself a corn dog and a Coke when I got hungry. I would hang out with friends all morning, and my parents would return in the afternoon to watch me play.

I remember my father bringing bushels of green beans home from work every year and asking me to snap them for dinner. He always allowed Mr. Davis to pay him in vegetables after the harvest, for orthopedic services provided throughout the year.

For the most part, my early life was charmed. I was loved. I did not know the pain of neglect or the worry of hunger.

But I was given a few things to carry and a road map to follow. Even at age eleven, I could see that the route was marked clearly and would involve long hauls over terrain that was not easy. But I had a head start, even if we weren't going to admit it.

A head start toward a destination I would try to make mine.

MAPS AND SEEDS:
HIGH SCHOOL INTO COLLEGE

By age eleven, my family map had become a clear guide toward certain identities and beliefs. This does not make me unusual. Most kids grow up amid cultural norms and familial expectations.

What made me odd (at least in the eyes of my family) is that I chose to carry those perceptions and expectations into some very unexpected places. While there, I noticed—and was drawn toward—unfamiliar perspectives and paths.

And while neither the girl I was then—nor the woman I am now—is particularly noteworthy, the people and places I encountered on my journey are remarkable. My hope is that revisiting them here—reviewing what it all taught me then—will both honor them in a way my current life doesn't and also help me figure out what to do now.

Still, before I introduce them, I need to issue a disclaimer.

These were not magical people and places. They were mostly unassuming. Easy to miss, especially for someone moving quickly along their own path or with their eyes glued to a map.

~

Have you ever gone out for a walk and strayed off-road just enough to feel wild grass under your feet? And then hours later, once you're back home, you realize your socks are full of those hitchhiker seeds that latch on like Velcro?

Well, in my teens and early twenties, I wandered off-road just enough to encounter, and unwittingly garner, some sticky seeds.

I was not particularly fertile soil back then. But sticky seeds travel with you. They take root later.

Most of mine took root just after I graduated from high school and college. In my mid-to-late twenties, growth from those seeds disrupted the manicured landscape of my personal, professional, political, and spiritual life. At that point, I had to discard my map and focus on navigating a living maze. It was *my* maze, full of twists and turns and dead ends and new leads and an abundance of sticky seeds that I treasured, newly aware of their potential and power.

But during high school and college, I was not focused on seeds. During those years, I was discovering that even though my mapped path was clear, it was not easy. Progress along it would require a tremendous amount of personal investment. So during high school and college, I invested in my mapped route, trying to adopt others' expectations as my own.

～

The three main messages I internalized during high school and college were *we love you, do not trust yourself,* and *stay on the paved road.*

My parents loved me.

As a child, I experienced their love in all sorts of positive ways. It is important to remember that love (and to know they truly had good intentions) as I focus on their next two messages (which turned out to be not so good for me): *Do not trust yourself* and *stay on the paved road.*

～

In my world, not trusting yourself was a spiritual directive.

Once my mother found God during my toddler years, there were lots of spiritual directives. We went to church weekly. We had family devotionals, nearly every evening. We prayed throughout the day (before meals, at bedtime, and every time we saw an ambulance). We listened to praise music in the car. We volunteered in our community. We spent vacation time doing medical mission work. And we studied our Bibles, well, religiously.

We were *faithful*.

Looking back, I realize how incredibly conservative it was. And how intense it was. And how much I ingested it. I actually remember praying privately to God (in Jesus's name) the night before the state tournament basketball games—not for victory, not for strength to handle whatever happened, not that we would all do our best and glorify Him, but that He would please delay His second coming until *after* the championship because I really wanted to win this thing before the apocalypse hit.

I also recall being targeted once by a boy I knew. I was at my family's country club, where I had no school friends. As a pack of his buddies watched, he said, "Kristi goes to that strange religious school. She's a *Christian* Kristi, isn't that right, *Christian* Kristi?" As he taunted, he picked up a handful of mulch and threw it at me. As I brushed mulch out of my eyes, picked it out of my hair, and listened to the laughter of his friends, I did not think, *I am going to toss this asshole in the pool.* Instead, I experienced a wave of relief. I had finally been "persecuted for righteousness' sake." That meant (according to Matthew 5:10) that I was headed to the Kingdom of Heaven for sure.

One of the strange things about it was that, at the time, my family felt religiously liberal to me. Spiritually progressive. And we were—compared to the only other people I knew. I knew my extended family (some of whom had refused to attend the "mixed wedding" of my Protestant dad and my Catholic mother), and I knew what was taught at my ultraconservative Church of Christ school.

I liked my school. I loved their athletic program. And almost everyone there was very good to me. But the school was next-level conservative: a strict dress code, no female pastors, no instrumental church music (because instruments are not mentioned in New Testament scripture), no spiritual celebration of Christmas (because the Bible does not declare December 25 to be the exact date of Christ's birth), and no dancing—not even a prom (like the movie *Footloose*). Our cheerleaders wore knee-length culottes instead of short skirts. And there were chapel services twice on Sunday, once on Wednesday evening, and every day while we were at school.

It was well-known that my family was on the progressive end of this community. Our church (the one with my grandfather's name on the stained-glass window) had a piano. This was sinful, according to the beliefs of my school. We did not attend services on Wednesday evenings (shocking). My family danced at parties (outrageous). We celebrated a spiritual Christmas (complete with a nativity). My parents allowed boys and girls to swim at the same time while wearing modern bathing suits in our pool. My mother grew up consuming real wine at communion in her Catholic church, and she did not agree with the school church's ban on all things alcoholic. Neither of my parents drank during my childhood, but we occasionally ate at restaurants that also housed bars. Together, all of this made us the liberal family at my school (which was *tiny*; there were only forty-two kids in my grade, so there was no flying under the radar).

Most of my teachers disregarded these differences. But school policies did not. This impacted my brother more than it did me. As a male, he would typically have been in the rotation to lead chapel. Instead, his name was removed from the list. (As a female, I was relegated to the pew regardless, so it wasn't as obvious that my family beliefs—along with my gender—excluded me from the pulpit.)

Still, there was the occasional teacher or classmate who felt obligated to point out the error of my family's ways directly to me. In elementary school, a classmate told me that her dad—a minister—prayed for my soul every evening at dinner. She wanted me to know that, as long as I was still alive, there was time to join her dad's church and be saved.

In high school, a Bible teacher in my Church of Christ school actually designed a course around what was wrong with other Christian denominations. (We didn't even discuss other religions, which were so remote they were not considered.) Each week we examined a different denomination, listed all of the things it got wrong, and memorized them so we could earn a high mark on Friday's quiz.

It was during this course that I finally cracked, on the day we discussed my family's denomination. My teacher knew I attended services there, and he told the class it meant I was going to hell.

"Hell?" I asked him, wanting to make sure I had heard correctly. "Me?"

"Yes, *hell*," the Bible teacher confirmed.

"Well, then . . ." I responded, finally putting down my pencil and raising my eyes to meet his directly. "I'll save you a seat by the fire."

By then I was known as a good student and a star athlete. I was well respected. I was relatively quiet in classes I wasn't leading (which meant, as a female, I was always quiet during male-led Bible). I *never* got in trouble in high school—until that day, when I pulled out all the stops on my very first transgression and told the *Bible teacher* I would see him in hell.

Cue a trip to the principal's office, where both of my parents would eventually join us for a conference with the administration.

~

"What were you *thinking*?" my mother asked me later.

"No," my father interjected. "This is *not* about what she was *thinking*. This is about what she *said*."

My words. My thoughts. Two distinct issues.

My father addressed the words.

He told me I needed to learn how to keep quiet and get what I needed out of situations without biting hands that could feed me. What I needed from this class was an A. So I was going to sit there and write down what was expected—even if it meant listing everything an ignorant teacher thought was wrong with our religion. And I was going to say nothing—even if it meant staying silent while our family was repeatedly condemned.

My mother addressed the thoughts.

I was not going to see my teacher in hell. I wasn't going to hell, and neither was he. Because we both believed in Jesus.

~

I need to pause here and issue about a thousand disclaimers.

I no longer believe what I was raised to believe as a kid. I still consider myself a Christian, but what that identifier means to me now is vastly different from what it meant during my childhood.

Back then, it meant following a Jesus who spoke through inerrant scripture and guided through horrific guilt and served as some sort of exclusive pass to eternal bliss. Back then, I was taught that exclusive pass was for those who embraced Jesus and denied everything else, including themselves.

Do. Not. Trust. Yourself.

As a child, I was taught that we must not trust our own nature. I was taught that we are evil at heart. I was taught the we-are-all-tainted doctrine of original sin.

I was taught that I had to choose between trusting myself and trusting Jesus. Either-or. Pick a side. Declare your loyalty. The number of ways this message was imparted to me would astound you. I was required to memorize verses, sing scripture, study theological terms, and live it out.

I learned that "He who trusts his own heart is a fool" (Proverbs 28:26a).

I sang a bit of scripture, which reminded me good disciples would

Deny themselves and
take up their cross and
follow [Jesus]

(La da dippity da, dee dippity da!)
Matthew 16:24 (NIV)

I was told that the path to *joy* was right there in the word, as an acronym: Jesus *first*. Others *next*. Yourself *last*.

I could go on and on. For example, 2 Corinthians 1:9 was quoted to teach me that "We should not trust in ourselves but in God who raises the dead." The message was clear, loud, and consistent: *Do not trust yourself.* Do you hear me? We do not follow our nudges or impulses or passions. We follow Jesus. We trust in Him.

These were not just words to me; I lived them out, especially during my teens and early twenties. And it impacted my life in every arena.

It led me into ascetic exercises, as I attempted to deny myself comforts.

It led me into medicine, as I attempted to deny my actual professional interests.

It led me into and out of relationships, as I tried—and failed—to make myself limit true marriage prospects to only Christians.

Eventually, I would reevaluate the entire concept of "self" in spirituality. But this didn't happen in my teens or my early twenties. In those days, I thought I had to choose between myself and Jesus, and I chose Him.

~

Self-denial impacted me in many ways, but it also had consequences well beyond my personal journey.

It is time for a confession.

Back then, I did not just deny myself. I also shrugged as people around me—people I cared about—denied themselves. This included members of the LGBTQIA+ community.

I was raised to believe that expressing LGBTQIA+ identities was a sin. In my hometown, LGBTQIA+ identifiers made some people preachy. It made other people squirm. It made a lot of people hide.

It made me shrug.

I shrugged because back then, and in that setting, it was a very ordinary thing—the idea that people should repress their natures. In fact, for the entirety of my youth, I was repeatedly and explicitly taught that every single person on earth had something in their nature they were supposed to spend a lifetime fighting.

My teachers helped me figure out what was problematic in my own nature. According to them, I was stubborn and selfish. And I refused to defer to men—even in church, where speaking up as a woman was a sin. And my instincts were terrible. I felt nudged into careers and places that were not for me (because I was female or White or Christian or could "do better"). I was told to ignore or fight those nudges—even the ones that seemed loving—because God wanted me to use my resources and my talents elsewhere.

I spent the bulk of my early life being trained to fight my own nature. Being told to ignore my inner voice. Being asked to trust someone else's map instead of learning to read my inner compass.

So I was not outraged when LGBTQIA+ persons in my town were asked to do the same. It was just part of it. I commiserated. I had to fight my nature—what was considered "unacceptable"—and they had to fight theirs. We all had our challenges.

Of course, the stakes were higher for members of the LGBTQIA+ community. I could go into statistics about depression and suicide rates among teens who are asked to fight such a big part of themselves (while simultaneously fighting what I now realize was discrimination and hate). I am not trying to say I understand what they went through. I ignored some parts of myself for too long, but it is nowhere near the same scale.

Once I left my hometown, I met members of the LGBTQIA+ community who were not fighting their true natures. *Good for them*, I thought. And then I stopped thinking about it. I was already proud of being color-blind. I would be orientation-blind as well. I would hang out with everyone. He's Black. *Shrug*. She's a lesbian. *Shrug*. I did not think of people in those ways.

I thought of them as friends. And I was too wrapped up in my own issues to think much about things I wasn't dealing with directly.

So, I continued to shrug.

Looking back, I see how much damage my shrugging probably did.

People knew I was a Christian. They knew I was from the Deep South. They knew the culture I grew up in. They probably assumed I harbored certain views. *Maybe parts of me did.* But I wasn't yet examining any of it. Instead, I thought I was so very progressive, just being friends.

I do not shrug anymore.

Instead, I am apologizing and declaring myself as an ally. I am writing about my own failings in the hopes that it helps identify the root of a very big problem and points to a potential solution.

Over the course of my life and the writing of this book, I struggled to accept some very simple truths about myself: my career interests, political affiliations, day-to-day encounters, and several other things that others might not see as a big deal but were significant to me and my family.

Learning to celebrate those things about myself freed me to be me. Freed *me* to celebrate who *I* am. It also freed me to finally—after years of shrugging—celebrate other people for who *they* are.

My point is this: Maybe the first step to stopping all the hate and judgment in society is to stop hating and judging ourselves. Maybe if we realize it's good to be who we are, we'll realize it's good for other people to be who they are as well.

～

When you do not trust yourself, you rely on pathways mapped out by others. You stay on the paved road.

～

What roads were paved for you in your late teens or early twenties, and what roads were restricted?

My parents paved the road to college and to medical school. If anyone tried to put up a roadblock on those particular paths, my family bulldozed the barriers. My mom's earlier experience with gender discrimination meant she was particularly eager to clear and pave a path for her eldest daughter.

For example, my folks hired a Latin teacher for our high school and anonymously paid her entire salary because they thought it would help us on the SATs. When, despite the new language program, our school still lagged behind others academically, my parents gave their children two options: Enroll at an elite boarding school during the school year or spend your summers taking classes at top universities. My brother transferred, finishing high school in residence at an elite private academy. I stayed but attended summer classes at Johns Hopkins and Duke.

Once my test scores and summer résumé were in place, we began touring colleges—mainly up North, even though it required more plane tickets and hotel stays and would eventually create geographic distance within the family. Location was important, my mother felt, because even though things might have changed, she could not risk her daughter experiencing the same discrimination she had felt twenty years earlier as a pre-med woman at a southern school.

So I was headed out, with my well-polished résumé, eventually to attend college at Princeton.

Yes, my access roads were paved, and the tolls were paid for me. But it came with a side of enormous expectations.

It was expected that I would pay close attention to the map in front of me.

That I would work extraordinarily hard.

That I would do incredibly well.

And that, more than anything else, I would stay on the paved road.

When I attempted to leave that road, I encountered resistance. There were guardrails put in for my own protection. There were also mile markers I was not allowed to eschew. I did not want to join a sorority. I did not want to have a formal (or any) debut. I did not want to take pre-med classes. Ultimately, each of these paved roads became battlegrounds upon

which I fought with my parents. I won some of the battles (no sorority), lost others (made my hometown debut), and discovered how high
the stakes could get when I announced, near the end of high school, as we
were touring colleges, that I wanted to become a *teacher* instead of a doctor.

My parents reminded me of my aunt's struggle, trying to raise two children alone on a preschool teacher's salary. They told me that if the dream
of being an educator persisted, I could eventually stop doctoring and teach
at a medical school. They told me that they would send me to Princeton
and pay for it all, but *not* if I planned to become a teacher. If I wanted
to teach, I could get my degree somewhere less expensive—and local. In
my mother's words, "It's not necessary to head North if you're going into
teaching; that profession has *always* been open to girls."

The bottom line was that I had a choice to make—and I didn't yet have
quite enough vision to see other possibilities. I was seventeen years old. I
wasn't sure what I wanted professionally, but I knew I would love to go to
an all-expenses-paid and faraway college. I agreed to the terms.

~

My parents wanted me to be happy (even if they were very misguided
about what would accomplish that goal), but it is important to note that
they did not focus exclusively on their own children. They could have
hired us a private Latin tutor; instead, they hired a Latin instructor for the
entire school and personally funded her position (without recognition or
fanfare). My dad also offered free counsel, glowing recommendation letters
and, on one occasion, résumé-building paid time in his office for a local
teen who wanted to attend medical school.

My parents cared.

Are we going to fault them for looking out for their own children,
when they also tried to help others?

Still, it's tricky—this whole idea of roadblocks and paved roads.

~

Pick a kid. What roads are paved for them? What roads are restricted?

I have now spent many years teaching, and I know how widely the answers to those questions vary. Some kids have a paved road into a gang. Others have a paved road into an Ivy League college. Others have a paved road into a trade or family business. Still others seem to have no paved roads; they are neglected, forgotten, and ignored.

Where are the roadblocks? Well, it depends. What color is the kid? Does the family speak English? Are there reliable mentors? Any time and money to develop skills? How about an awareness of opportunities?

Paved roads provide access. Eliminating roadblocks provides choice.

As a society, we need to eliminate roadblocks for more people. We need to have a much more diverse array of paved roads.

~

If you went back in time and told my parents to stop paving roads for me, they would have seen you as a roadblock and knocked you down.

But what if you went back in time and encouraged them to listen to their daughter?

What if you went back in time and encouraged me to listen to myself? Or my mother to listen to herself? To live out her own dream instead of foisting it upon her child?

Is there any chance we would have noticed earlier that expectations had become corrals? And that even our "nice" corrals imposed constraints that forced us to break ourselves in order to fit? And that society had lots of not-so-nice corrals that were breaking others?

Maybe.

~

Once, during my senior year, my father and I were in a school parking lot after one of my basketball games. Our team would soon be playing in its fifth straight state championship tournament. I was named the MVP in two of those state tournaments and was being recruited by several colleges. One evening, just after a big win, we were sitting in the car, waiting for traffic to clear so we could head home. As we sat there, my dad turned to me and said, "I want to say this at least once, very clearly. I love you whether or not you play basketball in college. So, if you don't really want to play, then *don't*."

It was one of the best moments of my life. It mattered. Even though I loved the game. Even though I wanted to play in college. Even though I was desperate to hear him apply the same sentiment to other arenas. (Hearing "I love you whether or not you become a doctor" would have been particularly nice.) But even hearing it in that one space provided so much air and light—and forged something really important between my dad and me: an uncorralled connection.

~

I have hinted at how much I loved basketball but need to really do it justice. I *loved* to play—anytime, anyplace, anybody. I was serious about the sport and about the training it required. I worked on my skills constantly. I even had a suitcase with a special compartment for my basketball. I once took it on a European tour with my family and did ballhandling drills on train platforms across the continent. My mother wasn't entirely sure it was appropriate to be bouncing a ball in such a setting. My father said if we attracted much more attention, he was going to put out a tip jar.

The high school I attended was private, but we engaged in the more competitive public-school league and were very successful. I practiced and played against older girls who were good, and I became good also. With that came state championships and personal accolades—including lots of state and some national recognition, as well as my jersey number retired and displayed on the gym wall—but what I really loved was the game itself. Years later, the passion I felt for basketball as a teenager would be the standard by which I measured other things. I would know what it was to be *all in* on something—and recognize when that was missing in careers and relationships—because I had experienced being all in for basketball.

My parents were my biggest supporters. They sent me to camps, arranged holidays around team schedules, and dragged my siblings to some truly hole-in-the-wall gyms to cheer me on. They also watched as I struggled through injuries and navigated sometimes tricky relationships with teammates and coaches.

One coach was particularly harsh, but I begged my parents not to confront him. My dad swallowed his words in a way that pacified his daughter, but possibly upset his stomach. My parents only spoke with this coach once about his methods, and they did it in the least aggressive way possible. They took him to lunch, said they had noticed he often seemed extraordinarily upset with me, and they wanted to make sure I had not done something disrespectful to prompt it. "No," he told them. "She's fine." No further words between them were exchanged on the matter. But plenty of words were hurled in my direction.

The worst moment was prompted by a mistake I made during the final five minutes of a game. We were winning, and during a time-out, my coach said, "Do not foul. Does everyone hear me? Play defense, but do *not* foul."

Well, of course, I fouled someone. Not on purpose, but still. My coach was absolutely livid. He pulled me out of the game, but when I went to sit on the bench, he stopped me. "No," he yelled. "After a mistake like that, you don't deserve to be in the game. You don't even deserve to be on the bench with the team. *You* can watch the rest of the game with *them*." He pointed to the small group of our fans who had traveled to this away gymnasium. I was directed—at full volume—to walk around the court and up several rows of bleachers to sit in my uniform with the crowd. So, amid jeers from my opponents and looks of horror from my parents, I walked over, climbed up, and sat down.

The coach's wife once told me she was sorry about his approach to me. She said he had a lot going on in his own life. She thought he targeted me because I was a player who wouldn't yell back, but also wouldn't quit.

One teammate—a player who played much less than me—offered a different perspective. After a particularly harsh diatribe was pointed at me in practice, she found me sitting in the locker room with my head in my hands. "If it makes you feel any better," she offered, "at least he thinks you're worth tearing into. He never yells at me. He doesn't think I have any potential, so what would be the point?"

Her position was worse than mine. I had an expert coach's attention, and if I could sift the instruction from the verbal barrage, I would improve immensely. That was all I cared about. But my parents cared about me, and it was miserable for them.

I only pushed back verbally once in my time playing for him, and I did it in the most respectful way I could manage—not because I was some bastion of decorum, but because he controlled part of the activity that I felt controlled my happiness. We were playing a game and had applied what's known as a full-court press to the other team. I was on the front of that press, closest to the basket. Our press was so effective against this opponent that we stole the ball multiple times in the first four minutes of the game. After each steal I scored a layup, which meant I had over a dozen points halfway through the first quarter.

My coach called a time-out to berate me at full volume. In a voice that bounced off the walls of our home arena, he called me a selfish ball-hog. How else could I have scored that many points only four minutes into the game? I would not be going back onto the court that evening, because if I was there, no one else would get a chance to play. I could sit on the bench and learn some respect for my team.

That night at home, my father—who recorded almost every game—sat with me and watched the first four minutes. He was clear in his assessment: I had scored on wide-open layups early in the game. Several were after stealing the ball myself, several were after teammates passed it to me because—due to the layout of our press—I was the person closest to the basket. None were inappropriate shots.

I told my dad I would talk to the coach. The next day, I gave him the film and asked him to show me which shots of mine he was upset about so I could adjust my attempts in the future. We arranged to meet in his office that afternoon.

As I arrived for our afternoon meeting, a teammate was leaving. I didn't think much of it until my coach grunted at me, "I saw the film; your shots were fine. We're done talking about it. There are people with bigger issues." I swallowed my irritation. A brief private acknowledgment after a public dressing down that could sow dissention among teammates? It was frustrating. But there was nothing to be done about it. Besides, it turns out there *were* people with bigger things happening. The teammate I had seen exiting his office as I entered didn't come to practice that day. Or go to her school ever again. She was pregnant at the age of sixteen.

~

Perspective is an interesting thing. I just told that story the way I experienced it as a teenager, focusing on the game I loved and a coach who taught me to play it, and being stopped in my tracks by the announcement that my teammate was pregnant. What I will realize later is that the one line of the story that will eventually matter the most to me is all but buried among the other happenings: *My dad swallowed his words in a way that pacified his daughter, but possibly upset his stomach.*

At the time, my dad's stomach pains were glossed over—certainly not dwelled on in front of the children. My parents did not dwell on my teammate's pregnancy, either. There was a brief mention of how hard things were going to be for her, but no outreach and no discussions about sex. Looking back now, I wish I had taken the initiative: called her, talked, listened, or asked what she needed. So quickly it seemed she was simply gone—not from our area, as she still lived one town over, but from every circle I encountered. And I never stepped far outside those circles, a stasis I have come to regret.

~

TV was different back then, in the 1990s. My family had four channels. All of them turned into "snow" (or images of a waving flag) at midnight. There was no Netflix queue. No DVR. No Amazon Prime or Hulu. No channels designed especially for kids or for teens (or for any niche, really).

If you wanted to watch something, you had to be in front of the TV when it aired. So did everyone else. This heightened anticipation for certain things (a new episode this evening!) and made debriefing more fun: There was no concern about spoilers, because anyone who was going to watch had done so last night.

On April 22, 1990, at the age of fifteen, I flipped on the TV and watched *The Earth Day Special*. It was on ABC, and it was remarkable. Over the course of two hours, famous folks told the story (through skits they threaded together) of an ailing Mother Earth. Folks like Bette Midler, Neil Patrick Harris, Danny DeVito, the Muppets, E.T., and Bugs Bunny discussed problems like pollution and deforestation. They also discussed solutions like recycling.

Back in 1990, this was breaking news to a girl like me—a high school kid in Alabama. For the first time, I heard the planet was in trouble, and there were things we could do to help.

The very next day, a friend and I cofounded a local environmental club and named it EARTH (Environmental Awareness Reaches the High Schools). Our focus was recycling. We were a low-tech operation, determined to reuse as many items as possible. This meant dumpster diving for cardboard boxes to use as recycling bins in each of our school's classrooms. One day, we loaded too many of the foul-smelling containers into the back of my family station wagon before slamming the door shut. A sharp cardboard corner was poking out and shattered the back window of my mom's car.

My mother was very gracious about it, and I really appreciated the support. It was the first of many recycling programs I would run over the course of my teens, twenties, and thirties, and it paved the way for the environmental activism I would continually engage in going forward.

~

Speaking of my mother, I was constantly learning from her. Not just because she was there establishing norms like "always have a book with you" and "it would be interesting to know how that works." And not just because she made us stop at every science museum and historical marker we passed, or because we kept a set of encyclopedias and vocabulary flash cards in the same room as the dinner table.

I learned from my mother because she was engaged, and she engaged her children—every day, and in every arena. She taught me how to thread a bobbin. How to change a tire. How to add a door to our previously open-air mailbox after we went to grab the mail one day and discovered a snake. She insisted that if we were going to use something, we should know how it worked. And if we were going to view something, we should do it with an educated eye. Back in 1986, we anticipated the arrival of Halley's Comet for months. Our enthusiasm was evidenced by the fact that when a new pet arrived around the same time, my siblings and I all decided together that "Halley" would be the perfect name for the dog.

But I also learned from my mother because she made a point to talk to me. Not about everything, and not always saying the things I wanted to hear, but the lines of communication were open.

I remember one conversation in particular. She wanted me to do something—maybe go somewhere with a group she admired or dress in a particularly popular fashion—and I was resisting. "Ughhhh" I remember her saying. "You are the most *predictable* person I know."

The comment struck me because it was so unexpected. I was OK being called rebellious or unreasonable. But *predictable*? Had I just been called "predictable" by the woman who seemed surprised by my choices at every turn?

Sheep were predictable. *Lemmings* were predictable. *My mother* was predictable. She would be in whatever outfit was most fashionable, whatever group was most prestigious, and whatever club was most elegant. I was the *opposite* of all those things.

"Exactly," she told me. "All I have to do is look at the crowd, and I know you'll be headed in the opposite direction. *Predictable.*"

Her words hit me like a ton of bricks. She was right. If I lived in defiance of the crowd (or in defiance of a mother who looked to the crowd for what was proper, fashionable, or expected), my direction was still dictated by others. If I defined myself in exact opposition to an entity, that entity was still controlling my path. *Defiance* meant *different*, but still *dependent*. If I wanted to be independent, I needed to think independently. My choices should reflect *me*, which meant they might sometimes—even by coincidence—align with the crowd.

And on occasion, they might align with my mother.

~

I was an odd mix of elements in high school: settled and successful on the surface, but restless underneath. I am not sure my itch to unsettle was visible to anyone except my parents and two closest friends. Everyone else saw the student with straight A's, the athlete setting records, and the kid in the right outfit with the bright future and correct answer. They saw a girl who was friendly—a bit on the fringe socially and spiritually, but seemingly by choice.

Did they notice the times I went quiet? I doubt it. But it is those moments of silence I remember most. I particularly remember those times I could have said something and chose not to.

I kept quiet for the remainder of my high school Bible classes. I kept quiet instead of supporting those who struggled with identity. I kept quiet when I saw discrimination or heard derogatory slurs.

And I kept quiet about an event that occurred a few weeks before I left for college, at a meet and greet for Princeton students.

I was driving to the event and was very excited. It was an overnight gathering hosted by a Princeton alum at his lake house, about three hours from my hometown. I wouldn't know anyone there upon arrival, but that was OK. The whole point was to ensure I would know someone when I arrived on campus in a few weeks. I spent a wonderful day meeting other students, riding on the alum's boat, and swimming in the water. While out on the boat, the alum showed us where they had church services on the beach the next morning and invited us to attend. I told him I would be up and ready.

During dinner, we turned on the TV to watch the 1992 summer Olympics. They were covering gymnastics, and the announcer mentioned that the next event would be the men's rings. The conversation turned to the difference between men's and women's gymnastics. Someone in our group noted that female gymnasts did not compete on the rings. Someone else pointed out the incredible arm strength those rings required.

Eventually, the host went to bed while several students stayed up swimming and chatting. One by one, folks trickled off until it was me and one other student—a male. He was attractive—smart, funny, and good-looking. He was also athletic, already guaranteed a spot on the varsity football team. Initially, I was flattered when he leaned in for a kiss. But then it progressed too far. He leaned into me, pushing me onto my back. When I used my arms to push back, he grasped my forearms and pinned them down next to me as his head dipped toward my swimsuit-clad chest. I struggled—told him no and considered the ramifications of yelling to stop him. Everyone would run back into the room. I would be safe—for now. But what would my life be like once I arrived on campus? I would be the girl who led on and then called out the varsity football recruit. I would be hated by the team and the people they knew, on a very small campus. And our host for the weekend—who thought the next time he saw me would be on the dock waiting to ride to church in his boat—what would he think when he found me on the couch in my swimsuit underneath the football recruit instead?

The football player held me there, breathing hot air on my chest and suggesting he could do whatever he wanted since I was unable to physically resist him. He was correct. I was pinned—unable to move either arm. The phrase he uttered before letting me go and leaving is the one that sticks with me: "Your arms aren't strong enough to move mine. And *that* is why they don't let women do the rings in gymnastics."

~

I have thought about that moment a lot over the years. In my thirties, I relived it while watching some *Law and Order*–type TV show that—on the surface—seemed to have little in common with my personal experience.

In the show, as a villain is interrogated, he experiences a flashback to his childhood. A girl from his neighborhood was missing, and the whole town was searching for her. He—alone—finds her, trapped and treading water in the bottom of a forgotten well. When she sees him, her eyes brighten with hope.

He can encourage that hope. But he chooses not to. Instead, as she watches, he musters a string of spit in his mouth. He lets that stream of saliva drop down . . . down . . . down between the walls of the well—and into the water that will eventually consume her.

The moment is clearly about exerting (his) and draining (her) power. As he relishes the memory, the villain explains that he loves seeing the moment when a girl goes from hopeful to helpless. He loves watching the light in a woman's eyes drain out.

It occurred to me that some light drained from my eyes that night at the party—and that the football player enjoyed watching it happen while he pinned me down.

~

I did not tell my parents about that moment. Instead, I went home, had a few more meals with my family, and packed my things. My parents bought me everything I needed, and as I was loading my things into the car my father handed me his olive-green sweater—the one I was always asking to borrow. It was the same color as those towels he covered me with as a toddler.

And with that benediction, I was off to Princeton.

Growth

COLLEGE YEARS

People sometimes make assumptions about me when they hear I attended Princeton. When I was seventeen, the mother of a friend in my hometown asked where I was headed to college. When I told her, she immediately responded, "Ohh, I guess you must think you're too good to go to school around here."

It bothered me. It still bothers me. Ever since, I have been careful to introduce myself in other ways before listing affiliations, including alma maters.

~

It is useful, having a Princeton degree. But that's not why I went there.

I knew I wanted to go away to school. To experience something different. To be around people who were excited about things that excited me. I wanted to be somewhere folks from all over the world gathered to read and think and talk about what we learned. I was—and am—idealistic and bookish. I was also a college kid who relished the freedom, the parties, and my first game of beer pong. It was wonderful to have a space where I could be all of those things.

I liked that Princeton was small, a place where I could read an editorial in the student newspaper and then realize the editor was sitting across from me at breakfast. I liked that everyone was required to write a thesis before graduation—that people living next door to me would be engaged in wildly different types of independent creation or research. But mainly, I liked that I could be all aspects of myself in all settings. I didn't have to be a student during the day, and a person after hours, and an athlete on the court. Everything bled together.

I had discovered that possibility during a recruiting trip to campus. It was part of a weekend-long visit, where I stayed in a dorm room and danced at a party and ate in a cafeteria and watched a basketball practice. Near the end of that practice, the team was hustling and exhausted, but not done. The coach told her players they had exactly sixty seconds for a water break, and the team manager started the arena clock, which measured the countdown: 59, 58, 57 . . .

The girls sprinted to grab their water bottles, all of which were department-issued and identical with one exception: Each orange bottle had a different jersey number written on it in black Sharpie.

One of the players caught my attention as she scrambled to find the bottle with her number. She picked up one bottle, realized it was the wrong one, and handed it to a teammate. She picked up another—also not hers—and passed it along. She picked up a third, and when she realized she still had the wrong bottle she yelled at the top of her lungs in thirsty frustration, "Water, water, every where, Nor any drop to drink!" It was a quote from *The Rime of the Ancient Mariner*, screamed across a gymnasium.

Hearing her, I felt the empathy any athlete would over the thirsty frustration. But I also felt instant delight. She was quoting *Coleridge*. During *basketball practice*. At full volume. In that moment I knew this was a place where ideas traveled with folks—and might explode in unexpected arenas. The concept thrilled me and drew me into the school.

～

Attempting to make good on the deal with my parents, I worked hard on my pre-med track at Princeton. That meant the bulk of my schedule was filled with science requirements, many of which had afternoon labs. I had just enough space left to major in history and take a few interesting electives. It was hard skipping over pages of philosophy and literature during course registration in favor of another chemistry class. But, for the most part, I focused on the positive. I was meeting people from all over the world, playing basketball with incredible athletes, laughing with friends in gorgeous, gothic dorm rooms, finding inspiration for unique summer experiences, and learning all the time—not just in the classroom. I liked it.

Still, there were hard moments.

~

Here is a hard moment, experienced during a college summer. One professor (not from Princeton) made a pass at me, touching me in ways that were suggestive. It was not an assault, but it made me uncomfortable, and we were in an environment I did not feel I could escape.

The summer after my freshman year, I took a French study-abroad class through another university. This school was closer to home. I visited my family, completed several weeks of coursework, and then traveled with this professor and a group of new classmates to France.

The professor was a well-respected married peer of my parents. When not sharing his language expertise with students, he shared an artistic ministry with several churches.

During the days, we traveled as a group through Paris. After hours, we were free to roam. After following my classmates to the Hard Rock Café one evening, I broke off. I did not want to eat hamburgers and listen to loud American music. Instead, I got a small table by myself at a bistro. It was not the Café de la Paix—where it is rumored that if you sit long enough you can see the whole world go by—but it was as close as I would get on this trip, and I did not want to miss a chance to see who or what the world might bring me.

My professor saw me there and admired my willingness to soak up a more authentic French experience. It was late, and since (in his words) "even the City of Lights has its dark corners," he offered to escort me back to the hotel. For safety. As much as I would have loved to stay at the bistro, I recognized the wisdom in accepting his offer.

Until he began rubbing my arms, up to my shoulders. He pointed out that in addition to being my professor, he was a "red-blooded American male just like every other." And me—well, I was "so smart and so eager to learn," unlike some of his students.

I was stunned. Moments before, I had been stationary and hopeful and curious and exhilarated about what both Paris—and life—would bring my way if I just got away from the noise, paused, and remained open. Now I was moving away from whatever this was at lightning speed, grateful to see a classmate near the hotel entrance and determined to spend all future Paris evenings at the Hard Rock Café with the group. *What the hell just happened?*

The next day, I purchased a phone card and broke away from the pack long enough to make a private international call to my parents—no small feat given the time change, language barrier, and unfamiliar phone protocols. I finally managed to get my parents on the line, relayed the story, and revealed that I was upset and very uncomfortable—and scared, to be quite honest.

My parents told me I would be fine as long as I stayed with the group, and that I couldn't make trouble for this professor because he determined my grade.

This experience is reminiscent of the one I had the previous summer with the football player. In both moments, the light in my eyes was at its brightest and most hopeful when someone more powerful did something to snuff it out. It is also reminiscent of the moment in my Bible class. An authority figure had come at me in a way that felt threatening, and I was told that if I didn't want to be punished by these men, I needed to keep quiet.

~

Years later, when Brett Kavanaugh was nominated for the Supreme Court of the United States of America, Christine Blasey Ford would come forward and state that Kavanaugh sexually assaulted her when they were both teenagers. My mother, who is staunchly pro-life (and therefore wanted Kavanaugh on the Supreme Court) said to me: "I don't believe her. Because if something like that really happened, she would have said something at the time."

Really? I thought. *You can say this to me, after telling my teenage self to keep quiet?*

It is difficult to comprehend—and to process.

~

It was during college that I learned a few things about feminine power— including its power to attract unwanted attention. It was also during college that I began to notice inconsistencies in my application of feminine strength.

On the one hand, I had been raised to shatter glass ceilings. I would be a doctor, and gender would not be an issue. I would also be a force on the basketball court. Although I never lived up to my high school hype, I did play on Princeton's Division I varsity women's basketball team for four years, and I could absolutely carry my weight on any coed recreational court.

I visited those courts frequently, looking for pickup games. On one occasion, when a large guy tried to exclude me, I felt very comfortable challenging him to a game of one-on-one.

"First to four by ones," I told him. "Winner gets to stay and play."

When he refused to play "man versus little girl" (his words), I pushed harder. "This 'little girl' is not leaving," I told him. "The fact that you're *bigger* doesn't mean that you're *better*, and the fact that you have a *dick* doesn't make you a *man*."

Those may sound like the words of a warrior. But I now realize that during those years, I only battled on the court, where I had been given permission to fight. Off the court—particularly in relationships and religious environments—I had been taught that women should submit.

Every day I code-switched and lived out the lesson learned in my childhood: I could walk onto anyone's court like a tiger. But when I left it, I became a gazelle.

~

One day, my college friend Jim invited me to attend a church service. Initially I was enthusiastic. But then I found out there would be a woman in the pulpit, and I decided not to go. I told Jim that I did not want to get into a big debate about it. I just wanted to go to a church where I would not be distracted. I told him the whole issue just made me uncomfortable. Jim stared at me. "Right," he said. Then he narrowed his eyes. "Just out of curiosity, do you think the first White students in integrated schools were ever distracted or uncomfortable?"

He was correct—and speaking a vital truth I had to hear and remember. Being comfortable doesn't mean you're in the right space, and being uncomfortable doesn't mean you're in the wrong one.

I went with him to the church, where I heard a woman who was both inspired and inspirational. Five minutes into her sermon, it was so obvious she had something to teach all of us that everything I had learned about limiting the role of women in ministry was completely erased.

How could I have ever thought the pulpit should be restricted to men?

~

Two years before college, I had asked my parents if there was a way to spend a summer living among the Amish. There was something about living more simply that drew me. My mother shook her head. "Do you really think you could keep quiet at a barn raising?" she asked me. "Stay with the women as they set up the potluck? Not offer an idea to the barn-raising men?"

She had a point.

A year later, I told my mother I wanted to spend time in a nunnery. There was something about living differently that felt right. And, I told my mom, I could handle the vows of poverty, chastity, and obedience. "I'm sure you could handle vows to God," my mother responded, "but could you obey Mother Superior?"

Touché. Again.

In college, I parried. I called home and linked my idea of an alternate lifestyle to medicine. It was 1995. I was a junior at Princeton, and I had an idea for my last summer before graduation. I wanted to escape first-world comforts by spending nine weeks with medical missionaries in a small village halfway around the world.

It was a dilemma for my parents. They were relieved I was finally embracing a medical opportunity, but this particular opportunity terrified them. They had served as medical missionaries themselves, but always in secure clinics on the other side of tourist-filled Caribbean destinations. Those spaces were well-guarded enough that my siblings and I had always accompanied them, entertaining local children with Christian crafts and skits while the medical staff worked.

This was different. I wanted to go to Nigeria, and my specific location would have dangerous elements and limited communication. I could be off the grid for months while surrounded by disease in the village hospital and political conflict in my home district. Even the large airport where I would begin and end my journey was red-flagged—the only airport in the world that year to which the United States recommended its citizens *not* travel.

My parents voiced these concerns as I planned the trip, and I dismissed them. I was leaving from an airport near my college campus, and they had flown up to see me before my departure. They took me out to dinner and, before the food arrived, my mother absolutely broke down. When I told her this was a spiritual journey into living differently that I had to take, she told me it was *not*. It was the opposite of spiritual; it was *selfish*. Did I care about how it was impacting my family, who would be consumed with worry? Did I remember my father's stomach ulcers? Did I know those ulcers had formed when he was stressed about *me* in high school, and that they would certainly get much worse now? Did I know my Dad had just elicited a promise from my younger sister that she would never follow in my international footsteps with this sort of madness? The climax of the conversation came when my mother stopped yelling and started crying. She told me they had been required to purchase *body bag* insurance for my summer experience. "Do you know what that means?" she asked me. "It means we think you might *die*. We had to make sure that if that happens, someone would go to that village, retrieve your body, and fly it back to us—so we can *bury* you in our hometown."

It was awful. There was so much in that fear-filled conversation that it has taken me years to unpack it. My dad's ulcers were *my* fault? My spiritual journey was *selfish*? My life (to be daily offered to God working in hospitals I disliked) was now too precious to risk (working in the one hospital that drew me)?

These three questions took root in me, morphing into a quest for answers that consumed me for years. How do I choose a course if pursuing my own path hurts people I love? How can I worship in a space where some spiritual expressions are celebrated while others are judged? And what happiness am I allowed in this life while others are struggling out in the world?

But I was not there yet, answering those questions. Instead, I was on a plane to Nigeria.

~

My first night in rural Africa, a car crashed near our compound, and I witnessed doctors without personal protective equipment helping victims soaked in blood. I was scared—literally paralyzed by fear of exposure—and then so incredibly ashamed at my hesitation to help.

The next day, the guilt got me moving. Just across the compound's dirt driveway was an orphanage; I played with the children. Just down the dirt road was the hospital; I assisted patients in whatever small ways I could. On the hospital lawn, I met their families, who often camped out during a loved one's convalescence. On that lawn, I also met grass cutters (with scythes) who had lost their Achilles tendons to on-the-job injuries—and then lost their jobs when a concerned traveling physician donated a lawnmower. When one of the mower's parts mysteriously went missing, the men and their scythes returned, grateful to resume their paid work.

There was a little girl who hugged me, an HIV+ mother who collapsed in front of me, and a soldier who pointed his machine gun at me after a high-speed car chase. I was riding with a hospital administrator who had become frustrated with officials who collected tolls but never used the money to repair roads. On that day, after hitting a particularly bad crater, he chose to protest by speeding past a tollbooth. The chase ended with me staring into the barrel of a gun thinking, "Well that's it. I am going to die here. Today."

There was another scare, when our hospital was tear-gassed by the government. The local village was the actual target, but the wind shifted. On this day, I learned that tear gas is terrifying when you don't know what you're inhaling. I also learned that medical missionaries sometimes cuss like sailors at soldiers holding semiautomatic weapons.

I spent long days in the hospital wishing I could do more. I was able to fan flies away from open wounds. I was able to comfort children during difficult treatments. I was able to donate blood. But I couldn't *help* the way I wanted to.

I did love the patients. And I loved every moment I spent in the nearby village. During my first visit, one child dared another to touch me. Soon we were all sitting together, with even the littlest ones reaching for my hand to try to rub the white off my skin.

I did feel God there, sometimes. I cannot share the story of the time I felt Him most profoundly, but I have been given permission to say that the day was gut-wrenching. And that when a caretaker's heartbreak was interrupted by a tropical rainstorm, it felt more like a baptism. That was my first-ever moment of spiritual *wow*.

—

I also met God in other moments that summer.

One day I was sitting on the steps of the volunteer compound, bracing myself for another shift at the hospital. The sun was blazing hot, and the day was so bright I had to shade my eyes as an African woman approached along the dirt road.

As I squinted into the sunlight, she stopped a few steps away from my perch and—out of nowhere—offered to pray for me.

"I believe in prayer," she told me. "I have found that whatever I ask for, I receive."

Right, I thought.

But what I said was, "Prayer doesn't work that way for me. Honestly, I didn't know it worked that way for anybody."

She looked at me for a moment. Then she bowed her head, raised her arms, and said out loud, "Dear God, please make it rain to show us your power."

Truthfully, in that exact moment, I was embarrassed for her. And uncertain about what to do with myself. I was still sitting. The sun was still blazing. And still, there was not one cloud in the sky.

Until there was. One cloud, which settled right above us. Where did that come from? And on cue, it began to pour.

I stared at her.

She shrugged at me.

And in my mind, two thoughts materialized.

The first was, "I still don't fully buy it, but maybe God thinks I need a lesson more than she does." And the second was, "If I weren't so worried about ruining this incredible moment, I'd get her to start praying at the hospital ASAP."

~

I was only there for a summer. But that time in Nigeria—combined with extra gratitude I felt for my dad's doctors once I began to believe his GI bleeds were my fault—personalized my commitment to medicine. I began filling out medical school applications. In their essay sections, I wrote about the pull I felt toward underserved populations. In interviews, I described the patients I hoped I could help.

Did I ever actually want to be a doctor?

No.

But I stayed on that newly personalized, always-paved career road. Around that time, I came across a quote by E. B. White that summed up my thought process perfectly. He wrote, "I arise in the morning torn between a desire to improve the world and a desire to enjoy the world. This makes it hard to plan the day."

I bought into his either-or approach. I thought I could either do good (as a doctor) or be happy. With those as my options, I chose to do good.

~

Perhaps I could find a happy space *outside* the professional arena. Maybe within a relationship.

Malcolm and I began dating when I was a junior in college (before my time in Nigeria), and we were in a committed relationship for over two years. We met at our shared "eating club," a social and dining option unique to Princeton. Malcolm's heart was kind. His mind was brilliant. His wit was both disarming and charming.

It feels strange to mention that he was of mixed race (half-Black, half-White, with beautiful brown skin), since we didn't focus on it back then. At the time, our shared view that race should not matter was one of many things that made us compatible. For the most part, even after my summer in Africa, I remained color-blind. Despite that overall lack of perception, I did notice moments when race had an obvious impact. I was there on occasions Malcolm experienced prejudice, and I saw him handle those encounters with a grace I could never muster. On those occasions, I attributed each incident to individuals who could be changed one at a time. It had not yet occurred to me that there might be a systemic problem.

Race was not an issue in our relationship. It was ultimately religion that drove us apart, post-graduation. Once again, I thought I had to choose between being good (in a relationship I knew would nurture my Christian faith) and being happy (with Malcolm). That is a gross oversimplification, but it does speak to the pulls I felt at the time. And within the nuance, there was heartbreak. We both wanted to be our best selves; we both wondered if we could do that while in a relationship with each other. Eventually, that struggle subsumed our spark. But for several years—before we (mutually, sadly, and amiably) decided to part ways—we searched for a path we could walk together. During those years, Malcolm and I were a hopeful and happy team.

I first met Malcolm in the dining room of the eating club, a beautiful space filled with tall windows, ornate woodwork, and golden chandeliers. He was president of the club. I was a year younger and not a part of the group's regular rhythm, partly due to my athletic schedule. Many nights after basketball practice, I would sprint to dinner right as the buffet line was closing. Malcolm noticed and began setting aside choice items so I was not left with scraps if practice ran long. We got to know each other over reheated pasta, an hour after most club members departed. I told Malcolm I was impressed with his presidential attention to detail, making sure every member received sustenance. He replied by saying he was impressed with me. He later confessed that he was drawn in once he realized the girl sprinting in after practice several nights a week was the same girl who recently attended a club event and left a balled-up pair of socks on the table designated for gloves. (I couldn't find my gloves and wasn't going to bike over without something on my hands. This Alabama girl was often freezing in New Jersey.)

Malcolm and I connected. He liked me, not my status, not my affiliations or affluence or aspirations. He liked *me*. And I liked him. I liked the way he talked about his sister, the way he talked about his classes, the way he talked about his childhood—taking pride in the company he started in elementary school, touching up street numbers on the curb in his neighborhood. I liked the way he talked about life. I remember once telling him I had to make a decision and didn't like either of my options. "Create a third option," he told me, "and be ready to sell or defend it." That approach was as natural to him as breathing. It was me on some core level—the girl who saw socks where only gloves or bare hands existed previously—but I had never applied it at such high levels. I credit Malcolm for planting the seed of an idea that would grow within me much later. He suggested I could create counteroffers when confronting life choices. More than that, I could just go my own way and let the chips fall.

～

One time, when Malcolm and I were strolling through campus, we exchanged casual hellos with a football player. Post-exchange, I was quiet for a moment. Then I whispered, "That was him."

"What do you mean 'him'?" Malcolm asked, then saw I was teary. "Wait. *Him?* The football player? I didn't even really see what he looked like. Where did he go? Are you OK?"

He collected himself, then said very calmly, "I cannot believe we just had a polite encounter with that guy. I cannot believe I *smiled* at him. *Never again.*"

I was initially shocked by his reaction, then realized he was having a normal response. What was shocking was my own. Why had I been politely greeting someone who had pinned me down and taunted me?

Why had I allowed conflict aversion or some default sense of etiquette to trump my self-respect?

But Malcolm respected me too much to let it slide. After that, I adopted his mantra: *never again.*

~

Malcolm graduated a year before me and moved to a new city. We had a successful long-distance relationship throughout my senior year, and we held out hope that we could eventually close the geographic distance and find enough common spiritual ground.

In the meantime, I was navigating my last year at Princeton. I had learned quite a bit during college—both inside and outside the classroom—so I was reflecting on that, while also focusing on next steps. I had submitted my medical school applications and been offered several interviews, including one in my home state of Alabama.

I booked a flight and prepped for the interview, while also juggling school and athletic commitments. The juggle got harder when I was injured during basketball practice. I was diagnosed with a torn interosseous membrane, which meant I was hobbling around a snowy campus with a cast on my foot. My coach was sympathetic, wanting to help however she could. She knew about my interview and offered to drive me, along with my bags and crutches, to the airport.

My thoughts were swirling in ten thousand directions as we rode. I was on the exact path my parents wanted, interviewing at the same place my mother had dreamed about for her own career, and I was literally dragging at least one foot. But my coach had other things on her mind: basketball recruits.

She told me about one she had spoken to the previous evening. "This new kid can play," she extolled, "and I don't think admissions will be an issue; she's good at school and apparently writes a great essay. Just yesterday she told me about something she wrote for her English teacher. It was in response to the question, *What is the most important decision you will ever make?"*

Well, that got my attention. And the recruit's response (as conveyed by my coach) was one I will never forget.

Apparently, this recruit dismissed common replies to the question. She anticipated that many of her classmates would write about deciding who they would marry, what career they would pursue, what religion they would embrace, or—given their current age and focus—what college they would attend. But, this recruit argued, all of those decisions were ultimately less significant because they were all reversible. People could divorce, switch jobs, convert, or transfer schools.

This recruit argued that the most important decisions we make are the ones that are *irreversible.* Then she gave several examples: You cannot go back in time and change your mind about whether to hold the door open for that particular stranger. Or how to interact with that driver you encountered on the road. Or how you treated the waitress or the cabbie or the older gentleman who was moving too slowly. This recruit argued that *those* decisions were the most important ones—because they were the ones we could never go back and undo.

I have been thinking about that essay on and off for over twenty-five years.

I thought about it recently (in my forties) when there was a weather event in our community that sent everyone scrambling to the stores. Predictions were that we would be housebound for up to a week, and I wanted milk for the kids—particularly for my child who was seeing a specialist in an attempt to get up to a healthy weight and relied on whole milk as one of the few consistent sources of "desirable" calories. Of course, the store shelves were empty. But I was undeterred, actually climbing onto the lower portion of the fridge to see the farthest corner of the top shelf. Bingo. One gallon of whole milk remaining, way in the back. As I pulled it down, an elderly gentleman congratulated me. "Well, your search is done," he sighed. And then we parted ways.

I am haunted by that moment. Why did I not give it to him? My son had inspired my search, but he would have been OK without it for a few days. And I have no idea what it might have meant to that gentleman. Maybe nothing. Maybe some important calories. Or maybe just a reminder that he wasn't alone during an otherwise isolating storm. The point is that I will never know whether it would have been a big deal in his world, and there's no way for me to find out or fix it.

There are lots of important decisions. Reversing those typically considered to be the biggest may be doable, but often comes at a price. I don't know if I agree with the recruit. I don't even know if I agree with the idea that a decision's importance can be ranked. But I do know that casual encounters matter.

And it makes me wonder if the real question is: *What most defines you? Is it really who you choose to marry? What career you choose to pursue? What religion you espouse? What college you attend? Or is it—maybe— how you treat people on a daily basis?*

I don't know.

I don't even know the name of the recruit who wrote the essay.

~

Here's what I did know: I was getting on a plane and heading to the first of many medical school interviews—including this one in Alabama, and another one in New York City.

And the following year, I headed to the Big Apple for medical school.

EIGHT YEARS,
SEVEN LESSONS

The next eight years of my life—from age twenty-two to thirty—would teach me some valuable lessons (and also provide seeds that grew into lessons learned a few decades later).

The real me came alive during those eight years, and I began opening my eyes to the real world. Everything important shifted (or began uprooting so it could shift later) over the course of those eight years. It was jarring, invigorating, isolating, emotional, hopeful, unsettling, scary, and wonderful—all at once.

I changed. My career, faith, politics, outlook, and more morphed into the unexpected. And while I learned something during each shift and turn, I want to start by sharing what I learned about change itself.

Change comes with a cost.

For me, the price was relationships.

I had a few relationships that ended. Friendships that didn't survive walking away from the arenas where they had thrived. Romances that didn't survive me seeing things differently. For the most part, I was OK with the closures.

What I found more challenging were the relationships I wanted to continue as a different version of myself, such as the one I had with my mother.

If I could go back to the era when I upended all sorts of expectations, I like to think that I would have approached her with clarity and calm. I would have said, "This is me. I know it's not what you expected, but this new version of me is worthy of respect. How do we move forward?"

But self-discovery doesn't work like that. I didn't go off on some mountain and come back fully formed as a self-assured person seeking a new dynamic. It was messy. *I* was messy. And my mother cared, so she was there during moments of uncertainty (when I wondered if I was doing the right thing) and sadness (when I cried over the cost).

There were moments when I needed support and got questions. There were moments when I finally announced clarity and was met with concerns. There were moments when I simply screwed up—and came off as rebellious and judgmental—and my mom attempted to *mother* me, which I didn't much like as an adult in my twenties. Finally, there were moments when my mother clearly felt something was wrong with me on a very basic level. She questioned my sanity (I am sane). She speculated about repressed trauma (I was not secretly abused as a child). These questions and speculations were very upsetting and damaged our relationship.

When my mother told me she loved me, I sometimes thought, *Me? Really? Or some version of me that doesn't exist anymore? That you hope will come back and stop stirring up controversy at the dinner table?*

Eventually, I just stopped sharing my adventure stories and changing political views, which were fodder for arguments. After a while these silences spread into other arenas (because if my new career and politics frightened my family, there was no way I was going to discuss my new take on spirituality).

Ultimately, the silence consumed so many spaces that familial relationships I valued became more superficial. I didn't talk about bumps I encountered on my new road because I didn't want anyone to say, "Maybe it's a sign you should reconsider your choices." And I didn't share the beautiful vistas because I wasn't sure they would be celebrated. Becoming me was a process. And during those eight years, from age twenty-two to thirty, I explored, I learned, and I grew.

~

These lessons didn't happen cleanly or chronologically, so I am going to categorize what I learned by theme. While that will require a bit of hopping back and forth between eras, my hope is that I can snag some threads from each time period and weave them together into some sort of rope. Maybe that rope can be a guideline through portions of text. Maybe it can also become a lifeline during portions of my current midlife crisis.

CAREER COMPASS

I grew up knowing I was bound for medicine. My parents often told me that the doctor in the delivery room, just moments after I was born, commented on my long fingers.

"She's got the hands of a pianist," he told my father.

"Those are the hands of a *surgeon*," my father responded.

I was less than ten minutes old.

There was only one problem: I did not want to be a doctor. I wanted to be a teacher, or maybe a writer.

Cue the head pats. Teaching is *great*, I was told. But it's not for *you*. Neither is writing. Maybe both could be side gigs someday. But as a career, *medicine* was the clear way to go. My parents tried to convince me with arguments about professional and financial security, and with promises of intellectual and social fulfillment. Still, I resisted, until the conversation shifted to *service*. Somehow, I became convinced that medicine was the best way to help people and the only way I could truly serve the world. That limited perspective seems crazy to me now, but back then it didn't.

At that time, the pink-coat incident had been haunting me for over a decade, in increasingly dramatic ways. It was not what my mother had intended, but that exposure was like a small fire built in a forest. It was intended to provide warmth and light, but quickly blazed out of control. The shame of that day, combined with the lessons I received from my spiritual teachers—that being selfish was bad, listening to yourself was bad, trusting your instincts over your instructors was bad—melded into one thought: *That shivering child is an example of what will happen if I am selfish; real people will suffer, and I will feel awful.*

As my parents watched with concern, I took being selfless to the extreme. I admired ascetics. I eschewed possessions. I challenged my parents about our lifestyle: How could we live in this house and have a maid and a pool and a boat and a country-club membership and take lavish vacations when people were *starving* in other parts of the world?

If there was a silver lining in all of this, from my parents' perspective, it was that the idea of selfless service pulled me toward medicine. No, they had not wanted it to pull me all the way to Nigeria back in 1995, just before my senior year in college. But they were very glad that experience had inspired me to submit my applications to medical school. And they were even more happy when I enrolled.

In the fall of 1996, I officially became a medical student. I was a naïve, White, wealthy, Southern girl who moved to New York City to study at what is now called the Columbia University Vagelos College of Physicians and Surgeons. I lived in a dorm near Presbyterian Hospital, which is in Washington Heights, just north of Harlem.

I loved the community. But did I love the future I was working toward? Not so much.

~

I actually tried to defer medical school for a year. I had a whole plan set up: I wanted to continue my exploration of an ascetic lifestyle—this time in an American setting.

I had discovered a place in inner-city Philadelphia that accepted volunteers-in-residence. I had visited, interviewed, and been invited to join them for a year. When Columbia said no to my deferral request, I was disappointed, but found a solution: I would complete my first year of medical school and then head to Philadelphia for a long summer stay before going back to Columbia for my second year.

My first year of med school was tough, but fine. Lots of work. Amazing friends. Some eye-opening experiences.

The summer after that first year, I moved to Philadelphia.

More specifically, I moved to Kensington, a poor but wonderful Philly neighborhood where residents live and love, but also struggle with a violent crime rate that is 30 percent higher than the rest of the city. Within Kensington there is a small Catholic Worker community that runs a free medical clinic, a soup kitchen, a women's center, and a community garden. I joined this community, accepting their offer of a bed in a halfway house. At that time, the household consisted of the two Catholic women who cofounded the medical clinic and three men who were transitioning out of homelessness.

I was invited in, and I was so very grateful to be there.

~

The Catholic Worker movement was founded in 1933 and was intended to radically change our world from "a society of go-getters to a society of go-givers."[1] I was drawn to the way the group integrated spiritual and corporal works, finding God among the hungry, thirsty, naked, homeless, sick, and imprisoned. There was also a focus on environmentalism: living simply, sustainably, and in solidarity with those who relied on shared community gardens for food. Finally, there was a belief in voluntary poverty that called me. The group lived with, and as, the poor—attempting economic equality and embracing the opportunity to put themselves on the same side of the struggle.

Going into that summer, I knew what would intrigue me the most was the voluntary poverty. But I thought what would inform me the most was the free medical clinic. In that clinic, I expected my professional identity would finally make sense. I would finally feel that resounding *yes* when I thought about coming back someday as a doctor.

However, the clinic was not what I expected.

In Nigeria my work felt medical, even though I was on the outer fringe of almost every procedure. As an untrained volunteer in an operating room without air conditioning (and thus, with open windows), one of my jobs was to wave flies away from patients during surgery. I organized the stock room so doctors could more readily access the donated, often-expired medicines. When my mentors asked for my attention, they usually wanted it for medical reasons. They wanted me to make notes in a chart while an HIV+ patient told us her husband had multiple wives. They wanted me to hold a small child's foot in a painful rinse to ward off post-surgical infections while she wailed.

In Kensington, it was different.

My mentors were two exhausted but content Catholic Worker women who needed me to work, but also encouraged me to spend time simply absorbing the *feel* of this community—outside of the medical clinic. They told me one of the best ways to do this was to occasionally stop running to meet needs—to stop helping so efficiently. To savor. To sit.

So I sat, in all sorts of nearby spaces. I sat in the community garden, pulling weeds. I sat in the women's center, listening to stories. I sat in the soup kitchen, sharing meals with our regulars. How were they? I sat on stoops with grandmothers, on curbs with kids, and at the reception desk of the medical clinic.

I do not want to romanticize what was a very tough environment. I did *not* sit outside after dark. But during the day, I worked and sat and listened and learned from so many within this community.

~

The three formerly homeless men who lived in the halfway house with me shattered my expectations immediately.

They welcomed me and made me feel at home. And they fed me dinner on that very first night. It was a wonderful meal in the kitchen of the halfway house. They had mixed a small amount of donated meat with a large number of community garden vegetables in an old cast-iron skillet.

I insisted on doing the dishes, and while everyone cleared the table, I began scrubbing that skillet with soap. One of the men saw me and begged me to stop.

"No," he told me, taking the pan. He was upset—not angry, but frustrated. He peered at me through his glasses. "You *never* wash a cast-iron skillet with soap. You'll strip all of the seasoning. You have literally washed years of flavor down the drain. Did you really not know?"

I really didn't know.

But I knew in that moment that I was going to learn a lot—including humility. And respect. And appreciation for people who deliver cast-iron truths straight and without holding grudges.

The truth was that those homeless men were far more knowledgeable than me in every way that mattered that summer. They knew the safest path through the neighborhood, understood how various systems and power structures within the community worked, and would occasionally tell me stories about how they had learned what they knew.

One of the men (my cast-iron tutor) was brilliant but had lost several jobs due to bipolar episodes. He was incredibly well-read and served as my docent through several Philadelphia museums that summer. We spent many hours discussing art, history, and culture. He was well-spoken and willing to expertly expound on almost any topic except his life on the streets.

The second man was staying there in hopes of resting his eye enough to avoid optical surgery. He was quiet. I respected his boundaries. I was left wondering what that worn eye had seen.

The third gentleman shared a bit more about his life, perhaps eager to use his voice after it had been spared during surgery for esophageal cancer that had threatened his larynx. He told me he had become homeless after losing his job at a church when he missed work due to chemotherapy sessions. According to him, there had been six chemo sessions in total, and he had missed three days of work during each round. Those eighteen days off had cost him his job, despite having been a reliable employee the previous ten years. I had trouble believing it, but it wasn't the only story like that I heard over the summer.

~

I met people as I sat in the medical clinic. I had thought I would be sitting, taking their medical histories for the doctor. Instead, they came in for the most basic of physical needs.

They needed to use the clinic's shower. Its washing machine. Its address, so they could give it to a potential employer. I set up voicemail for them on our system so they had a number where people could reach them. Being able to provide an address and phone number greatly increased their chances of being hired. It also gave other vital communications—mailed Medicaid forms, chemotherapy appointment updates, results from biopsies, and plenty of nonmedical notices—a place to land, without the price of a P.O. box.

We did provide some medical services. The medical staff did their best to assist addicts in detox. They gave medicines to patients who couldn't afford them. Still, I quickly learned that some people needed me to read their prescriptions for them as much as they needed them filled.

~

Within the realm of medicine, there was one primary complaint: bug bites. This sounds small, but it was not.

Several of the residences in our area—including the abandoned buildings where so many homeless slept—were absolutely infested with insects. Imagine the discomfort of sleeping on the floor of a swelteringly hot, abandoned building while being crawled on and bitten. Imagine the itching.

And now imagine a bite that is then repeatedly scratched with a dirty fingernail (since an abandoned building is not going to have running water, and certainly not soap). And now imagine fifty bites repeatedly scratched with a dirty fingernail. The infections were awful, and people were suffering.

~

I met Joe, a small, older, Caucasian man with a quick laugh, as locals greeted him on the sidewalk. As an exterminator, Joe spent his daytime hours working for a company that paid him the going rate. But in the late afternoons, Joe used his spare time and his own old personal equipment to fumigate crumbling complexes. Of course, everyone was extraordinarily grateful to him, but what struck me most as I saw him deflect their thanks was how genuinely he was able to state that it was his pleasure.

Joe *loved* his job. He was so expressive about his enthusiasm that it was hard not to smile as I heard him talk. He spoke about his "battle against the bugs" as if it were a war, and he was a frontline soldier. I cannot remember his exact words, but I remember the feeling they gave me: inspiration.

I thought of Joe recently when I saw a rendition of the speech Coach Knute Rockne made to show the world how his Notre Dame football team could be inspired to victory. In my mind, Rockne's words to his team became Joe's words to our bug-bitten men. He told them the biters would be *gone* by the end of the day because

> We're gonna go inside, we're gonna go outside—inside and outside. We're gonna get 'em on the run boys and once we get 'em on the run we're gonna keep 'em on the run. And then we're gonna go go go go go go and we're not gonna stop til we get across that goalline. This is a team they say is . . . is good well, I think we're better than them. They can't lick us. So what do you say, men?[2]

Joe! My hero in so many ways, and I wish I could tell him. What you did to those bugs, what you did for those men, what you did for that community, what you did for our spirits, and what you did for a young girl who recognized two things in that moment: I did not have to be a doctor to make a difference, and I wanted to feel about my work the way Joe felt about his.

Something changed the day I heard Joe talking. I began to wonder if maybe I didn't have to choose between improving the world and enjoying it. I began to wonder if I didn't have to choose between self-actualization and service. Thanks to Joe, a small off-ramp appeared along my paved route on that metaphorical map. And in October of my second year of medical school, I would use that ramp to *exit*.

My actual moment of departure from med school was a bit dramatic. The night before, I had been studying histology slides and had the rare-for-me occasion of being unable to focus on a task. I recall shoving my notebook aside and pulling out a piece of paper. On it, I listed everything I would rather be doing with my time—all of them distinctly *not* medical.

I carried that list around with me until it was in tatters, but I remember several things that were on it: teaching, writing, learning to cook from my grandmother, getting to know my little sister (who had been only eight years old when I left for college), traveling anywhere, traveling everywhere. Breathing without all of this *weight*.

I went to bed that night without completing my homework. I woke up early and tackled it the next day before class. But as I sat in the auditorium waiting for that class to start, I found I just couldn't. I had the sensation that I had just slammed into a brick wall or run into a dead end. I could not be in med school one second longer.

I collected my things, loaded them into my backpack, and told the classmates on my row that I was sorry to disturb, but I needed to leave. As one slid his bag off the narrow aisle to make more of a path he asked, "Are you OK? I mean, this is a *mandatory* lecture."

"Only for people who want to be doctors," I told him. And I walked out.

~

As I walked up the steps of that auditorium, I felt lighter. Happier. Like something was right.

I didn't realize I was crying until I bumped into a classmate who was rushing into class late. "Are you all right?" he asked me. "Yes," I told him, "but I have to leave."

As I did leave, there was a crisp fall air blowing cool over my tearstained cheeks. I felt awake. And mobile. I needed to go. I needed distance from that setting that had sucked me in for so long.

But go where?

Anywhere. I could go anywhere.

I spent the day in the travel section of a Manhattan bookstore looking at progressively smaller maps. I started with a map of the world, then the United States, then Colorado. I was mapping *my* route.

~

My first call was to my parents, whose disappointment was overshadowed by their terror. My mother was so convinced I had lost my mind that she kept telling me to stay inside—specifically to avoid walking anywhere near the George Washington Bridge. She was afraid I would jump. She called me every hour late into the evening, just to make sure I had not committed suicide. She did not believe me when I told her I felt better than I had ever felt.

I had to tell my roommate, who could have lived with another group of friends, but chose me. She was amazingly supportive, and found someone else quickly, but I hated what I'd done to her plans.

I had to tell friends who were struggling with their own choices. One approached me to ask if her own doubts had underscored mine. "No," I told her honestly. The classmates with misgivings had made my own doubts seem normal. It was the classmates who fully loved what they were doing who affected me—I knew I could never feel that way about medicine.

I was required to complete an exit interview with a med-school psychiatrist. I was more relaxed than I had ever been. I even cracked a joke as I walked into his office. I noted the many different types of chairs he had in the large space (including the traditional sofa) and asked if I would be evaluated on which one I chose. He laughed and said, "Now you will be."

I looked at the doctor, sitting behind his formal desk, and told him that walking into his office reminded me of walking onto an empty New York bus and being able to sit anywhere except the driver's seat. "It's ironic," I revealed, while plopping down onto the nearest chair, "because I am only here because I am *finally* in the driver's seat of my own life."

At the end of the hour, the psychiatrist told me I was free to go and cracked what might have been his own joke. "You have to get out of my office," he told me, "because if we talk any longer, I might leave medicine also."

The true test came at the bookstore, where I had gone in hopes of getting some money back by returning my textbooks. As I handed them to the clerk, he cocked an eyebrow and said, "Couldn't hack it, huh?"

This, I realized, would be my challenge. Some people were going to think I quit because it was too hard. Why did I care what they thought? I don't know. I was fully aware that this random person behind the counter would not think of me at all past this moment, and that even if he did, it shouldn't matter.

But what *I* thought of me mattered, and he was verbalizing the part of my pride that had to be confronted and swallowed. I could not tell my childhood stories anymore without an asterisk. I was not the educational culmination of grandparents who made sure everyone went—and stayed—in school. I would not break the portion of the glass ceiling my mother had eyed for decades. I took pride in never quitting—took pride in my stubbornness. But now the toddler who would not quit the pool deck, and the girl who would not quit the oatmeal, and the player who would not quit the team had become the student who quit medical school. That part of it stung.

But I had to shift my perspective. I had to realize that it was either quitting this career or quitting me. I would not quit me.

~

I remember the day I finally left New York City. I had turned in my textbooks, said goodbye to my classmates, and packed up my apartment. Malcolm and I, who had been on and off since college, had ended the romantic relationship for good. I had put my things in storage and planned to have them shipped to wherever I landed. On my way to catch a bus out of the city, I decided to take one last stroll past the hospital, where I saw James, the man who sold flowers on its front steps.

James was at least seventy years old, Black, and always sitting on an upside-down bucket that matched the right side up ones that held his well-watered flowers. He was always positioned near the main entrance of the hospital, where he often saw groups of medical students in their short white coats heading to class. James was one of those guys who was so much a part of the landscape—and so congenial—that I could not be angry at him, even though for the entirety of my medical career he had greeted every white-coated girl in my class with the words "Hey, pretty lady!" and every guy with "Hey, doctor!" On occasion he even told the guys to "pick a pretty lady and buy her some flowers!" For over a year, I had felt that all of this *should* irritate me, but it hadn't. Maybe because, during all that time, James had literally brightened a dimly lit patch on my path with daisies and roses. I lived in Manhattan; I didn't see enough flowers.

Anyway, as I saw him there, I stopped—and for the first time, I sat and chatted with him. I told him I was leaving and that I wanted to do something for him before I went. I had gotten to enjoy seeing his flowers every morning without ever buying any. And today, I wanted to purchase whatever kind were his favorites.

James selected the flowers thoughtfully, explaining that he liked the ones with the brightest colors and the biggest blooms. I listened and watched as he chose each one, then arranged and wrapped them. Finally, I paid him, tipping extra. And then I told James I wanted *him* to have this gorgeous, tailor-made bouquet.

James was confused. What was it I wanted?

"I'm giving you flowers," I told him. "You provide flowers for tons of people—I see them next to half the beds in this hospital. But *this* bouquet is not for them. Or for me. I am buying it for *you*."

James's eyes watered over. "Did you know," he asked me, "that no one has ever done that? I have been sitting in this spot for twenty years telling people that flowers are the way to make someone feel better, and in all those years no one has ever bought *me* even *one*?"

"Well, it's time," I told him.

And as I turned to go, it struck me that James had just given me a gift. The bouquet was his, but symbolically it had felt appropriate to mark this moment at the entrance to this hospital.

My medical identity was no longer. There had been a benediction, almost a burial. Complete with the flowers.

CHARACTER(S)

Did I really just make my med-school departure sound like a funeral? I didn't plan to when I began writing that section. But now that it has come out, I recognize that it did feel that way for some of my loved ones. And I did have to head back to Alabama and deal with that perspective before heading west.

But at that moment—that happy moment with James—I was not one of the mourners. I was the spirit—the one being liberated.

I was alive, exhilarated, and free.

I was also in no rush.

My parents wanted to buy me a plane ticket to Alabama. It was important for me to be there—for a bit. But I shocked them (again) by telling them I wanted to take the bus.

I didn't want to zip to destinations anymore. Some part of me was beginning to recognize that the journey itself would be important. I wanted time to breathe, process, and be. So I bought myself a book, a bus ticket, and a few quiet weeks on a slow Greyhound that meandered me past friends (where I hopped off and visited for days at a stretch) and fields (which I viewed for hours through the windows) and gas stations (with tiny convenience stores where I bought prewrapped sandwiches and Snapple iced tea).

After several days on the bus, I was happy, but I was also disheveled and in need of a shower. I was also in a bit of a psychological watershed, between the exhilaration of my exit and the aftermath that awaited me in Alabama. Still, I was in the moment, on a bus, paying attention. And my curiosity had been piqued by a fellow traveler who reminded me of my homeless friends in Kensington.

For over two hundred miles, this gentleman had been seated in the back of the bus, near the bathroom. He was wearing several layers of clothing, including a full-length tattered wool coat that didn't smell great. Every single time anyone approached the facilities, he yelled out "Well, when you've got to go, you gotta go!" He had made people uncomfortable enough that most had stopped using the bus bathroom. That meant our gas station stops took longer, because everyone lined up to use the public restrooms. This—along with the privy pronouncements—had caught the attention of the driver. This passenger was clearly a bit different from the rest of us. This worried the driver and intrigued me.

At one stop, I saw him counting out pennies to purchase a pack of Nutter Butters. After waiting my turn at the register, purchasing my tea and two sandwiches, I reboarded the bus and moved to sit across from this gentleman. I greeted him with a simple hello, and before I could say anything else, he surprised me by offering me a Nutter Butter.

I took the cookie and offered him a sandwich, which he refused. "Are you sure?" I asked him. "If you take it, we could have dinner and dessert together."

He shook his head no. Go figure. Then I asked him where he was headed. "To see my son," he responded. Then he pulled out a photograph and told me his story.

It was not a photo of his son. It was a polaroid of my new bus friend—I'll call him Nick—holding a large fish. Nick had somehow entered—and won—a fishing contest. This, he informed me, had been his greatest accomplishment in years. And he was hoping it would impress the adult son who wanted little to do with him.

Nick told me that he had been an American soldier in Vietnam. He had sustained a minor physical injury—and a major psychological one—when his buddy had stepped on a landmine and died in the explosion. Seeing the death up close had affected Nick in all sorts of ways. And when his commanding officer had later ordered him to shoot a child who was suffering from exposure to napalm, he had refused. When the officer had persisted, Nick had thrown a punch, catching the officer off guard.

He had been dishonorably discharged and come home to his family but could not get a job. In addition, he could not get the images of the buddy or the child or the war out of his mind. Altering that mind with alcohol and drugs had helped a bit, then became its own problem. His wife had soon given him a dishonorable discharge also. He went years without seeing his son.

But before all of that, he told me, before the war—he and his son had gone fishing. His son had loved fishing and was always begging to be taken. So, decades later, Nick had devised this plan to get back into his son's good graces. He had gotten a rod, entered fishing contests, and eventually won first prize. Here was the photo! He was certain seeing this picture would make his son very proud. And then they could go fishing again.

Nick became so emotional while telling this story that he excused himself to go to the bathroom. He stayed in there until our next stop, when the bus driver banged on the door until he came out.

Our conversation resumed. When I asked him if he had any advice for someone my age, he told me to give first without waiting to receive, because "if you can't give to others you ain't worth shit." He also said that we should respect and honor other people; it had been respect for life that made him refuse the officer's order and a sense of honor that made him throw the punch. Also, he told me, never let anyone tell you that life is bad or that other people are bad. Give both a chance.

Then he said, "You know more about me than my own family, and I wish I were twenty years younger because I'd be over there trying to pull your drawers off."

This statement made several close-by passengers squirm, but it was clear to me that Nick was physically harmless. I was more aware of the emotional upheaval he might soon trigger within himself and for his son.

Nick and the bus driver had several more conversations. Eventually, he disembarked and did not get back on. As our bus rolled away, I thought about the child who lost his fishing buddy and the soldier who lost his friend. And I hoped that, somewhere, both of those victims could find a corner of the world that is *kind*.

~

You cannot grow up in a small Southern town without learning how to sit and listen. The hours I spent at picnic tables, in church pews, on parlor settees, or sipping lemonade on a porch swing would astound you. I loved hearing the adults tell stories. And when there was a lull in the conversation, I always had a book.

I missed that part of my childhood self—the one who had been slightly revived in Kensington. The one who made time to sit and listen, or to sit and read. So on the bus, I sat. And I listened. When there was a lull, I read. It had been years since I had consciously carved out time to do those things, but this trip was going to be all about shuffling priorities.

The book I bought for my bus trip from Manhattan to Alabama was Henry James's *The Portrait of a Lady*. I chose it because, eight years prior, one of my high school teachers had written a quote from the book on the board in her classroom, and it had stayed with me: "I don't want everyone to like me; I should think less of myself if some people did."

I had no idea when I picked that book up how relevant its story would be. Isabel Archer, its twenty-three-year-old heroine, begins the book as a free-spirited woman, who shares my age and is on her own journey, determined to discover who she is and choose what she will do. I engaged with her, cheered for her, and cried over her final choice. I found relief only when I read an essay on the book that reminded me that in her ultimate decision, Isabel had shown independence from even me, as a reader. It was *her* story. Ultimately, what *I* thought of it didn't matter. I had to respect that—and perhaps take it as a lesson in independence.

The book was also a lesson in character development. In its preface, Henry James speaks about how he tried to discover Isabel's character. On the bus trip, I rushed through his explanation, eager to get to Isabel's story. But decades later, during a midlife crisis, I would read that explanation closely. I would listen to James as he considered whether a story's plot and setting really mattered, or if they were simply there to serve the development of what is actually essential—character. The midlife me would appreciate that question, and I would wonder if I could switch my own focus from a plot-driven to a character-driven life. And if I could do it in my current setting—right where I am—or if I would need to go elsewhere.

~

But that midlife crisis was decades away.

For now, I was twenty-three. I was on a bus, headed from New York to Alabama. I was happy. I was thinking. I was exploring. I was going to be whatever I wanted to be, and the idea was exhilarating—to me.

Now, consider a different perspective on this journey.

Imagine you are the mother of this young adult. This daughter who dated outside your comfort zone in college. This student who required body-bag insurance on her summer break. This young woman who loved living with homeless men in Kensington. Your child who has just called you and announced that she is quitting school. She has also announced that she will not come directly home on a plane. Instead, she will travel by bus, so she can see friends and meet more of the world's people. There were no cell phones back then, so you will hear from her whenever she bothers to call. In these conversations, she will talk about coming home for a few weeks—until just after Christmas—when she will enact some vague plan to "head west to Colorado." She has no job, no specific destination, and no fear.

That last piece terrifies you. Does she not realize what can happen to young girls traveling alone? Specifically *this* young girl, who thinks nothing of connecting with adult male strangers in unfamiliar arenas. Her aunt—your own sister—is stunned when she picks this young lady up at the downtown Atlanta bus depot, at night, for a short visit. Nothing about this seems safe.

You had thought your child would outgrow these impulses. Instead, she keeps surprising you with fresh deviations from your norms.

You ultimately acknowledge that your attempts to protect her aren't working, so you shift gears. You cease constructing roadblocks, give up on guardrails, and begin building safety nets.

When your daughter offers to pay back her tuition in installments— she knows she broke her part of the professional bargain—you dismiss hundreds of thousands of dollars in debt without blinking. You want every dollar she has to go toward making this journey safer.

When your daughter talks about her next bus trip, you loan her the spare family car. She is shocked at the support, but incredibly appreciative. She knows a car means *freedom*.

Maybe, but what you are really offering is an olive branch of acceptance. With a side of security, if she will please, please take it. And maybe a small dose of *I really don't understand this*. Why is she rejecting everything you worked so hard to give her? Things you were denied?

Meanwhile—during this whole time, as you are fighting back the fear and wondering what on earth is going on in that head of your child—there is something else happening.

Your other daughter—her little sister—is watching.

~

The week after my medical school announcement, when I was still dismantling my life in New York, my mother called me. Without even a hello, she yelled into the receiver, "I hope you're *happy*!" She continued and—in a tone of exasperated frustration—proclaimed, "Your little sister has just announced that someday she wants to move to Barbados and get a job training *dolphins*. Where do you think she might have gotten the idea she could do something like that?"

It did make me happy. I had cracked something—maybe a window, maybe something more structural—but the idea that those openings might allow my sister's imagination to breathe was affirming.

Despite many opportunities to jump on the "Kristi is crazy" bandwagon, my sister has always been my unconditional supporter. She has always seen me. When I came home for that six-week visit, I told her one of the main reasons I had come was to see her. When I left for college, she was only eight, an elementary school student who loved being "twins" in our one set of matching pajamas. Now she was fourteen, and this visit was a chance to connect in a different way. I knew, at her age, the best way to ensure time together was to serve as her chauffeur. I had the best time driving her to and from practices and driving her and her friends to see movies. Listening when she was with her buddies, chatting when we were alone. When she asked me why I was going West, I told her I just felt like I needed to. It felt like the right place to write uninterrupted until the words helped me figure things out. As my parents begged me to load the loaner car with blankets in case it broke down on a snowy Colorado mountain, Ashley sent me off with a journal. She wrote a note on page one that said, "Follow your heart, chase your dreams, and let your soul be your inspiration. Writing is a gift—use it for all you can." I still have the journal and feel so lucky to have the sister who inscribed it. As adults we live far from one another, but she is my best friend. She is the godmother of my eldest daughter, and my younger daughter's middle name is "Ashley" as a tribute. We communicate at least every week, sometimes every day.

Of course, it's interesting that we recall very different childhoods with very different parents. She was not enrolled in etiquette classes (where I had been told my fingernails were too important to sacrifice for my athletic passion). She was not trained to walk like a model on the catwalk where I threw up. She became a writer and says she did not encounter any family resistance. She did feel the familiar pressure to please others, the pressure to marry for the sake of it (pressure she overcame, as she cared less about timing and more about finding her wonderful husband, Brian)—but Ashley attributes those pressures to our hometown. She says she felt none from our family.

I am not quite certain what to do with that. Examine it? I have. Resent it? I don't. Appreciate it? I do. Take credit for it? No. I don't want credit for breaking anything connected to our parents. Part of me knows that in shattering their expectations, I damaged our relationship and broke a piece of their hearts. My sister had more freedom—typical youngest child stuff. My mother loves us both, but she likes my sister better. I've made my peace with that and appreciate the way they care for each other. They now live in the same city, just two hours from our hometown, and I am grateful that my sister is there for my mom in all sorts of ways on a regular basis. I am thankful that my mother and I have the freedom to find the exact degree of closeness and breathing room that best serves our relationship. Ashley connects well with both of us, and it has helped us connect with each other. For that, I am so very grateful.

And I hope my sister realizes that the message I was trying to internalize and convey with my destruction, my temporary exit, and my lifelong journey is very similar to hers: "Follow your heart, chase your dreams, and let your soul be your inspiration. Life is a gift—use it for all you can."

~

Something snapped when I pulled out of my parents' driveway after that six-week period. I knew, when I left that day, that I would never be staying there for another extended period unless my assistance was needed. I had uprooted, and I was headed West.

~

After a week of driving, I crossed the border into Colorado. It felt like a finish line I had worked so incredibly hard to reach. I had cut so many tethers to be there.

It felt so much like a finish line that I wanted to stop. Right there. Just over the border, near Trinidad. This was a place I wanted to stay.

I pulled into what looked like a campground. I saw empty tent sites and cabins scattered in the distance. I parked in the gravel parking lot and walked up to a cabin that had an "office" sign on the door. I entered and was greeted by a woman and her young child. I told her I was looking for a place to stay and was informed that they were closed for the season.

But after revealing that, the woman hesitated.

"Are you low maintenance?" she wondered.

"No," I told her, honestly. "But the maintenance I need is emotional, and I'm going to take care of it myself."

She laughed and handed me a key to a cabin. "It's $125 per week. There's water, heat, and electricity. There's a TV, but you'll only be able to see whatever channel we have ours tuned to because they are all connected to a satellite that I rotate to pick up different shows. There is a pay phone at the end of the parking lot."

I thanked her—she had made an exception for me—and headed to my cabin. I was greeted by a quilt-covered bed, a small table, and a bathroom.

It felt empty. Uncluttered. Unassumingly expectant. What would I make of it?

It occurred to me that I was at the point in the movie where the credits were supposed to roll. I had literally driven west into the sunset. Future scenes were unscripted.

~

Over the next few days, I felt defined by what I was not doing: I was not studying. I was not dating. I was not driving—literally or metaphorically.

Most significantly, I was not listening to anyone's expectations.

When I used the pay phone to let my parents and a few close friends know that I had arrived (and that they would not be able to reach me on this unmanned phone, I would have to call them), my mother exhaled. I think it was a sigh of relief—I was safe. But it also felt like a sigh of release. Maybe she had given up control.

For the first time, I was asked, "What are you doing?" in a tone of inquiry instead of incredulity. It was a significant shift.

And it was my question to answer.

~

I only stayed in Colorado for two weeks.

One purpose of my trip West had been to prove—to myself and to others—that I could create my own map and follow it. Another was to be free.

I accomplished the first goal.

I thought I had accomplished the second, but I realized that I was still constrained. I had cut ties. I would be *what* I wanted (professionally), and *where* I wanted (geographically). But the question remained, *who* did I want to be (in terms of spirituality, politics, etc.)?

I had to go elsewhere—explore a few more interests and expectations—to find those answers.

I decided the first place I had to go was Ohio. There was a guy there who had always encouraged my wild introspection, and the relationship seemed full of possibility.

MARRIAGE—OR NOT

I had actually met Luke, a White American medical student, in Nigeria. I was in a serious relationship with my college boyfriend, Malcolm, at the time, and there was nothing romantic between Luke and me for years. But Luke and I became friends and stayed friends—even after we left Africa and resumed our separate lives in the United States.

Given that Malcolm and I had ended our relationship over faith, I thought that a relationship with Luke, a fellow Christian, would be easy. I called Luke from the pay phone near my Colorado cabin, expressing my interest. He was happy to hear from me, and equally curious about whether our relationship could evolve. Since he was temporarily tied to Ohio, finishing his last semester of medical school, I drove to Cincinnati.

Luke and I began dating, embarking on a romantic relationship that would last almost two years. During our first two months as a couple—in Ohio—I volunteered at a local school while waiting to hear about a summer teaching opportunity. Luke finished his last rotations at the hospital while waiting to hear where he would match as an emergency medicine resident. All the while, we eyed the month of May on our calendars. It was a free month for both of us, and we wanted to spend it together, before any future career commitments began.

Ultimately, Luke and I pooled our money (including my old childhood savings) and planned a backpacking trip. We both loved those planning sessions, which enlivened dinner discussions and left our tables littered with maps and travel guides. We also both loved the trip, which ultimately materialized as a month of museums, cafés, hostels, churches, mosques, memorials, train cars, and river walks all over Europe.

Luke and I were kindred spirits, and it was such a relief to be on the same spiritual page: Christians, but not Bible-thumping evangelicals. We were quiet congregants, but still inspired by our faith and enthusiastic about any moments of religious *yes*. We were also both ascetic at heart, which simplified the lifestyle questions immensely. One year, we went Christmas tree shopping. I was thrilled when we both immediately reached for the scrawny $5 one. (It was even labeled "The Charlie Brown Tree," which we both thought was fantastic.) The one arena we both wanted to spend more on was travel. Still, we tried to do it as frugally as possible. As we backpacked around Europe together, we thought nothing of downgrading from hostel to hovel and giving whatever we saved away.

So much about our life together was easy. There were no negotiations. It was like we shared the same brain. This was so extreme that in certain arenas we actually had to develop some systems to move us from identical to compatible. I recall one occasion, when we were both Christmas shopping in a mall (before cell phones) and did not have a clear meetup plan. When I couldn't find him, I simply found a bench, sat down, and began reading the book I had brought. I figured if both of us were wandering around looking, we would miss each other. If one of us sat still, we had a better shot. Over an hour later, he sat down next to me, chuckling. "We think too much alike," he told me. "I've been reading my book for an hour at the other end of the mall. We have to figure this out, because we can't both be the sitter."

Sure, there were a few bumps. We were both extremely introverted, which was great 90 percent of the time. We wanted to stay home and read books, declining invitations. But when we did go out with friends, I missed having someone who wanted to occasionally take the conversational baton. We would both emerge from these evenings drained, and with me a bit frustrated that he was so content sitting quietly, when I wanted a chance to do it too.

We both wanted to live off the paved road, but we were each accustomed to being around friends and family who at least kept us near it: people who made sure living differently never morphed into living dangerously. With just the two of us, neither had any experience drawing those lines. One day while we were driving, we saw a prison. A mile later, we passed a disheveled man on the shoulder of the road holding his thumb out. Neither of us hesitated: We both wanted to pull over and pick him up. It turned out he was from the prison, and his life had been rough. It also turned out that he was very nice to us. Still, it was an interesting new experience for us to be together and realize that no one was going to stop us from doing anything.

~

Luke didn't talk much about faith; he just lived it. I admired that. I also admired his commitment to radical generosity. I had seen it in Nigeria, where he gave away his favorite hat. He had *loved* that hat, partly because it celebrated his favorite team: the University of Kentucky. And perhaps partly because he had enjoyed aggravating me, a girl with other SEC loyalties. Every time I had seen him wearing it, I had groaned. So one day, when he had come home from visiting patients without it, I noticed. Where was the hat?

Luke had looked sad, then strong. "A kid asked me for it. I didn't want to give it to him, so I knew immediately I had to."

It had been radical generosity, practiced by a guy who had no interest in preaching about it. But he would talk to me about it, if I asked.

After our summer in Nigeria ended (almost three years before we began dating), Luke and I shared the occasional phone call. One of those calls occurred just a few months after we returned to the United States, when I was at Princeton and he was in medical school. During that call, we realized we were both struggling with cultural readjustment and spiritual stasis. I was also struggling to make sense of what I had learned in Nigeria. I recall telling him: "I naively thought life would be simpler in our rural village. I feel so dumb." How had I not understood that life there appeared uncluttered because "simple" things—like accessing clean water—were too complicated to allow time for anything else?

Luke listened. We talked more. And after our conversation ended, I took a walk around Princeton thinking. I thought about the pink coat and the Kentucky hat and the village children and the whole concept of radical generosity. As I walked, the hour grew late, and the campus grew quiet.

I do not pray regularly—I have always felt kind of weird about it—but I whispered a question to God during that solitary stroll. My question was, "If I give it all up—*everything*—and live out this idea of *radical generosity*, would you, God, take care of me?"

In a flash, I was struck with a feeling. Exhilaration. Assurance. Absolute *awe*. The sensation was so overwhelming that I collapsed down to my knees, ultimately moving into a seated position just off the path, with my knees drawn to me. I remained there, on the grass, in the twilight, for close to an hour, simply breathing. It was like the boundaries between me and God and rest of creation were *gone*. I felt both tiny and vast—small but connected to everything.

I eventually staggered back to my dorm room and climbed into bed. When I woke up, I was still awed by the experience. I ate breakfast, tried to study for a few hours, then gave up. Instead of fighting my brain, I decided to do something physical and think about what had happened. It was a Thursday—the day I collected recyclables from three local businesses and transported them to a larger bin on campus.

I had begun this program my freshman year, and once a week for the past three years I had engaged in the same routine. Always the same: walk in, empty the business bin into my own rolling cart, thank them, and leave.

But this day felt different. The question I had asked God about provision—about whether I could live out this idea of radical generosity and just trust that He would meet any needs—was lingering in my head. The assurance I felt was present but fading.

I walked into the first shop, a stationary store. As I emptied every last scrap of paper from their recycling bin, the manager approached me. "You've been doing this for years," he told me, "and I don't know if anyone has ever really thanked you. Pick out something you'd like from the store today. No charge."

I stared for a moment, then collected myself, expressed my appreciation, and selected a postcard from their display that depicted a beautiful

Van Gogh painting called *The Siesta*. "Would this be OK?" I asked him. "I really love the picture on the front."

"Sure," he told me. "You're welcome to pick out something larger, you know. It doesn't have to be just a postcard."

I thanked him and said, "The card is perfect. I'm going to frame it and keep it on my bookshelf." He had no idea that over twenty-five years later, as I write this, it will still occupy a place of honor in my office.

I moved onto the next store—a sandwich shop. As I emptied their recycling bin, the manager approached me. "You've been doing this for years," he told me, "and I don't know if anyone has ever really thanked you. Let us treat you to whatever sandwich you'd like today. No charge."

I stared for a moment, then collected myself, expressed my appreciation, and asked him if a turkey and cheese would be OK. "Absolutely," he told me. "Enjoy."

It was the same experience at the next store, where the manager told me to pick out a drink and offered me one of their famous soft pretzels.

On that day—for the first and only time in those settings—I was gifted unsolicited sustenance and beauty.

In other words, I was provided with everything I needed. And as I saw it, I had been provided with an answer from God.

~

But do you know what God never provided me?

The desire to marry Luke.

I don't know why.

Maybe it's because I was born to question, and with Luke, I never had to.

Regardless, after a friendship that lasted through my forays into medical school and Kensington and Colorado, and after a relationship that lasted through time together in Ohio and backpacking through Europe and career explorations that required many long-distance phone calls from several states apart, we decided to end it. We were both sad, but when a spark isn't there, you can't force it. So Luke and I parted the way we started—as friends.

~

My parents were not thrilled. Because after Luke, I began ping-ponging through many relationships. There was a pattern.

I always had religion in mind and felt my childhood faith demanded I marry a Christian. But I kept falling for guys who didn't believe in God. They were great guys: caring, charismatic, and dedicated to making the world better. Dedicated to me. Energetic engagers who made the world seem bright and inviting and fun. Until—in the midst of that positive energy—my soul would begin to squirm. They didn't believe in Jesus. How was I supposed to partner and prioritize and raise children with someone who rejected that piece? The idea of it terrified me.

So after a year of being with someone who made my heart sing, we would end it. Religion was always a factor. And I would rebound into a relationship with a Christian.

Over the years, I dated some great Christian men. Guys to whom my core seemed magnetically drawn. Guys with incredible vision. Guys who made me feel seen and made me see life so very differently. Guys who left my soul breathless and peaceful and awestruck and inspired. But I wanted more laughter and more energy in our day-to-day interactions. They warmed my heart, but I wanted someone to set it on fire. I believed there was a Christian guy out there who could do it, but I couldn't find him. I kept thinking this would be such an easy gift for God to bestow on a relationship. That one day, with one of these Christian men, I would wake up and find a spark in my heart. But I never did.

So after a year of being with someone who recharged my soul (and got me talking to God again—although sometimes in fury), we would end it. My lack of enthusiasm for next steps was always a factor. And then I'd rebound into a relationship with a really fun, spark-igniting guy.

Back and forth, back and forth, back and forth. Hurting good people. Hurting inside.

~

My mother began to wonder if, as a parent, she had done something wrong.

One day, she asked this aloud. I had recently ended another relationship, and I was upset. This upset her. There was definitely a problem, she insisted, but what exactly was it? Why could I not commit? Maybe I needed to see a psychiatrist who could identify an issue or diagnose a disorder, she suggested. Because there was clearly something wrong with my wanderings in every arena: professionally, geographically, and now even in terms of relationships.

My dad stepped in during that chat and told her to stop, that this particular line of questioning was over forever.

But she is my mother. And to her, it looked like I was flailing. So, several years later, my mom decided she had to say something more. She told me—during an intense conversation—that if I continued on my current path, I would someday end up old and alone, which was the surest way to become selfish. She compared me to the family villain—my great-aunt Adine. The final hammer came down when my mother looked at me and said, "It makes me wonder if I missed something when you were little. I mean, is there any chance you were sexually abused as a child?"

Something snapped when she asked me that question. No, I was not sexually abused as a child. But when the person who was your primary caregiver and protector for your entire childhood asks if it happened, it stops you. "What do you mean 'was I abused'? You tell me! Was I ever alone with someone who would have done that? At an age I was too young to remember? Why are you asking? Is there something you know?"

No, I was not abused as a child—sexually or otherwise. It would ultimately be my wonderful sister-in-law Betsy who would bring me some peace about that suggestion. She would say, "Kristi, she just doesn't understand you and is searching for anything that will explain why you chose a path different from hers."

Still, it was clear that I was in a space where being unmarried or where I couldn't commit was seen as a symptom of some sort of horrific problem. I was not sure exactly what to do with that.

The final conversation about my relationship status came a few years later. It was a tough weekend. I was visiting my folks in Alabama, taking a break from my wanderings on the day I would have been graduating from medical school. And instead of toasting to a new doctor in the family, we were discussing my new boyfriend. I asked my mother what she thought of him, and she responded, "I don't even bother getting to know them at this point. Whenever I meet them, after they leave, I stand in the yard and holler 'OK! We're done with him! *Next!*'"

When my dad heard this, he asked me to take a ride with him. So we got into his car and drove to his favorite local place—Walmart.

My dad's affinity for the large store was well-known in my small town, but very few understood why he visited Walmart so often. It was because my father, a former college athlete and eternally proud man, was having an increasingly hard time walking. A neuropathy in his lower legs had made him unstable, but despite being an orthopedic surgeon himself, he had absolutely refused to use a walker or a cane. So my dad would go to Walmart almost every day to shop. In reality, this was his daily walk, taken without a cane but with a stabilizing grocery cart. (As a bonus, at Walmart, my introverted father got the exact amount of social interaction he wanted. He saw people, but everyone was mid-errand so nobody lingered. "So great to see you! Glad to hear all is well. I'm off to buy tomatoes. Goodbye!")

When we got to Walmart, my dad asked me to sit with him in the car and watch people exit. He told me to focus on the couples: not the dolled-up ones I saw when they had their best feet forward—instead, just regular couples, out in the world.

We began watching, in silence. He occasionally tapped my arm to make sure I had noticed a particular pair that he found unattractive (in looks or behavior). After about twenty minutes, he said, "You've been watching, right?" I nodded in affirmation. "Good," he told me. "Here's what I want you to take from it. *Anyone* can get married. Anyone can find *someone* who will marry them. It's not an accomplishment."

It was an objectionable delivery (and certainly offensive to the unwitting couples he noted), but my father was not really looking at those couples that day. He was looking at me—seeing me—and trying to make sure that I understood something very important.

My dad wanted me to know that I did not have to get married. He was lifting that pressure.

And I took his words as a blessing on whatever lifestyle or timetable I chose.

THE WORLD IS UNJUST. THE MERITOCRACY IS A MYTH. I AM PART OF THE PROBLEM.

While I was in Ohio with Luke, I was also exploring my new professional goal: teaching.

I approached a local elementary school and asked if they needed volunteers. They did, so I spent my days there, grading papers and working with small reading groups. I really liked what I was doing and wanted to explore it further. I was specifically drawn toward programs that would help me work in low-income environments. Ultimately, I decided to apply to Teach For America, and I was accepted.

I had a few months before the program began. During that time, I left Ohio, backpacked with Luke around Europe, and helped him move to Georgia for his emergency medicine residency.

All the while, my anticipation and enthusiasm grew. Soon, I would begin to learn how to teach.

~

My Teach For America (TFA) preservice summer began in June of 1998. The training took place in Houston, Texas, where I met hundreds of other new TFA Corps members. We were divided into groups of four, assigned a mentor teacher, and placed in a Houston summer-school classroom. Barely a week after my arrival, I was standing with my team at the front of a classroom, meeting a group of eighth graders who needed to pass middle school history before starting high school. It was like being thrown into the deep end of a pool filled with struggling swimmers while trying to learn how to lifeguard. I was overwhelmed, invested, anxious, inspired, exhausted, and surrounded by energetic mentors who cared and knew so much that I was overly optimistic no one in this crowd could drown.

My first job on my first day in my first classroom was to take roll.

Curtis was the first name in my roll book, and he revealed he was "here." Next was Kashay, who said she was "here" too. But student number three, Melinda, did not simply announce her presence. Instead of letting me know she was here, she told me to "go to hell."

I was absolutely unprepared for that moment. I am not sure I even managed to raise an eyebrow before stammering out the next name on my list. But even as my facial features froze, my insides adjusted and my focus shifted. In that moment, it hit me like a tsunami: I was not here to teach *history*. I was here to teach *students*. And to learn from them.

That moment was pedagogically powerful, but it not only altered my perspective as an educator, it also made me feel something as a person. Because as Melinda glared at me—with eyes full of challenge and words full of venom—the part of me that had wanted to love my job finally stood up and screamed *Yes*.

Everyone who warned me this would not be easy had just been proven right—but I didn't care. I found Melinda's challenge inspiring. It would not be easy—but so what? For me, it finally felt like the right kind of hard.

~

Teach For America has been celebrated for its work and criticized for elements of its approach. I could quote either chorus, but I won't do it here. I will, instead, express my gratitude to the three communities that welcomed me: Teach For America; Houston, Texas; and, most of all, the site of my actual two-year TFA teaching commitment, Warren County, North Carolina.

I was placed in Warren County, North Carolina, because they needed teachers. But one of the things I appreciate about TFA is the emphasis on the exchange at work during the two-year commitment. While teaching, I was also tasked with learning a tremendous amount about life in areas facing economic challenges, both out of respect and to inform my future work as an advocate.

I certainly learned a lot about Warren County, a rural area with many large tobacco fields and a few tiny towns. Those relatively quiet spaces belied a telling history that included slavery, antebellum freedmen, temporary industries, extended economic decline, and a crisis that birthed the environmental justice movement. The stories both jarred and occupied me.

But it was the students who drew me in and captured my heart.

~

I loved my students. There was Kiara, the shy girl who refused to read aloud because she was embarrassed by her stutter. There was Darnell, the captain of the middle school football team. There was Larissa, sleepy because she spent last night in juvenile detention. It seemed her uncle thought she would be the perfect one to deliver the drugs he was dealing. He never imagined the police would search someone with such a youthful, innocent look.

I worried about Jamal, who, as an eighth grader, already felt pressured to follow his sister to an Ivy League college. His father called me often to discuss how we could turn those A grades into A-pluses. When I taught him, Jamal was thirteen and had already taken the SAT twice.

There was one student who threatened to stab me with scissors, actually lodging the sharp blades in a door. He ended up in the conference room with me and the principal. His father was called, and the dad blanched when he saw me. Apparently, a female relative—someone extraordinarily close and important to this child—had died the year prior, and I was her spitting image. I looked exactly like the photo of her in the father's wallet. As I stared at it, the child stared at the floor. He was expelled—he had threatened a teacher in a public and violent display and our hands were tied by a zero-tolerance policy—but oh, how I wish we could have done something more.

The following spring, we had a bomb scare. It was a week after Columbine, when everyone was on edge, and one of our students anxiously reported a ticking sound coming from a locker. The principal and assistant principal were both out of the building, and a newly hired administrator was in her early months on the job. When she made a panicked announcement over the loudspeaker that everyone needed to *run*, the halls became a mob scene. I actually opened my first-story windows so students could climb out and start sprinting. We later found one of those kids more than two miles from the school. Meanwhile, most gathered in the football stadium, creating a chattering cacophony until one word got everyone's attention: *"Look!"*

I looked, and I saw a lone custodian walking back toward the school. Without any protective gear, he entered the building, found the ticking locker, and opened it. I remember wondering: Did he volunteer to go? Was he asked to go? By whom? Was he feeling heroic? Expendable? Protective? Or pissed? I don't know. I do know that he emerged from the building moments later holding a battery-powered Walkman attached to a headset. It turns out a book had fallen and pushed the play button. The music had apparently played quietly until the device reached its end and began clicking, which a student heard and feared was the terrifying ticking of a bomb.

Throughout the school year, I made mistakes. My first semester, I requested that school supplies be in class by mid-September, without knowing that the local factory did not pay parents until the end of the month. I learned that, even then, school supplies would not be a priority for many of the families. If my students really needed things, I had to buy them and distribute them quickly. I learned the hard way that things stored in my classroom, like my camera, might disappear.

I learned that my job entailed much more than being a teacher. I was also a coach, janitor, arbiter, disciplinarian, and friend. I was an amoeba, changing shape quickly and without complaining. During my first year, I taught North Carolina History in Room 120. Three days before my second year began, I was moved into the auditorium and told I would also be teaching Character Education to a selected group. I had no desks, no filing cabinet, no key to the often-locked room, and no curriculum, books, or guidelines for the new class. Instead, I had three days, challenging students, and a list of words around which the administration wanted me to design a new course.

What an epic failure it was at the beginning, as I threw away the history curriculum to teach responsibility, respect, caring, and fairness to kids who had been labeled *disruptive*. But once we also trashed my expectations, those kids were amazing. They were the brash, unbridled bunch who taught me that if we could channel teenage rebellion, it would be a world-changing force. One day, I stood in the classroom, completely exasperated, and asked, "Why are you wasting your time rebelling against *me*? Pick something real to target! Reroute your energy. You could be such a *force*."

In that moment, something shifted. These kids knew they had been identified as disruptive. What they had not been told is that they could do whatever they wanted with that label: reject it, ignore it, or use it. Most world-changing heroes are disruptive, after all, but a hero's aims are not arbitrary.

Finally, we had found our groove. I altered my lessons. Instead of trying to teach this group fairness, I acknowledged that things were not fair. Instead of trying to teach them respect and responsibility, I gave them both. Instead of trying to teach them to care, I asked them what they cared about. We started reading the local newspaper and tackling a few things in the real world.

One time I posed the question, "My generation is destroying your planet—what are we going to do about it?" They began a recycling program for the school. Later, we read an article about a homeless shelter whose residents needed clothing. My students coordinated a sock drive, walking a lap around the gym for every pair that was donated.

When Hurricane Floyd hit North Carolina, hurting our region while absolutely devastating neighboring areas, these kids galvanized an interstate effort. They wrote letters to my hometown in Alabama offering a partnership. If folks in Florence could send donations, my kids would get each donation exactly where it needed to go. My younger sister, then a junior in high school, shared those letters in my small Alabama community. Together, these kids and their classmates collected thousands of pounds of food and medical supplies. It *mattered*. It mattered to the recipients. It mattered to the students. It mattered to the community, who put a photo of their students—including those disruptive leaders—on the front page of the local paper. Those kids earned that recognition, as well as the respect of their own hometown crowd.

~

Speaking of that hometown crowd, I have gotten ahead of myself, detailing events throughout my two years of teaching without describing my first encounters in a new locale. Why?

Because I need you to care about this community before viewing its underbelly. *Every* community has an underbelly. To avoid dismissing towns and entire regions as underbellies are exposed, we have to know and connect with the people who live there. We have to see the good happening amid the struggles.

In North Carolina, I saw middle school teachers open the building early every day so kids who did not have running water could use the gym locker rooms to shower. I saw staff who earned incredibly little money donate their own dollars to provide graduation dress clothes for the most needy kids. They wanted those kids—who had worked so hard to graduate—to walk across that stage feeling nothing but pride. There were White, and Black, and Brown faces on both sides of all those exchanges. This was a *community*.

Except when it wasn't. Racism is real, and I now realized it is everywhere, including in all the places I lived before moving to North Carolina. But still, when I first arrived in Warren County, it shocked me. For the first time, I entered rooms as an adult and was spoken to plainly. I was in a place where, initially, no one knew anything about me except what appeared on the surface: my gender and my skin color. Based on those characteristics, assumptions were made about how I viewed the world.

In other words, some bigots were very honest with me.

For example, when I moved to rural North Carolina, I had heard there would be a number of housing units available to rent, but when I looked at listings in the paper, I could only find a few options. The best was twenty minutes from my teaching job, and when I stood in the front yard, I could see a prison at one end of the street and a cemetery at the other. Where were all of these available units?

I was told I would need to ask locals—that real estate was more of a word-of-mouth business here. I was informed that the best place to talk was at church. So I went to the church recommended to me (the White church), asked random congregants about housing, and began touring spaces.

I was directed to one man who met me at his rental property and, as he unlocked the door, apologized that he could not list his properties in the paper. "We can't," he told me, "because that would tell the Blacks they're ready and legally we'd have to rent to them." As I absorbed that, he continued, urging me to see past the pile of boards and rags on the floor—and to ignore the fact that all the appliances were unplugged and pulled away from the walls. "We just keep it like this so we can tell any Blacks who see the place that we're not physically prepared to put it on the market," he explained very easily. "But I could have it cleaned up for you in less than an hour."

So I found another landlord—I would not rent from someone I knew was racist. Instead, I ended up living in a cinder block apartment in the back of a store. A neighbor who came over to introduce himself actually told me that if anyone bothered me there I should shoot them, but warned me to make sure I dragged the dead body over the threshold into the house before anyone came to investigate. "That will eliminate any dumb questions about whether a young White woman really needs to use force to defend herself," he said.

At the time, I believed the problem was confined to a few racists. I thought the solution was to punish those who discriminated and to make sure my classroom was a safe space with a color-blind teacher. I would serve my students by making sure race was never an issue in our classroom. I would devote myself to providing an equal opportunity for every child, making sure the American Dream was open to all.

It was—and is—a pervasive mentality. Lots of good folks believe punishing racists will eliminate the problem. Lots of good-hearted teachers tell students that hard work is sure to get them to the top. If that is your belief system, I understand you. I was you. And then I learned the hard way that *I was wrong*.

I learned the hard way that I could not ignore race while also engaging in the actual lives of my students.

I learned the hard way that I could not convince poor minority children (the ones without adequate housing or money for school supplies, the ones whose curriculum I was asked to throw out in order to focus on their character) that they lived in a meritocracy without causing those kids immeasurable harm.

~

It was a spring day, during my first year of teaching. The year was going OK. Those initial months were bumpy—I was overwhelmed—but things improved as I settled into a rhythm. And things really improved when basketball season started. Kids viewed me differently once they realized I could coach, and that I was always willing to play.

Columbine had not happened yet. We had not had our bomb scare. My character education class would not convene until next year. At this point, I was steadily working my ass off, determined to teach North Carolina history to the best of my ability.

I was still so completely color-blind that, as I moved my class through historical eras, I prepped my lesson on the Civil Rights Movement without hesitation. The official North Carolina Standard Course of Study stated that I was supposed to "explain the impact of human and civil rights issues throughout North Carolina and United States history." And so I would. Even better—I would do it with enthusiasm.

On the spring day designated for that lesson, I stood at the front of my classroom and celebrated the impact of racial protests during the 1960s. The peak of my impassioned speech came when I asked the students, "Can you imagine how different our classroom would look if it had not been for the Civil Rights Movement? If they segregated us by race? *Can you imagine if skin color was what opened doors?*" As I made the point, I looked at my class—for the first time—with race in my conscious line of vision.

And I realized that every single student in class that period was a person of color.

Every single student was either Black, Latinx, or Native American.

Every single one.

How different would our classroom look if society was segregated? The answer hung there, heavy, like a ton of bricks that would hit me a split second later: *not much different at all.*

My students had bused in that morning from housing that was still largely segregated. The schools were still mostly segregated as well. I was a White teacher, but I was up there spouting gibberish that helped no one— teaching social studies while being blind to the actual world.

I had not *seen* my students. I was not paying attention to *who* was facing the academic, economic, and (many) other challenges that had led a national nonprofit to place me in this struggling school. I had ignored race, which meant that in addition to ignoring—failing to celebrate—an aspect of each student's identity, I was blind to how challenges disproportionately impacted entire communities of people. I was blind to the fact that my celebration of the civil rights movement—my speech about how it changed everything—was taking place in a significantly segregated school.

Until that one moment—a powerful moment of horrifying, humbling awareness that I experienced in a room full of students.

I will never forget the look on my students' faces in that moment.

They saw it all happen. They watched those bricks of realization hit me. They saw the scales on my eyes dislodge, and then fall. They bore witness, and as they observed their teacher, the glazed expressions they had worn during my ignorant ramblings became raised eyebrows during my stammering epiphany. Then they sat there with crossed arms, cold stares, and shaking heads—tinged with a tiny bit of hopeful relief—as I finally caught on.

~

So I began paying attention to skin color. I wanted to recognize it, applaud it, and note spaces in which representatives of different races were absent and ask, "Why aren't they here?"

Unfortunately, I would answer that question incorrectly for two additional years.

I would erroneously continue to think that all of the absences, all of the problems, all components of all racial issues our country faces, were the result of one persistent problem: racist bigots.

Some of these racist bigots were assholes, so I confronted them. Some of these racist bigots were ignorant, so I educated them. I did this everywhere, in all sorts of situations, even when Black allies did not want me to (making my ignorance both disrespectful and extraordinarily dangerous).

I felt it was important to address individuals because, in my mind, the problem was individual racism. I did not yet understand that racism is systemic and institutionalized—and also in all of us, including me.

~

Two years later, I was a student at the Harvard Graduate School of Education (HGSE). This next step in my professional development felt right because I loved teaching and I wanted to learn more about how to do it well. Also, Harvard had just announced a new focus on urban education, and I was drawn toward the socioeconomic settings it intended to embrace and examine.

I entered HGSE with a few enormous misconceptions. Despite my time in North Carolina, I still believed racism was an individual issue and that once we dealt with all the overt racists, things would get better. I also still held fast to the idea of the United States as a meritocracy.

Both of these beliefs fueled my passion for education. In the classroom, I could address racism by educating the next generation. I could also ensure a functioning meritocracy by making sure a good education was accessible to all.

That last statement implies an understanding I need to make explicit: If there is not fair access to equitable education, there is no meritocracy; it is simple logic and clear common sense. But somehow, back then, I managed to believe things were fair enough. I embraced my assumption that if any individual was really willing to work hard, the system would not only support that effort, but reward it.

Then I met a child. I will call him Antonio.

~

As part of my coursework in the HGSE Teaching and Curriculum program, I was required to student-teach in a public school. I was excited about that opportunity, and I asked to be placed in the most under-resourced urban school setting in Boston. Most of my classmates requested the same, so not every request could be honored.

My request would not be honored.

Instead, I would do my student-teaching in a very wealthy suburb of Boston: Brookline.

Brookline was a revelation. I took a tour of its campus the first day and was absolutely amazed at what I saw. The resources were incredible. Brookline—a public high school—had a swimming pool, tennis courts, and a teacher–student ratio that was infinitely better than what I had seen in other school settings. As the tour continued, I discovered that the environmental studies class had its own greenhouse. The dance class had its own studio. The shop class had its own cars.

I should not have been shocked. Over the course of my life, I had been given plenty of chances to notice the gap in educational opportunities. But somehow, I bumbled along, not really compare-and-contrasting until I began student-teaching at Brookline, where it was glaringly obvious that these kids were getting a *lot* more than my other students.

Still, to be fair to these Brookline students, I must acknowledge that they were working very hard. And one of those hardworking kids was a fourteen-year-old Latino freshman: Antonio.

Antonio was a quiet kid who paid attention. He carried a huge backpack that was always filled to the brim with really good work. I was in his history class regularly because I was assigned there. As a student-teacher, it was my designated spot to observe. I was not teaching yet, but I was present. Watching the class. Watching the teacher. Watching all of the kids. Taking notes.

If I am honest, I must confess that Antonio was not any more on my radar than the other students—until the day I was told to keep an eye out for him.

Why was I asked to do this?

Because Antonio had been told not to come back to this school.

It turns out that Antonio did not live in the Brookline school district. He lived in a different district—one with a much poorer school. His parents had used his grandmother's Brookline address to register Antonio because they knew he would get a much better education. So every morning, for several weeks, Antonio had risen, ridden the train across town, and worked hard for his Brookline teachers.

Until yesterday, when Antonio had been told to leave.

I was looped in the day after his dismissal—just a few moments before the bell rang to begin class—because if he showed up, action had to be taken. Someone would need to notify the administration that he was on campus. My mentor teacher could not do it; she was busy teaching our students. This left me as the obvious option.

And so I did.

With a quick word, I notified an administrator that Antonio, with his big dreams and his big backpack full of big Brookline assignments, was in class, right on time, just like always.

And during that private word, Antonio worked. And he kept working, until the administration responded by sending security. And when security arrived, a humiliated Antonio was escorted out of the building, and then off "our" campus. And he never came back into the school.

〜

Antonio. Gone from the building. After my notification.

But I had just been doing my job, right? While the teacher did hers, and while the administrators and the security guards and the folks in the central office did theirs.

None of these individuals were bad, right? We were all public educators. Humble public servants. We had chosen this career in public education because we loved kids and knew what an education could do for them. It could open so many doors.

But in that moment, a key access door slammed shut on Antonio. And as it did, I am sure something shattered in him and his family. I cannot even imagine.

But I can tell you what shattered for me: my belief in a meritocracy. My identification of the problem as an individual issue. And any semblance of self-righteousness. *The problem is in me. And I am part of the problem.* And this problem goes well beyond any one person, or any one school.

What kind of system tells a kid like Antonio—and so many others— that they are not allowed to access this level of education? And then will tell them—years later—that we live in a meritocracy and any lack of progress is their own fault?

A system that is chock-full of problems.

Problems that are systemic and institutionalized and in all of us.

~

I could spend the rest of this book talking about the problems. I could detail discriminatory lending practices that segregate neighborhoods. I could highlight the inequity that results when those neighborhoods are then property-taxed to pay for their own local schools. I could show you pictures of the school in this town versus that one and ask where you would like to send your six-year-old daughter, who is too young to be responsible for any of this, but whose life trajectory will be enormously impacted by systems beyond her control. I could tell you which states step in to try to level the playing field a bit and why it isn't nearly enough (I see you, North Carolina). I could tell you which states leave it up to the local officials, offering no state-level assistance at all (hello, Alabama). I could tell you what it is like when a child from one district goes to play in a gym in another and is confronted by the ridiculous disparity. I could tell you what that moment does for his or her sense of self-worth.

But maybe just try looking right out your front door.

Seriously. How far do you have to look for the nearest school bus stop?

Peek out your window sometime and pay attention to the age-order of your school district's pickups.

Most school systems have different grade levels share buses, which means elementary, middle, and high schools must stagger their start times. In your community, which age group uses the buses and goes to school first?

In the wealthy and predominantly White school districts I have visited (and within which I now live), the buses pick up the elementary school students first. After running their routes, they come back for the middle schoolers, then the high school students. This is an enormous advantage. Kindergarteners are in their rooms learning by 7:50 a.m., when they are naturally awake and ready. Teenagers sleep in longer and are more alert a few hours later when it's their time to learn.

In poor and predominantly minority communities, the order is often reversed. I have taught in these communities. I have been charged with teaching exhausted high schoolers world history at 7:50 a.m. because they have that early bus time. I have seen kindergarteners fatigued as their afternoon rolls into what should be their nap time. It just doesn't work. So why don't they flip the order? Because they can't. In poorer communities, the teenagers need to get home first so they can meet younger siblings at the bus stop. The adults—who cannot afford a stay-at-home person or other after-school option—are at work.

A solution to even that one problem would require tremendous alterations with attention to social and educational necessities. Still, I believe it can be done. But not if we refuse to acknowledge the problem—and the systems—at work.

I owe Antonio an apology. We collectively owe him—and all his classmates, in both schools—an apology, for so many things.

~

But I did not get the chance to apologize to Antonio back then. I never saw him again. But because of Antonio, I began seeing other things differently.

The world is unjust.

This meritocracy is a myth.

I am part of a systemic problem.

ASKING THE RIGHT QUESTIONS

During my year at Harvard, I lived in a tiny basement studio with a floor so lopsided I had to take my computer table off its wheels to keep it in place. I loved it. Part of the appeal was the location. It was walking distance to my classes at HGSE. It was also walking distance to a bus stop, which came in handy after the city dropped a large dumpster on my car. Another part of the appeal was the address: 2 Ware Street, a homonym for "to where?" that I found appropriate and funny.

I also loved HGSE, right from the start. I was enrolled in the school's TAC (Teaching and Curriculum) program, which prepared educators to work directly with students in classrooms. With all my various wanderings and involvements, I really thought I had seen everything when it came to orientations. But HGSE and its faculty won me over almost immediately.

The TAC professors knew we were all there to become teachers, and they were determined that we would internalize two messages that very first week: Our social location impacts what we can see, so we should pay attention to it and work to expand our vision, and teachers need to know their students, which requires helping students know themselves.

The professors had each of us complete and discuss a Myers–Briggs assessment. I had never even heard of the tool and was fascinated. My responses identified me as an INFJ: Introverted-Intuitive-Feeling-Judging. The INFJ type is often labeled an "idealist" and "advocate." In addition to being creative and caring, with high moral standards, INFJs like to translate their ideals into action. It's hard not to enjoy that characterization—until you realize there are also some serious draw-backs. Those include being stubborn, overly sensitive, uncomfortable with confrontation, perfectionist, and private to the point of seeming aloof. In addition, we tend to overanalyze everything and have a blind spot in our worldview, missing moments of simplicity as we look for connections everywhere. Finally, we can become melancholy, since our tendency to search for meaning can spiral into an existential crisis that makes us world-weary, while our empathetic instincts can lead to emotional exhaustion.

As I sat in that HGSE classroom, reading through those descriptors for the first time, I felt both stunned and relieved. It was jarring to see so much of myself there on the page. At the same time, I was so grateful to have something external I could point to and say, "A lot of this feels accurate." It helped to have a starting point in a conversation with an entire community that believed it was important that each of us feel seen.

INFJ is the rarest personality type, making up only 1 to 3 percent of the population. Also, based on our tendencies, even if two of us did manage to find each other, it would be difficult to get to know each other. And then we'd both need time apart to recharge.

Fortunately, I didn't need carbon copies. What I needed were friends.

~

I remember the exact moment I began hoping Liz A. would be one of those friends. It was during that first week of HGSE, as the faculty continued to model how we should enter our classrooms. They staged a mock math class—asking us to play the part of middle school students—and began the lesson with a question designed to grab our attention. That question had been written by a professor on the board. It read:

Find four odd numbers that, when added together, equal the number sixty-three.

The professor gave us a few minutes, saw everyone looking quizzical, and then provided the answer:

Since adding four odd numbers will always equal an even number, the task cannot be done.

Everyone looked relieved except my classmate Liz A., who raised her hand and told him it *could* be done, and that she would be happy to reveal the method. In response, the professor launched into a mathematical explanation intended to convince Liz that you simply cannot get sixty-three by adding four odd numbers.

Liz responded by insisting it was possible and asking if she could write her answer on the board. The professor agreed, and Liz wrote the following:

$$60 + 1 + 1 + 1 = 63$$

The professor looked sympathetic and told Liz her answer was wrong because sixty was not an odd number. Liz, who still had the dry-erase marker in her hand, simply continued writing until something like this emerged on the board:

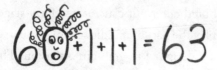

Then she turned to that Harvard professor and told him he needed to expand his definition of "odd."

Unable to restrain myself, I approached Liz immediately after class, introduced myself, and told her she needed to decide whether she wanted me as a friend or a stalker.

I am so very grateful she chose friend.

~

Friends like Liz were a big thing I appreciated about that year at HGSE. Another thing I appreciated was how frequently I had my perceptions rattled. So many of my friends and professors and advisors rattled me in ways I absolutely did not expect.

For example, one advisor pulled me aside and told me to stop working so hard on every element of every lesson for every class period.

Was he joking?

No, he wasn't. He was looking at a twenty-six-year-old student-teacher who had decades in front of her and had to learn how to avoid burnout.

The week after he told me to relax, he watched me crash and burn in a ninth-grade classroom. While trying to teach students how Aztecs could elevate their social standing by earning spoils of war, I actually said—out loud, to an audience of fourteen-year-olds—"after the war, the most successful soldiers got booty."

I heard myself, immediately blanched, and began stammering. With a look, I dared any of those teens to comment.

But what I could have done—my advisor suggested later—was *relaxed*.

I could have stopped and laughed at myself, giving the kids permission to laugh along with me.

"You chose the wrong word," my advisor acknowledged. "It's embarrassing. But it's also funny. And really human. Those human moments are opportunities to connect. If you had laughed at yourself, the student who whispered 'so *that's* why the Aztecs fought so hard' could have cracked the joke out loud while you face-palmed and begged to rephrase. It's not about running a tight ship; it's about creating a classroom community—a space where it's OK to mess up, then learn something."

He was right.

Another thing I appreciated was the constant attention to how our social location influenced our perceptions—and others' perceptions of us. I knew I was privileged. I knew my money and education greased big wheels. What I didn't realize was how my color and carriage greased small ones, every day, all the time, allowing me to slide effortlessly in and out of situations that would demand an energetic and emotional toll from others.

I began to realize how frequently I took advantage of unjust systems. Back in Manhattan, when I needed a change of study scenery, I would put on a nice outfit, pack up my medical textbooks, and take the subway to a fancy downtown hotel. I would sit in the lobby, spread my books on a table, and enjoy complementary lemon water, soft music, twinkling lights, and people-watching during climate-controlled study breaks. Never once did it occur to me—even as I dressed the part—that I was taking advantage of a system of privilege. I was White, well-clad, and welcomed. And never once was I asked to leave.

The same thing had happened in Colorado, in a cluster of cabins that were closed for the winter. Until an exception was made. For me.

It was during my twenties that I really began to realize how many of the doors I slid through were closed to others. It was during that year at Harvard that I saw that door slam on Antonio.

No—I am lying to myself. It is so easy to lie to ourselves. I did not see the door slam on Antonio. I helped slam the door.

Something in me fundamentally altered the week of Antonio's exit—several things, actually. I have already addressed alterations in my understanding of privilege and justice and merit and my own culpability.

But something else altered, too.

My idea of what it meant to be a student shifted during my time at HGSE. Prior to that year, I had always worked for my professors. That year, I felt like my professors were working for—and with—me. They did so while I worked for myself and for my future students. The program was only a year, which seemed like so little time to examine cracks in my foundational beliefs, realize much of that foundation wasn't worth saving, and begin constructing a new one.

I tried to take advantage of every resource HGSE offered, and I paid attention when they pointed to gaps in their own program. One of those gaps was diversity within our cohort. I learned a ton from all of my classmates, but as a group, we acknowledged that voices were missing. There were students of color in our class—a handful of Black, Latinx, and Asian American peers—but having such a small number placed an unfair burden on them. In addition to working on their own education and learning how to educate their own future students, they were generously taking time to educate me.

All of these experiences and thoughts came to a head one day as I engaged in a weekly "Urban Education" seminar with our cohort. This seminar was everything that was impressive about HGSE. It had been thoughtfully constructed, with attention to environment and exposure and impact. In stark contrast to our mornings in public schools and our afternoons in Harvard classrooms, this was an evening around a buffet table. The spread was incredible—particularly for students who had consumed to-go breakfast on buses and bites of lunches while on the job in public school cafeterias. As we ate, we relaxed and chatted with a parade of incredible thinkers. I wish every educator in the world could savor a chocolate treacle tart while chatting with Howard Gardner about the multiple types of intelligence students possess. I wish everyone could chew on the idea that we should celebrate all those intelligences—not just the ones schools tend to measure—while admiring both the brilliance of Gardner and whoever made that mouthwatering tart.

But as I looked around that impressive setting, I began calculating the cost of this event and environment, and an idea was born.

What if we skipped the buffet and just talked? What if our entire cohort told HGSE we would eat on our own before we arrived if they would use the money they saved on the spread to do something? I had just been part of removing a minority student from that classroom in Brookline—I had to do something. What if I could be part of helping a minority student enter a classroom here?

I proposed the idea in the form of a question. Would our class be willing to forgo the food typically served at the weekly seminars and ask Harvard to redirect the budget for those meals toward a grant for a minority student at HGSE?

Eventually, a hardworking committee of classmates would draft a mission statement that explained the idea in more detail. Our class voted unanimously to approach the administration with the idea, and the administrative response was incredibly supportive.

I had only one classmate approach me with concerns. It was not a concern for herself; she had money. She was instead concerned for our classmates who depended on that meal. Was it OK to ask them to give it up?

I understood her concerns, but when I explored the situation, I discovered the same thing I had encountered before and would encounter again many times over: Our classmates who struggled the most financially were the ones most committed to making this easier for a future student. Their empathy and investment were absolutely off the charts. They were particularly keen to help a student who had obstacles beyond those with which they were dealing.

And so the Teachers of Color for Urban Education grant was born. It was not an earth-shattering amount of money. We sacrificed our eight remaining dinners. Meals for fifty at $12 per head for eight weeks meant we had $4,800 to give. So we gave it, with the hope that it would make a difference financially (especially after my friend Laura penned a letter to Harvard alums sharing the story hoping to inspire gifts through other channels), but also psychologically (a demonstration of investment) and symbolically. We were determined to acknowledge our own culpability and to do something—now and in the years ahead.

~

It is important to highlight how immersed one can be in these issues and still not see them.

In the midst of the grant development process, I sent an email to a Harvard professor. The entire purpose of my note was to finalize details on our grant, which was intended to challenge the social structure. Still, in the last paragraph, I asked a personal question that revealed my blind-eye view of that stagnating structure at work. I told the professor that although I wanted to teach in an urban school, I was only receiving interview offers in suburban settings. How long did they think I should wait for an urban offer before looking elsewhere?

The professor, God bless them, had to explain to me *again* that this was part of it. They told me that struggling schools were going to be late on everything for a myriad of reasons. Those schools faced obstacles on all fronts, including hiring. Their delays meant they lost teachers who weren't willing to—or could not afford to—risk the wait.

I waited. And eventually, I was offered an interview at a public, urban institution: South Boston High School's Excel Academy.

~

South Boston High School, "Southie," was among those schools court-ordered to desegregate by busing in 1974. It became infamous for the resulting violence, which included assaults on Black students, KKK marches in the streets, and Boston police officers in riot gear. Ultimately, a National Guard presence was required to keep the peace.

Race was the most obvious issue, as White students were bused to Roxbury and Black students were bused to South Boston. Economics and politics were also at play, as both schools were impoverished. Southie—a White, Irish-Catholic community—included some wealthier families, but many lived and schooled apart from poor Whites until the issue of busing brought them together. At that point, they rallied against common enemies, namely Black students and anyone who supported desegregation and busing.

The result was "White flight" to private schools and into the suburbs of Boston, which essentially resegregated South Boston High School.

This resegregation persisted, but by the time I was hired at Southie in the fall of 2002, two significant things had happened: First, just a year prior, in 2001, the school had been restructured. Inspired and funded by the Bill and Melinda Gates small-school movement, Southie had become three separate academies with three separate principals. The three schools (including the one that eventually hired me, Excel Academy) shared the original building, a well-documented history, and a sports program—all still under the name of South Boston High School. Second, on January 6, 2002, the *Boston Globe* published an exposé on sexual abuse of minors within the Catholic Church's Boston archdiocese. These crimes had the potential to impact parochial school (and by extension public school) enrollment—particularly in a largely White, Catholic neighborhood like South Boston.

So, by the spring of 2002, it was natural for administrators at Southie to begin preparing and to wonder what might unfold if more White families began sending their children to what was by then a predominantly minority school.

And it was in the spring of 2002 that I interviewed at Southie.

I had all of this in mind when, on the day of my interview, I took the T (subway) from Harvard to South Boston. I walked up the streets I had seen filled with rioters and police in 1970s photos, and I met an administrator of Excel Academy. I thought the meeting went well, but later discovered that they were hesitant about me. Post-interview, they expressed that hesitation in a conversation with one of my Harvard professors. Specifically, they called to ask why on earth Harvard had sent a young, sweet, fragile-looking, Southern-accented White girl into an environment that required tenacity and grit. They mentioned a fight that had broken out while we had interviewed, during which—in addition to being worried about the students—they had been worried about me. They needed assistance, not someone else they had to protect.

My professor told them, "Behind Kristi's sweet smile is a will of steel. Hire her. She can handle it."

And just like that, my plans for the next year were set.

~

I should clarify that my big-picture plans were set. My actual classroom lesson plans, on the other hand, needed some work. For assistance with that, I turned to my friend and classmate Betsy B.

Betsy was a powerhouse in our HGSE program. She enlivened us, inspired us—and held us accountable. I recall two specific moments in class where she got my attention. The first was when she raised her hand during one of my class presentations and admitted she could not see anything on the overhead. She was legally blind, able to view all of us and most presentations at close range, but the tiny font I had chosen rendered my posted notes absolutely illegible to Betsy. Did I have a copy of the overhead notes she could borrow to follow along?

On that day, Betsy taught me a valuable lesson about viewing my own teaching from the students' perspectives. Betsy had raised her hand, admitted a struggle, and—in an extraordinarily kind way—suggested how we could fix it. I was lucky to have made the mistake in a graduate-school classroom where a student had the courage to stand up and say, "If it's done this way, I can't." I could not expect the teenagers in my classes to demonstrate that willingness. I had been thoughtless, but Betsy's bravery that day made me much more thoughtful about my teaching going forward.

The second was during a class we took on adolescent development, within which Betsy shared a reflection on her own teenage years. She said, "I remember looking at these sweet, quiet, well-mannered girls in high school and wanting so much to be like them. I tried, disappointed myself, and finally had to acknowledge that, for me, that persona was never going to fit." As she revealed this, I stared at this vibrant, edgy, quick-witted, caring, hilarious ball of loving exuberance that was Betsy, and I was so grateful she was who she was—and had not spent a lifetime trying to be someone she wasn't.

As luck would have it, Betsy and I were hired by different Boston public schools to teach the same ninth-grade world history course, so we decided to plan together. We began this process one Saturday in a room at HGSE. The room was full of tables and whiteboards and all sorts of resources—but the only resource I needed in that room was Betsy.

Because Betsy knew how to ask the right questions.

~

So far, this section of the book—subtitled "Asking the Right Questions"—has danced around several, including *Who am I? Who are my friends? How is my social location limiting my vision? How am I culpable? And how do I make amends?*

But Betsy taught me that sometimes, we don't have to dance around questions. Sometimes, we can just ask whatever it is we really want to know. Part of this approach is simply and instinctively Betsy. Still, it is worth noting that Betsy—like all teachers—is trained in the art of asking questions. Educators are taught to ask questions that are thought-provoking and demand high-order thinking—questions that will continue to inspire ideas, even if asked over and over again.

Betsy and I were incredibly excited to craft these types of course questions. We were teaching world history! There were so many valuable lines of inquiry. Oh, the lofty questions we could have our classes consider: questions about historical context and present-day impact. We considered sample questions such as, "How does the legacy of earlier groups and individuals influence subsequent generations?" We were *into* it. That day, Betsy and I shared high-level discourse, delved into deep thoughts, and used a lot of big words. At a glance, it probably appeared impressive.

But Betsy was not impressed with our efforts. She was frustrated. In fact, she was getting pissed. She wanted the question to be essential not only to our world history course, but to our *students*.

"I wish," she told me, "I *really wish* we could toss out all this garbage and ask something truly important. Something like, *Why does the world look like shit?*"

Both of us stilled in that moment, as her words hung between us. The air around that question felt different. The question itself felt different. It was authentic. It was important. It was something we—and our students—wanted to know the answer to.

Maybe it wasn't *exactly* the right question—but hearing it out loud liberated us. We could ask anything. We could make sure there was a tone of authenticity and import, and "*Enough* with the bullshit; let's learn what *matters*."

And we were the teachers.

It was a tone we could set.

～

Betsy and I eventually designed a course that focused on four essential questions, which we printed in huge letters and hung on our classroom walls:

1. What does the real world look like?

2. What do you want it to look like?

3. Why doesn't it look that way?

4. What are you going to do about it?

Our final assessment would require students to answer those four questions from their own perspective in an essay and complete an action project that moved their vision for the world forward.

To prepare the students to complete this assessment, we would explore the world's history. In each era, on each continent, we would examine how different people and cultures had answered those questions. As we learned, we would print out all the different responses (correctly attributed to their authors) and hang them near the questions on the walls. By the end of the year, it would be obvious to our students that China and India and the United States and Muhammad and Confucius and Buddha and Jesus and Gandhi and MLK and immigrants and landed gentries and dishwashers and ancient Aztecs and *everyone* had different answers to those questions.

We would insist that these responses—formulated throughout history— be used to inform and challenge each student's thinking as each drafted his or her own personal response to the questions. There would be no right or wrong answers. But if you wanted to pass the class, you had to answer them all thoughtfully and then do something to enact your vision for the world.

Our final lesson would be a celebration of the process and a reminder that it was not over. Throughout their lives, our students would need to ask and answer those exact same questions—over and over and over again— not only for themselves, but for the world.

~

Betsy and I learned a lot from our students that year. Students are incredible teachers, if we are willing to listen to them. They will tell us what works, what doesn't, and what the school needs.

They will also tell us about themselves, if we ask.

The most vivid example I saw of this came in a classroom of mine a few years later (after I had married, moved, and was teaching in a different community). A few months into the school year, I felt something shifting in my new high school classroom. My students were becoming less engaged and more disruptive. I had to turn things around. One way to attempt this would have been with punishment—demerits for sleeping in class, detention for disorder. But I wanted to try something different. So instead of telling the principal that some troublemakers were headed his way, I asked him for a favor. I asked him to hire a substitute teacher for two days that I would be in the building. For those two days, the sub would monitor my class while the kids completed work at their desks. As they worked, I would call each of my students—one at a time—into an individual five-minute conference.

The goal of that five minutes would be to let each student know I was listening. That I really wanted to hear whatever they really wanted to say.

The principal, initially hesitant, ultimately agreed. I then broached the idea with each of my classes. I told my students that I thought we could become a stronger community if we knew each other better. I wanted to really *see* each of them. To get that process started, I was taking two days away from teaching. For two days, I just wanted to learn: about them, from them. To that end, each of them would have five minutes of uninterrupted time to say whatever they wanted. Their homework for the next few nights was to think about this one essential question: If you knew someone really wanted to get to know you—and you had five minutes to start a yearlong conversation—what would you say?

I tried to take the pressure off by telling them they didn't have to say anything. Maybe what they needed was five minutes to rest—they could have it. Maybe they needed five minutes of fun; we could play a short game. Maybe they would tell me their best memory or their craziest dream or simply how I could do a better job for them as their teacher. Maybe they wanted to use their five minutes to ask me a question. If so, I would do my best to answer it honestly. Or maybe—if they knew someone was truly listening—they had something else they really wanted to say.

So I tried to truly listen.

And those kids had *a lot* of things they wanted to say.

I spent the rest of the year following up on all of the stories and ideas and requests I heard—always with my students' permission. Conversations with families and counselors and learning specialists. More conversations with kids. The vibe in our classroom improved immediately, but honestly, accomplishing that goal had become secondary. These were not *students* anymore. They were *people*, with challenges, in need of adult assistance. Needing to be reminded that the people around them truly cared. Some of them didn't actually need anything from me, but it still changes the dynamic when someone gives you their full attention for even five minutes and says, "The school has invested in this moment because you matter. I am listening. I see you, and I really do care."

Those moments can be harder to come by in a busy, crowded classroom. I never had two days like that in South Boston, but I still tried very hard to get to know my students. That girl who always came in late, looking exhausted? Her mother had cancer. I only discovered that when I asked her if there was a story behind all the tardies. She spent each morning making sure there was food within easy reach of a mom exhausted by chemo. She broke down in tears as she described going to take a shower and discovering that the bathtub contained several clumps of her mom's hair.

There was also the girl who tried out for the basketball team, then heard me say that practice every afternoon would be mandatory from 3 p.m. to 5 p.m., no exceptions. She approached me after that tryout and told me she wouldn't be able to play because she had to be in line with her family at the homeless shelter by 5 p.m. every night in order to get a bed. *Right.* You're on the team. And we'll make sure you have a bed.

Finally, there was the kid who simply stopped showing up one day—then was back two months later—and then appeared at my door during her lunch block. I cannot share her story. But I can tell you that she needed assistance, and an entire team of people would help provide it. It would require out-of-school intervention. And kindness. And understanding. And investment. And connection with a kid who needed someone to ask her how she was doing and then pay attention to her answer.

The truth is, all sorts of connections happen when we take time to care. And to listen. And to ask ourselves and others essential questions.

~

With that in mind, how can this section end but with a couple of questions? The first is a version of the one I asked of my students. The second is one I had to learn to ask of myself.

If the world (or someone safe in your world) was really listening, what would you say?

Also, *is there anything your inner voice is trying to say to you?*

A BIG GOD AND A MINUSCULE MOLD

The ideas I explored during Teach For America (from 1998 to 2000) and at HGSE (from 2001 to 2002) were closely connected. I spent time during both experiences asking questions about teaching and race and justice and identity and access.

But chronologically, there was a yearlong gap between the two programs. During that gap, from 2000 to 2001, I lived in St. Louis, Missouri. I moved there, at the age of twenty-six, because I wanted to explore a relationship with a guy I will call Logan.

I had met Logan in Houston, during the Teach For America summer training program. We became friends, but we knew it would be a long-distance friendship. That TFA summer was preparing me for my two-year commitment in rural North Carolina while Logan was training for his two-year placement in the Mississippi Delta.

Logan and I remained friends during our TFA experiences by occasionally connecting on the phone. For the bulk of that time, I was either in a serious relationship with Luke, recovering from the emotional toll of that breakup, or—eventually—casually dating guys I met in North Carolina.

Logan visited me once during the second year of my TFA commitment—he was traveling to a school nearby so we seized the opportunity to connect—and during that visit, we wondered if the friendship could become something more. It was a weekend full of meaningful conversations about teaching and coaching and life and family and students and perspectives and thoughts. There was also laughter, so much simple, joyful, this-guy-gets-me-and-I-get-him-and also-every-joke-he-cracks *laughter*. It was good, and soon we were dating long-distance.

I liked Logan—a lot. He was not a Christian. Instead, he was an incredible person who made the whole world, and then my world, brighter with all kinds of sparks. Still, I knew the religion piece would weigh on me, and then on us. And I knew that my pattern would typically be to spend a year, get soul-angsty, and end it. But this time, I was determined not to let it simply play out that way. This time, I decided to take a year and set aside all my other identity crises and really *focus* on religion and spirituality. If the faith of my childhood wanted me to sacrifice another relationship, it was going to have to stand up to some serious examination.

I moved to Missouri in July of 2000 and rented an apartment near Logan, who was enrolled in a program there. I actually worked two part-time jobs that year, but the main requirement for each was that they not distract me in the mornings, which I kept clear for religious study. Every day, I rose, prayed, read, reflected, wrote, grappled, and fought my way through readings from, or about, the world's religions. I had many questions about all types of faith, but the two that were most pressing with regard to my current relationship were *Am I a Christian? And if so, can I marry a non-Christian?*

~

Fun fact: As I entered this period of existential crisis, Malcolm—the college boyfriend with whom religious differences had proved insurmountable—affirmed a conversion to Christianity and married a minister. It was the ultimate irony, but at least I was not caught off guard since we had stayed in touch over the years. He had even visited me once after his Christian conversion, but during that trip we discovered that our spark had been subjected to too much and had died. He met his wonderful and gracious wife while she was a seminary student. Anyway, one weekend—during my year in Missouri—I went to their wedding. At the reception, Malcolm's bride told me a guy named Chris had been key in her own spiritual development. Malcolm told me that I—with the similar name of Kristi—had been key in his. We all smiled over shared paths and departures and reconnections. Then we all hugged and said goodbye.

~

My mom once told me she knew God had a sense of humor because of something that occurred when she was a young mother, wrangling children into clothes, wrangling breakfast into children, wrangling children into the car . . . crazy mornings where she managed the bulk of the home front while my dad prepared for work. During my mom's first break of the day—while my dad was at work, my older brother and I were at school, and my younger siblings watched an episode of *Sesame Street*—my mom would head into her bedroom to touch up and regroup. And there, she would see my dad's empty coffee cup.

And every day, that cup made her angry.

Why could he not carry his cup to the kitchen? She'd asked him hundreds of times. Every day, during what should have been her first moment to breathe, she fumed. Did he not remember? Not care about the space she had been asked to occupy? Not care about her?

She said she finally reached her breaking point and kneeled down to pray. "God," she prayed. "I am begging you. Please, please show me you are listening by having him never leave a dirty coffee cup in this bedroom again."

That very evening, my dad came home from work and announced he was giving up coffee. He had decided he didn't need or want the caffeine. My mother was stunned. The next morning, she made a beeline to the bedroom after he left for work, just to smile at the empty spot where the coffee cup had frustrated her on so many occasions.

And in that spot was a dirty glass sporting the remnants of orange juice.

My mother laughed. She said she laughed so hard it brought her to tears. She picked up the glass, carried it to the kitchen, and loaded it into the dishwasher. And for many years, she continued to do exactly that. But she maintains that the experience gave her a new perspective. Instead of a dirty cup making her feel angry and isolated, it made her smile.

~

I am not sure what to make of that story. But I can tell you that, at Malcolm's wedding, and during my year in St. Louis with Logan, I did not find God funny. I fought with Him. And—even though it scared me—I tried to cast everything I knew about Him aside.

At the start of that year in Missouri, I tried to be a blank slate. I cleared my desk, attempted to clear my mind, and started reading. I began with a book called *The World's Religions* by Huston Smith. I liked that he focused on the values each religion espoused, instead of their institutions and historical moments. I liked that he wanted to listen carefully to seekers around the world, "lifting their voices in the most disparate ways imaginable" in their attempts to address the divine.[3]

From there, I picked up other pages ranging from those in the Torah, the Qur'an, the Vedas, and *The Analects* of Confucius to those in *The Tao of Pooh, Siddhartha, The Alchemist,* and *Zen and the Art of Motorcycle Maintenance.* I read scientific articles that attempted to explain away the spiritual moments of awakening that had anchored my more recent version of faith. Attempting to keep an open mind, I read with one purpose, asking one question: What are these voices saying?

Eventually, I realized I needed to shift my perspective. I was looking outward, hoping to see something with a big red arrow above it reading "TRUTH" or maybe a giant red dot, like those you see on maps in national parks or near hotel fire escapes that say "YOU ARE HERE."

I realized I was not going to find that in these external sources. To discern "truth," I was going to have to use these sources as various lenses and informants while I looked *in*.

~

Houston, we have a problem.

I had been told my whole life not to trust what I found when looking "in." Not to trust my "self." As I sat at my desk in Missouri, I realized I was *not* a blank slate. As a child, it had been ingrained in me that there was a fork on everyone's spiritual road demanding they make a decision between being *selflessly good* or *selfishly bad*. As a twenty-six-year-old, I could not remove that lens. Even as I took spiritual roads through different faiths, I always looked for the fork, knowing that—as the girl still haunted by pink coats and Kentucky hats—I would choose some version of selfless. Depending on the faith I was studying, I would attempt to deny myself, or transcend myself, or sacrifice myself to whatever lifestyle or practice or outlook was required. Regardless, with my childhood lenses on, being good always came down to being *selfless*.

I learned several key things about faith during this period—and every faith I explored would earn my admiration and respect—but my real religious revolution did not actually come until twenty years later when, at the age of forty-six, I read a page in Glennon Doyle's book *Untamed*. Glennon shocked me when she said that selflessness is *not* the pinnacle of womanhood—that the ideal is actually a woman who is *full of herself*.[4]

This wording was so diametrically opposed to everything I had ever heard or read that it stopped me in my tracks. And as I sat there trying to sort it out, two truths hit me like a ton of bricks. The truths are that

Doyle's idea that *full of self* = *good* is the exact opposite of what I have heard my entire life, and the exact truth of what I have experienced.

My most beautiful, authentic, and generous moments—my most spiritual moments—came when I finally embraced my authentic self. My pilgrimage became personal—and much more powerful—once I acknowledged and appreciated myself as a teacher and a writer and a feminist and an activist— all the things I was told for decades not to be. Those identities are parts of *me*. And embracing them was not just a relief in terms of my professional and personal and community authenticity. It was also a *spiritual* experience. I felt like I was finally becoming the person I was *created* to be.

I no longer believe selflessness is a spiritual ideal. Instead, I now believe that knowing and growing your true self is central to a spiritual journey. I believe that the divine is within each of us and speaks to us through our instincts and passions and identities. I believe that in discovering ourselves we uncover something about the divine. Not everything about the divine, but something. And if we ask other people what *they* have discovered about *their* most authentic selves, we get to know *that* piece of the divine also. What a gift we can give to each other if we look within and share. And what a tragedy if we reject what others are sharing. A loss for us. A cruelty to them. A disregard for divinity.

I also think that exploring inward—and nurturing what I find—is the *opposite* of selfish. I have to know and grow parts of myself before I can share them. I have to get them strong enough to survive on the outside. I have to become so full of myself that the most authentic parts of me can spill over and offer connection. This connection involves generosity of self, not selflessness. Knowing myself, growing myself, and generously offering my authentic self to the world—believing that the real me is good on some core level and could learn something from the authentic you— well, that feels way more spiritual to me than constantly fighting against my own nature.

～

But I did not understand any of that as a twenty-six-year-old. Instead, after a year of study, I ended up only a short (but significant) distance from where I started, a Christian who was slowly discovering herself in some arenas (professional and political) and denying herself in others (material things, relationships, and happiness).

My perspective on a few of those things, including happiness, would shift drastically during my upcoming semester at Harvard. But that story is on hold for a moment, while I wrap up life in St. Louis. As I packed my theology books into moving boxes I would carry away from Missouri, I knew that during my year there, I had reinforced a few—but also laid some new—spiritual foundations.

I had recommitted to the idea of a Creator. I felt the genius and artistry of the world could not be explained otherwise.

I believed that creation revealed something about its source. To me, our world suggested a Creator who enjoyed beauty, admired diversity, respected free will, and was emotional, powerful, and moral.

It made sense to me that a Source would create because He or She wanted expression and connection. At the time, I believed that connection would require me getting over myself.

I had accepted that the question of self was central to my study of spirituality, even if I had no idea my answer to that question would change drastically twenty years later.

And finally—in a significant shift—I came to understand that my childhood vision of God was too narrow.

~

The God I grew up with was thin. He lived in a very small fold. That tiny fold had narrowed spirituality to include only religion, and narrowed religion to include only Christianity, and narrowed Christianity to include only people who think and vote and even dress in a particular way.

After that year in Missouri, reading widely while asking, *What are all these voices saying?* I was *done* with those narrows. And as I expanded my vision, the amount of God I could see grew.

One sentence from Smith's *The World's Religions* kept creeping into my psyche. While exploring the natural pluralism of the Hindu faith, he shared a perspective that "to claim salvation as the monopoly of any one religion is like claiming that God can be found in this room but not the next, in this attire but not another."[5]

To claim salvation as the monopoly of any one religion *limits* God. I was willing to do a lot of things during that year of spiritual study, but I was never willing to limit God.

Creation is awe-inspiring. And complex. And magnificent. I will not limit the Creator of all that to one room or one outfit. That meant I was done with evangelism (including within my romantic relationships) and done with conversion-centered mission work (in any part of the world). I would not tell anyone they were required to enter my room—or my even smaller closet—to meet the Creator of the universe. No. Even if God met me there willingly, why would I try to keep something so vast in such a limiting hold?

~

Let's expand the image. Picture multiple rooms, each representing a different religion or spiritual starting point, and picture each of those rooms in a different spot at the base of a mountain. God is everywhere on this mountain, but some seek Him at the summit, where God feels vast, and it is the air (and everything else we rely on) that feels thin. Each religious room will prepare you differently for the ascent and put you on a different path to the summit. But a God without limits could certainly find His way into all those rooms—onto all those paths—if She wanted to. And I imagine a Creator would want to, since His or Her children are there.

But if any of those children want to meet God where the air (and everything else they rely on) feels thin, they have to climb. I wanted to climb. And, since I had just spent a year studying spirituality and my own interface with it, I knew that I personally needed a religious base camp to begin an ascent.

At the age of twenty-six, I chose Christianity as my home base. I chose it because it was one of the options. And because I was already familiar with its panoramas and pitfalls. And because, if I am being completely honest, I was afraid to leave it. I tried to excise that fearful part of my faith, but it lingered.

And finally—I hope I am being honest with myself here—the real draw to Christianity was Jesus. Not the Jesus I had grown up with—the Biblical bouncer who either opened the gates of heaven or didn't—but the Jesus I met in Missouri.

As I surveyed all types of faith that year, I felt drawn toward religions that maintained the world was *real* and we were supposed to *engage it*. I liked the idea that God is not just sitting on top of the mountain. God is manifesting in us and in others and elsewhere—including as teacher or prophet or on-earth deity that assists with the climb.

I really appreciated that about Christianity. God himself comes down—in the form of Jesus—and gets in the *muck*. If I truly look to Jesus as an example, I am not supposed to transcend the world. I am supposed to engage it. I think it gets lost that Jesus prioritized love for the poor, and that he pursued justice, and that He offered—to any who were struggling—hope, assistance, and grace.

I discovered that Jesus back in the year 2000, in Missouri, and then discovered a particularly powerful description of Him years later, in an article by Craig Warren Greenfield, who wrote, "Jesus was all about turning things upside down. He overturned cultural norms, challenged the authorities, undermined the establishment, and generally shook everything up." Greenfield reminded me that "as far as the ruling authorities were concerned, Jesus was a *huge* pain in the ass. That's why they killed him."[6] Another author I admire, Jen Hatmaker, highlighted that Jesus "loved outcasts and shunned power."[7]

That was the Jesus I found in my Bible back in Missouri.

That was my Messiah.

~

I have been in Christian circles long enough to know what some Bible folks are now thinking.

Some are thinking, "She has succumbed to a false, pluralistic prophet of peace." Some are going through their mental rolodex of Bible verses, choosing one to remind me that Jesus is the *only* way to God. Some want to tell me that if I really loved other people, I would try to save them.

I could get into a theological debate with them about an inerrant view of scripture. I could ask how they think the Holy Spirit has shaped post–Pentecost Christianity, and if they believe that Spirit can still shape interpretations today. I could throw other verses back at them, and we could discuss what it means to accept that others can be "a law unto themselves" (Romans 2:14). I could tell a funny joke about why Saint Peter makes us take our shoes off in certain parts of heaven (OK, just the punchline: "No, it's *not* because we're on holy ground. We just have to walk quietly past this room because the folks in it think they're the *only* ones here").

Instead, I want to describe what I experienced after I released God from His or Her Christian container. I still felt connected. I still loved Jesus. I still wanted to climb that mountain. And I loved that my pathway on that mountain had Christ connecting Heaven and Earth. But I also loved how it made my heart feel to look at people on other pathways, as they bowed in reverence or climbed over spiritual boulders. I saw beauty there. I saw divinity there. And when I saw it, my heart swelled. I felt like the Grinch after his heart grows three sizes.

Here were my three leaps: I would not narrowly define spirituality as religion. I would not narrowly define religion as Christianity. And I would not narrowly define Christianity as requiring me to think and vote and even dress in a particular way.

Because a big God deserves better than our minuscule mold.

GOOD VS. HAPPY

My heart felt bigger as I packed up my St. Louis apartment and made plans to rent a studio near Harvard. But big hearts can be filled with sadness. Logan and I had decided to end things. It turns out reading religious tomes every morning for hours seeking permission to partner isn't the best way to nurture a romantic spark. Also, my ideas were too new; I didn't yet trust them. I didn't yet trust myself. I wanted a companion on that Christian path up the mountain. And Logan deserved a companion who was less in her own head. He also deserved a companion who didn't take pride in denying herself all sorts of things, including happiness.

At the time, I denied myself happiness in several ways, but always for one reason: I thought I could be good or be happy, but not both. I still carried (and displayed and cited) that E. B. White quote about the choice to improve or enjoy the world, and I was clear on my own personal decision. For me, it just didn't feel right to be happy when there was so much pain in the world. I thought I should *stop* dancing, *find* the problem, and *fix* it. And if a problem could not be fixed, I should stay in there and at least try to help.

I no longer believed I had to be 100 percent miserable. I allowed myself, for example, to focus my fixes within a professional arena I actually liked (goodbye, medicine; hello, teaching). But within that new arena, I believed I had to exhaust myself while focusing on what was needed. I believed I would know I had done my part when I collapsed in a heap.

I shared this mentality with my older brother. Today, he is a brilliant orthopedic surgeon whose sharp mind (and tongue) mask an incredibly soft and generous heart. He cares about his family, his community, and his patients. He will verbally cut the system to ribbons, all while using those ribbons as ropes to lead patients to health and safety. He is tireless in those professional efforts. He is the only person I have ever met who came out of his own open-heart surgery with a resolve to spend more time at work. Still, he makes time for family. When I was eventually diagnosed with cancer (in my forties), he made two calls within forty-eight hours, the first to tell me he loved me and was on it, and the second to communicate what he had learned and to offer anything—childcare, medical connections, anything—he could provide. His love language is provision, and he loves well. And he will exhaust himself to do it.

When my brother was in high school, he ran cross-country, and I recall him telling me, "I know I am doing my best when I feel like I am going to throw up the entire time. *That* is how I know I am running fast enough."

I accepted this viewpoint without question—it was identical to mine. We both knew we were working hard enough when we felt *ill*. And if one of us collapsed in a heap? Well, sometimes that was part of it.

Over the course of my life, I will collapse in many heaps. These are literal, physical collapses—within athletic arenas, after tough days in the classroom, and while acting as a martyr mom in my own home. My work-horse I-must-give-until-there-is-nothing-left mentality will make me very effective, right up until the point it threatens to kill me. And I am not as tough as my brother, so that point will come earlier than expected and deliver an important message: that I have to *relax*.

But I will not hear that message at the age of twenty-six. I will not allow myself to relax. I will, however, decide—over the course of that next year at HGSE—that it's OK to be happy. Maybe, just maybe, I do not have to deny the part of myself that wants to enjoy the world once in a while.

〜

Did I really—before that year—think I was not allowed to be happy?

Not exactly. I actually thought it was important to be cheerful ("God loves a cheerful giver." 2 Corinthians 9:7). But carving out time and space to focus on happy? Well, it kind of felt like being told to clean the kitchen (help others) and then deciding to take a break to watch television (something for *you*). You want to keep the volume low because you're not sure it's allowed.

I recall a conversation where I shocked someone with this *meh* perspective on happiness.

I had just arrived at HGSE, and an advisor had asked me about my future plans. I revealed them, and he responded, "That sounds like decades of *miserable*."

I shrugged and replied, "It's only a lifetime."

It sounds strange, but it was a normal perspective for me back then. I was choosing *service*. I was going to *work*. Enjoying myself too much meant I was not working hard enough for others. Plus, after Missouri, I had a renewed spiritual outlook. I was focused on eternity. Surely, I could spend a few decades here devoted to *good* without getting distracted by *happy*.

~

Three things changed my perspective on happiness, and they all occurred around the same time.

First, I was jarred by my HGSE advisor's reaction when I shrugged off a lifetime. He did not admire my commitment. Instead, he was appalled. He put down his pencil and spoke emphatically. "*Kristi*. That is a *horrible* thing to say. Aren't you a history teacher? Don't you know how many atrocities have been committed by people who casually dismissed a life?"

His words surprised me. I had not been talking about anyone else's life; I had been talking about mine. But I recognized a slippery slope when I saw one—and we INFJ's know everything is connected. His response unsettled me and became a seed that grew into much food for thought.

Second, I happened to be reading the Bible's book of Ecclesiastes. And in chapter three, verse twelve, it said: "I know that there is nothing better for people than to be happy and to do good while they live." *Both*. What a concept—wrapped in Biblical permission. Soon, this verse replaced the E. B. White quote on my wall.

Third, I was challenged by a course I was taking. Each student in the Harvard Teaching and Curriculum program was required to take two electives—both outside the school of education—while we were on campus. I chose to take one offered through the Harvard Faculty of Arts and Sciences and cross-listed at the Harvard Divinity School, a course titled "Personal Choice and Global Transformation."

This particular course listing was brand new, inspired by events that had occurred just before my arrival on campus. The previous spring, a two-year, student-led campaign to provide Harvard workers with a living wage had culminated in a three-week sit-in on campus. Harvard students occupied Massachusetts Hall, which housed the office of the university president and other administrators. The protest drew national attention, and Harvard ultimately agreed to the demands.

This "atmosphere of engagement and hope" inspired professor Brian Palmer and teaching fellow Kate Holbrook to design a course.[8] The class would acknowledge enormous inequalities, introduce changemakers, and engage students with difficult questions including, "What are the obligations of those who are comfortable to those who suffer?"

Our very first class meeting was scheduled for September 12, 2001.

One day before—on September 11, 2001—four planes were hijacked, one crashing into a Pennsylvania field, one into the Pentagon, and two into the Twin Towers. As the horror unfolded, I was student-teaching at Brookline, in Antonio's ninth-grade world history classroom. Two of the hijacked planes had originated from nearby Logan Airport, personalizing an international tragedy as students and staff waited to hear if any of their family members had been on the flights.

After a day that included a stint in the auditorium where hundreds of high school kids were told the nation was under siege, I bused home in a daze. I worried about friends I had in New York City whom I could not contact, about Muslim friends everywhere who were now afraid to go out, about my parents who were traveling abroad, and about my classmates—particularly my good friend Liz M.—who would soon confirm that her close friend had died in one of the towers.

The next day—shaken and heartbroken—I entered the course nicknamed "Idealism 101."

You would think, in the midst of all of that, what I would have taken from the class would have been ideas for action. And I did. But the moment that altered me the most came from an unexpected element of the course.

It came from a week devoted to beauty.

Every other topic in the class made sense to me and thrilled me. Even the format brought so much alive. Instead of lecturing, Professor Palmer invited guests in to answer our questions. And by guests, I mean the rock stars of social activism who stood there and answered students' questions—my questions—about their personal lives, their viewpoints, their accomplishments, their self-proclaimed failings, and their plans for changing the world.

We met the founding pastor of a religious homeless community. We met a homemaker who led a convoy of relief trucks from England to Bosnia. We met an attorney who prosecuted perpetrators of genocide in Rwanda. We met an intrepid human rights journalist. We met over a dozen incredible, inspiring, world-altering individuals and had the opportunity to ask them when, why, why not, and how?

One of the rock stars we met was Elaine Scarry.

In our syllabus, Dr. Scarry was identified as "a leading intellectual on questions of war, torture, beauty and human creativity." *Well*, I thought while preparing for the interview, *that's an interesting juxtaposition of interests*. I assumed we would focus largely on how to combat the injustice of torture or the horrors of war.

But as Professor Palmer introduced Dr. Scarry, he surprised me by highlighting her interest in *beauty*. He said today's discussion of beauty would make this week a linchpin of the course. This topic—beauty—would connect to every other person and idea introduced in our classroom.

This unexpected emphasis on *beauty*, and the idea that it could connect with every element of such a powerful course, left me rapt with attention. Professor Palmer then focused that attention by asking a question. He encouraged us to think about each activist we had met during previous sessions. What did they all have in common?

Later, in a book about our course, Professor Palmer would write that these speakers "shared only a seriousness about the need to confront the world's violence and injustice."[9] But that day in class, he emphasized something more.

Each of those activists was working toward something. Each of them was fueled by something. Each of them had encountered obstacles that required them to take a moment to somehow recharge. What provided their inspiration, their energy, and their renewal?

Beauty.

As Dr. Scarry explained it, beauty is not at odds with a fight for justice. Nor is it a distraction. Instead, it is essential. In addition to the ways mentioned above (providing inspiration, energy, and renewal), beauty renders abstract ideals (like fairness and justice) concrete by providing positive examples of symmetry. It demonstrates equity by making itself accessible to all. It increases our capacity for empathy by nurturing our ability to imagine. It prompts the creation of more beauty as we attempt to replicate a portion of what we felt or saw. Perhaps most significantly, beauty decentralizes us. Many things make us feel good. But beauty makes us feel good while we stand outside the center, sparking positive power while each of us considers and then forges a connection between something *within* and something *outside* of ourselves.

I entered the course confused about whether considering our own happiness—our own experience of beauty—is a luxury that compassionate citizens of the world can actually afford.

Yes, said my advisor.

Yes, said Ecclesiastes.

It is not a luxury, said Elaine Scarry, in this inspirational course.

~

I just related, perhaps even conflated, beauty and happiness. For me, that absolutely works. Consider this list of things I find beautiful:

The faces of my loved ones. The colors at sunset. Ocean waves. Flickering firelight. Van Gogh paintings. A wooded hike. A perfectly executed athletic offense. The "Carol of the Bells" coming on the radio unexpectedly. Cinnamon-scented candles. Any interesting idea. The moment when a travel plan I have worked hard on becomes a reality—when I can hear the kids squeal as gravel crunches under that first turn of the tire. Well-chosen words. Really hot showers. Giant redwood trees. Fuzzy blankets. An engaging book. Anything purple. Flea markets full of antique treasures. Quiet. Irish dancing music. And a day in a museum with someone who can make me laugh, knows when to let me be, and can teach me something new about art.

All of these are things I find beautiful. And they are all things that make me happy.

After that class, I finally knew—in my mind—that I should stop feeling guilty about taking time and spending money to enjoy them.

I did still occasionally need to remind my heart.

~

I actually began displaying a visual reminder.

Once, when Luke and I were dating, a friend asked us to watch his children for an afternoon. During a break in the wrestling, tag, and dodgeball action, one of the kids peppered us with some Disney trivia. We did pretty well until he came to a question about Snow White and the Seven Dwarfs. Could we name them all?

We racked our brains but could only come up with six. We racked our brains some more and came up with lots of names they *should* have given that seventh dwarf (why not Stinky? Or Drippy?). Funny, the kid told us, but absolutely not correct.

Finally, to the delight of our small audience, we gave up. Waved the white flag in surrender while his youthful eyes danced.

"*Happy!*" he yelled. "You forgot *Happy!* I win!"

Honestly, what the heck?

The very next week, Luke gave me a present. It was a tiny figurine of Happy the dwarf. He delivered it with a note that said, "So you don't ever forget Happy again."

After we broke up, I tucked Happy away. It didn't feel right to display him as I dated other people. But after that class with Professor Palmer and Elaine Scarry, I dug around in my memory box and found him. I regifted him—from me to me this time. And that tiny reminder that we cannot forget Happy still sits on my shelf.

Blooming on a Floodplain

RELATIONSHIPS

George and Denise joined Teach For America in North Carolina the same year I did. They were husband and wife to each other—and very good friends to me. They actually lived with me for a month in my tiny, cinder block, located-in-the-back-of-a-store apartment. I liked them immediately. They had easy laughs, sharp wits, good hearts, and quick minds. But even more than that, they had the ability to discern paths that were meaningful to them—as both individuals and a couple—and then navigate those paths while packing so much wisdom for, and from, the road. In addition, they were among the most down-to-earth people I had ever met.

Denise and George met in New York. Both had a dream of living in Alaska, so they packed up and moved there, working toward their separate master's degrees. I recall that Denise was hard at work on a biology paper when she realized a few animals would be injured in the study. She immediately switched topics, then programs, becoming a botanist. In *Alaska*. Cue the greenhouses. In addition to being scientists, George and Denise were both teachers at heart, so they eventually applied for TFA and were placed in rural North Carolina, where I met them.

Eventually, they found a house to live in and moved out of my small apartment. Their house was far from school in a beautiful, wooded area, and it had a basement where we hunkered down together during hurricane season. I remember one winter evening when our community got four inches of snow in one night, which was unheard of in North Carolina. I woke up that Monday morning, looked out my window, and immediately turned off my alarm and went back to sleep. There are no snowplows in much of the rural south, and I knew we wouldn't be in school for a week. Forty minutes later my phone rang. George and Denise were calling from a pay phone near our school buildings wondering what they had missed. Where was everyone? This was before email. Before cellphones. Our school faculty had a phone tree: I received a call, then called Mrs. X, who called the next person on the list, and so on until everyone had received word. But George and Denise had received no cancellation call, so they had assumed there would be school. Had I received a call, they wondered?

"No," I told them. "I'm guessing no one called because they thought it would be obvious. It's impossible to drive in all of this snow." Of course, I realized as I spoke, it had probably not felt impossible to people who had driven here from *Alaska*.

I think that is what I liked best about Denise and George. They saw possibility everywhere: in their students, in the schools, and in their own lives.

George and I taught in the same middle school. We shared a parking lot and a principal with the high school that hired Denise. George was a straight shooter. I once heard him tell a class they were a smart group. When they resisted, saying they had been told they were the dumb section, he stopped everything. One by one, George looked them in the eye. He said, "I don't lie to my students. There are times when some of you are lazy, but *none* of you are dumb. You can do this. Let's get to work."

George was a teacher who realized that students—even the ones who initially refuse to do anything—want to be successful. A refusal to do work often means a kid is scared of failing. There are so many students who refuse to try because they would rather be labeled "defiant" ("I *won't* do it" can feel powerful) than risk being labeled "dumb" ("I *can't* do it" brings feelings of shame). George skirted this issue by teaching high school science to our middle schoolers. He did this by recycling one-sided papers from his wife's high school class. There was no risk—his students weren't actually supposed to be able to grasp concepts that were years above them—so they had no fear or shame in failing. And there was huge reward: pride (and bonus points) for those who could go beyond their middle school studies and get the high school questions on the exams. He taught the middle school content, too. Once you had proved you could answer an eleventh-grade question, the eighth-grade ones didn't seem so scary. His methods and his classroom were inspiring. His students *loved* him.

The administration? Well, not so much.

George was worried about our students. They were facing many challenges that required adult attention. One issue in our community was that the principal's attention was literally divided. She was the principal for both the middle school and the high school. George felt strongly that each school needed its own principal, and he said so. As our time in North Carolina wound down, he became concerned that this view had not really been heard. He approached me one day and asked if I wanted to write a joint letter to the editor of the local paper informing parents about the concern.

I agreed with his position, but not the process. I felt strongly that we needed to talk to the principal first. If that didn't work, we should approach the superintendent, then the school board. If all those efforts failed, I would sign the letter, using the media to reach the parents and express our view that this system put students at risk.

George initially agreed with my point, and we made an appointment to meet with the principal. It was a frustrating encounter, to say the least. She never made eye contact with either of us. We were dismissed through distraction. She shuffled papers. Filled out forms. Filed unrelated notes as we talked. I left the meeting disheartened. George left furious. He was writing the letter, process be damned.

George, Denise, and I had lengthy discussions about the following questions: When attempting to enact change, what is our role? If I am passing through a community, how long must I observe before it's OK for me to identify something I see as a problem? Before proposing a solution? Must I commit to staying before advocating for change? Is it OK to start a revolution if you aren't remaining there to fight with your allies? What if you are only leaving this particular battleground but are committed to fighting the same war on another front wherever you go? When attempting to enact change, how long do you go through proper channels before abandoning them for something more drastic? What if you believe those channels themselves—or the people within them—are part of the problem?

Ultimately, George could not leave his students with the situation as it was. He wrote the letter, expressing his concerns about student safety to the community. I respected his course of action—and very much appreciated how it focused the community's attention on what was happening in the schools. Within a year, each school had its own principal. We were not there to see it, but it only makes sense that this would enhance adult attention, safety, and instruction—at both schools.

I did not sign the letter. Even though I was not optimistic that running our concerns through the proper chain of command would do anything, I felt like attempting it would preserve relationships, garner credibility, and ultimately add weight to our claim that the larger community—not just the officials to whom we had already appealed—needed to keep a closer eye on what was happening in both school buildings. George agreed with all of those things, but rightly noted that we were out of time. And he could not leave without doing everything in his power to make sure someone was watching the students we left at the school.

I still don't know if I made the right decision. I do know that I am grateful to have been a part of that community and faculty for two years. I know I am grateful to everyone who advocated and worked for those students, and I am so grateful to have had teammates like George.

~

George and Denise supported one another—sometimes standing shoulder to shoulder, sometimes cheering one another on from the sidelines, and sometimes cheering from another field entirely while they each did their own amazing things. I appreciated seeing how they made all of it work.

When George wrote his letter, Denise decided not to sign it. She worked at the high school and could have added that perspective, but she did not feel the call for that type of action. She wanted to focus 100 percent of her energy on her classroom, and she served her students brilliantly in that capacity. And that was great by George.

When Denise decided to hike the Appalachian Trail right after our TFA commitment ended—a hike that would require six months, two thousand miles, substantial gear, and an extended period of unemployment—George was thrilled for her. He encouraged her, assisted her in the planning, provided support along the way, and occasionally kept her company for a few dozen miles at a stretch—but he did not hike it with her. The trail was her thing. And that was great by Denise.

George and Denise both had tremendous respect for animals and expressed concern about how animals in our food chain were treated. This core value led George to become a hunter who killed and processed his own meat. It led Denise to become a vegetarian. They respected one another's choices and shared a kitchen. Same core values, different expressions, mutual respect.

I was in awe, and knowing them raised the bar for what I wanted out of a marriage even higher. I wanted a partnership like the one they shared.

We kept in touch after TFA ended. Even though there were stretches where life took over and communication lagged, none of us needed constant chatter to feel connected. Still, sometimes greater forces conspire to recharge relationships right when you need them. There was one moment—fifteen years after they had moved away and too many years past our last phone call—when I met someone from their home state of New York and jokingly said, "Oh, you're from New York! You must know my friend Denise!" And—I kid you not—it turned out she was Denise's *sister*.

Well, that prompted me to call Denise to check in. During the call, when I asked if she had anything new going on, Denise replied, "Yes! Well, kind of an *old* new thing. Did you know that I have always been interested in the cello? When I was a little girl, I always wanted to take lessons, but my mother said no. She thought it wasn't ladylike because you have to play it between your legs. Anyway, I realized recently that—at the age of 40—I was still blaming my mother for the fact that I did not play the cello. And that seemed really dumb. So I signed myself up for cello lessons and now I play."

Well, that little wisdom drop from Denise made me rethink my own perspective, path, and familial relationships. It made me start taking ownership of my own here and now. And it reinforced that I was very lucky to have friends like Denise and George.

~

Friendships matter to me. So does family. I love my family, and it's OK that we don't always see things the same way. Still, during my twenties (before my sister came of age), I felt very lonely within my own family. I was different: my relationships, my politics, my career, my spirituality . . . all different.

And lonely was the least of the emotions. At various points, interactions left me feeling devalued (the family joke), dismissed (as an outlier perspective, too far from the norm to be considered legitimate), misunderstood (as actions I considered spiritual were seen as selfish or crazy), and dumb or discouraged (when I did a poor job defending my views).

I am owning my part in this. I am the one who changed—I took more life risks, became more liberal, lived in unexpected places—and I know those changes offended and scared people who loved me. Also, I am not a person who can engage in a healthy debate without feeling drained. Some people enjoy the banter, but I don't. And it stays with me. After one family dinner, I was so discouraged by how poorly I had represented my new political perspectives that I asked my HGSE Equity in Education professor if I could forgo the actual final assignment and instead write what I wish I had said to my family. He agreed, and it turned into a twenty-five-page paper. The next time our conversation turned political, I was going to be ready.

The arguments that ensued were fraught. My parents had been immersed in high-level conservative discourse for decades. I was a newly minted liberal who met with Harvard professors to fine-tune arguments during office hours, and who also issued emotional reminders that *those are my students you're talking about.* It was exhausting for everyone.

At one point, my dad offered me anything I wanted if I would stop responding to statements about race and religion and politics around the dinner table. He actually sent me a cartoon that depicted a family Thanksgiving. The father figure had called for the table's attention, produced a long sheet of paper, and read its contents to everyone gathered. It said something like, "We will begin the meal by reviewing the list of topics no one is allowed to discuss: politics, religion, Aunt Linda's friend . . ."

The cartoon made me feel less alone: this was happening in other households, too. And it was a point of connection with my dad, who wanted to lighten the heaviness that was beginning to descend.

Because families are also a source of light. This was my family. And there were other things to talk about.

We talked about my grandmother Mary Sue and my great-aunt Adine, who were both struggling as they aged. Those conversations reminded me of how much there was to admire in my family. How much we could pull together when needed. How much laughter there can be through tears. My mother became an instant legend when she took my octogenarian grandmother to an appointment, where a doctor told Mary Sue to eliminate sugar from her diet. "No," my mother told him, "absolutely not. She is almost ninety years old. She cannot hear. She cannot see. She cannot walk. Her one joy is sweet treats in a warm kitchen. She will have them, and the rest of us will ask her advice on what we should eat if we want to live ninety years."

My father became an instant legend when he had to visit my great-aunt Adine's nursing home, called in (as if to the principal's office) because she was disturbing other residents. Now in her eighties, Adine was having loud sex with a man on her hallway. In addition, when another resident had reached for a piece of toast off her plate in the cafeteria, she had stabbed his hand with a fork. I could not help but whoop when I heard these stories. My great-aunt was an inspiration! May we all be so spirited during our twilight! My dad shook his head. He had been called in to deal with forking and fucking, all in one horrifying afternoon.

I think it's easy to advise people to set boundaries with their family, but it's tricky in practice. It is hard to transition from having the people who know the most about you as a kid know the least about you as an adult, especially when there is so much love there on so many different levels.

~

The most exhausting part for me was deciding what to say when.

Did I speak up when someone made a political comment, or let it go? Did I smile as jokes were cracked about the revolving door on my dating life, or let it go? Did I defend my wanderings, or just let it all go?

I took different approaches at different times.

Sometimes I laughed along. Sometimes I spoke up. Sometimes I sat silently.

Eventually—for my own mental health—I let the silence take over. The silence began in the realm of politics and religion and then spread into other arenas. I simply stopped revealing anything about my life that I thought might become fodder.

But that tension-free environment came at the price of intimacy.

~

The toughest relationship was with my mom. I was a disappointment to her. More than that, for years she thought there was something fundamentally wrong with me.

In her eyes, I didn't just leave medicine; I had some sort of breakdown. She saw it as such a self-destructive move that she assumed I was—at that point—suicidal. Hence those phone calls, to make sure I hadn't jumped off the George Washington Bridge.

In her eyes, I didn't just end relationships. My refusal to commit was a sign of a serious psychological problem. Hence the inquiries to discover if there had been any abuse.

In her eyes, I was not exploring my faith. I was toying with *damnation*.

I was not becoming more liberal. I was saying things that were *dumb*.

I was not only hard to understand, I was *unlikable*. This is not hyperbole. It was her actual perception. During my HGSE graduation weekend, we gathered for a private celebration with the families of my friends Laura, Liz A., Liz M., and Betsy. As we left that group, my mother said to me, "I didn't realize you had such close friends." The comment struck me as odd, and I said, "But I've told you all year how much I like these ladies." My mother responded, "I knew how much you liked them. I am just surprised at how much they seem to like *you*."

Years later, when the man who will become my husband asks both my parents (separately) for their blessings before offering a ring, my dad responded by saying, "I know you could get someone younger, but you won't ever get someone better." My mother hesitated, then offered, "If you are the one Kristi chooses, I will pray for you." She reminded him that marriage is for life and cautioned that "the things you think you love about Kristi now may be the things that you find you cannot live with later." When he told me about my mom's reaction, it bothered me enough that I approached her directly. "It sounds like you were *warning* him," I said. She replied, "I just think it's better for him to really think about what he is getting. Honestly, it would be better for him to leave you now than when you have children. I was trying to protect you from a greater pain down the road."

Although *protected* is not what I felt in that moment, I knew my mother loved me. But I also knew that for a long time, she just didn't like me—or understand why anyone else would—because I was different. It's a hard thing to make peace with. No one wants to be loved "even though."

~

There are two things that offer me comfort. The first is knowing my mother.

I know she did not put a lot of thought into any of those statements. She is all about motion. The likelihood is that she verbalized fleeting (but apparently recurrent) thoughts.

I know she really believed rejecting parts of me was in my best interest. Moving me toward happiness. Saving my soul.

I know she is a perfectionist. Recall her childhood, wanting to be perfect to earn approval from an alcoholic father. Recall her decades-long faith, based on the idea that God will perfect her. This is someone who is going to be viscerally uncomfortable if her child's life goes offtrack, so she will do whatever it takes to keep it on track. She will advise her daughter to keep quiet and collect As, even from professors who condemn or harass her. She will continually point to a well-thought-out map. She will warn a future son-in-law about perceived imperfections and potential deviations from the road. And when her daughter rejects the whole concept of perfection as not only unattainable but also undesirable and subjective, the relationship is going to rattle.

I also find some peace in knowing there are larger forces at play—that things are not always personal, that there is something about mothers and daughters in general that is far larger than our one dynamic.

A line in the movie *Spanglish* spotlights part of this gendered generational problem. In the midst of a climactic confrontation, a mother asks her daughter, "Is what you want for yourself to become someone very different than me?"[1]

The mother even identifies it as "the basic question" of her daughter's life.

Is this a question all mothers ask? Do daughters need to identify themselves as "like Mom" or "not like Mom"? Must there be association or disassociation? Why can I not just be me, without that being a commentary on my mother? Why can't I make my own choices without it seeming like I am passing judgment on hers?

If I meet a new friend—and she is different from me—I do not take her distinction as a personal affront. Can you imagine if I met someone in a different profession and thought, *She must think there is a problem with my choice. Why is she careering at me?* It would be ridiculous. But mothers and daughters do it to each other all the time, and I think there are several key reasons.

The first is confusion about defiance and definition. If I am defying my mother, I am openly resisting her. If I am defining myself, I am pointing to parts of us (two people standing close to one another) that could be conflated and saying, "That part is you, but I have a line there. It's not really me."

Another is how we expect mothers to erase themselves in service to their families. If—when asked to point to her identifiers—a woman points first to her children and says, "there I am," everyone is going to feel pressure. The mother is going to feel the kids' choices reflect on her not just as a parent, but as a person. The kids are going to feel pressure to transform from a child into a proxy—to become their parent's do-over. I could have been the doctor my mother wanted to be.

～

My friend Sarah is the mother of two children. When one of her girls was in third grade, her daughter's homework was to list the hobbies of everyone in her family. She listed her dad's hobby as playing ice hockey, her sister's hobby as riding horses, and her mother's hobby as *doing dishes*. Sarah was horrified, but then realized that not only did she not have any hobbies, she could not even remember what she liked to do before having children. She began running, not because she liked to run, but because she felt her daughters needed to see her doing something on her own, ASAP. There was no time to remember or explore or simply be.

I am not saying men have a lot of that time either. I am only saying that I know more women who eventually wonder, *When did I become defined by my relationships? Am I only seen as a mother, a wife, and a daughter? What happened to* me?

Finally, we have to admit when we are judging and adjust when appropriate. For example, are we blaming mothers for things? Because if so, it is understandable that they would become more heavy-handed.

In a different vein, are we celebrating some mothers for keeping their daughters close to tradition while judging other moms for the same? In the movie *Spanglish*, when the question of whether a child wants to become someone very different from a parent is asked, we applaud the daughter's answer. We cheer as she recognizes and appreciates that her "identity rests firmly and happily on one fact: I am my mother's daughter."[2] And the movie makes it so easy to celebrate. The teenager is expressing appreciation for her mother's culture, hard work, and values, and she chooses to embrace her Latinx roots and a beloved community.

But what if you are asked that same question by a wealthy, White, conservative, evangelical mother? We do need to acknowledge the privilege and power at play, but we must also note that there is no cheering.

Let's not pretend our only issue is with the process. Does my mother feel judged partly because she—and her values—have been judged? In some ways, yes. We should at least be honest about it, if not apologetic.

~

My mother and I eventually reached an equilibrium. We prioritized our relationship and let lots of conversations go. We will have to find a new equilibrium when I have children, another when my father dies, and then another when Trump appears on the Republican campaign trail (a development that feels so high stakes it brings politics back to the dinner table).

We will have loving moments and bumps.

My brothers will marry wonderful women who are both Christian,

Republican doctors. Lloyd marries Holly, a confident, quick-witted, caring pediatrician. Todd marries Betsy, a devout, joyful, altruistic MD who leaves the career path to homeschool their eight children.

They are incredible ladies I am lucky to call sisters. My mother feels lucky also. In fact, I remember the phone call I received from my mother after she visited my younger brother's fiancée. My mom was thrilled. My future sister-in-law—in addition to being lovely—was leading a Bible study, heading to medical school, and supporting conservative candidates. All of a sudden, my joy turned to jealousy. This new addition to our family could be her authentic self—and her expression of self would inspire easy affection from my mother. My expressions—spiritual exploration, working in Nigeria and Kensington, voting for candidates who supported environmental and social programs—were seen as silly and selfish and negative.

As my mom got older, she wanted to whitewash our history—and I could not let her erase it. She will apologize.

As I get older, I will see the spaces where I was judgmental and defiant instead of defining—and I will recognize all the ways I took my mother for granted. I will apologize.

She will begin to like me. I will wonder why. Because she is different? Because she finally accepts that I am different? Or is it because as I married and raised children, parts of my life scared her less—and finally looked more similar to hers?

We will decide to just let some questions go and focus on forgiveness.

And throughout it all, we will love each other.

And we will recognize that our struggle is not just born of difference, but also of similarity. We are both strong, independent women who engage.

We respect and *like* that about each other.

~

One final thought, before describing a nice moment with each of my parents: If you have a child who surprises (disappoints) you, be careful. They probably surprise you because you have an idea of what is "best" and what is "true." Remember that what is best and true for you is not necessarily what is best and true for everyone. There are all sorts of beautiful lives that don't look like yours. If you deny that, you could miss out on a lot of beauty, including the most beautiful parts of that person—and the most beautiful parts of a relationship with them.

And please do not tell yourself that you are trying to protect them from a world that will not accept them as they are. If *you* do not celebrate them as they are, it is possible you have given them a deeper emotional cut than they would ever get out in the world.

—

Now, back to those two nice moments I mentioned. The one with my dad occurred on Father's Day. It was 2000, the year I could have been graduating from medical school. Instead, I have just finished my two years with Teach For America and am in Alabama for a brief visit before heading to Missouri. It has already been quite a reunion. I am spending time with my parents while packing for another vague adventure, applying to start a different degree, and researching health insurance for the unemployed, because the two part-time jobs I have taken in Missouri do not come with benefits.

My car is loaded with boxes. Most will come with me to Missouri, but some will be stored here in Alabama. My parents' stability has provided me with a reliable place to stash things I want to hang onto, but not carry. Their stability has also provided me with a permanent address. I have taken advantage of that, giving their address to all my students during my last week of Teach For America. In the era before cell phones and email, this is a big deal—a means of staying connected while bounding from town to town instead of settling down.

When I wrote that address up on the chalkboard in my North Carolina classroom, just weeks before this Alabama visit, I would never have predicted that one of my students would use it so quickly. Nor would I have predicted that a student would use it to write a letter *to my parents*.

My dad revealed the letter in a fairly dramatic fashion. The date was June 18. We were sitting around the table in my parent's home, celebrating dad. There was an ice-cream cake (his favorite), peach tea Snapple (another favorite), and presents from all of us. I don't remember what I gave him, but I remember when he opened his cards.

He read cards from my siblings, my mom, myself, and my grandmother, and then he produced another envelope that was already opened and read it aloud. It said something like this:

> Dr. & Mrs. Johnson,
>
> My name is Eliza. Your daughter is my teacher. She gave us your address so we could write her, but I want to write a letter to you.
>
> One day in our class, when we were talking about jobs we wanted when we were older, Ms. Johnson told us that she had thought about being a doctor. She said you wanted her to be a doctor because you thought it would make her happy.
>
> I just wanted to tell you that she looks really happy when she is teaching. And I hope she stays a teacher because she's the best teacher I ever had.
>
> Stay cool!
> Eliza

What a gift my father gave to me on that Father's Day, when he read that letter in front of my entire family, then smiled and placed it back in the envelope. That sign of respect—even admiration—from my father.

And what a gift Eliza, an eighth grader, gave to us all.

~

I also received an extra-special gift from my mother.

She gave it to me about a year after my father read the letter, as I was finishing up my time in Missouri and packing (yet again) for another adventure. She told me that she saw it in a store, thought it was a fair representation of what my guardian angel must look like, and just had to buy it for me.

This tiny doll might be the craziest, most exhausted-looking angel ever manufactured. It is a troll doll, less than two inches tall, wearing a white robe and bearing golden wings, but no halo. It has a wrinkly face, fiery red, gravity-defying hair, and wide-open, slightly shocked-looking eyes. Its arms are spread, offering a blessing, a benediction, or a hug.

I love this angel. It is a symbol of both release and care. Go, and may angels go with you. It has clearly lived through some hair-raising episodes but come through them with its arms still wide open. It is a wonderful posture for—and gift from—a mom.

~

In terms of romantic relationships, by this point I've become a pro at serial monogamy. Malcolm, Luke, Logan, and several other relationships are behind me. I am OK being single but would prefer having a partner. As a result, I am dating.

I do not enjoy dating.

There was the guy who invited me to a *Spiderman* movie, then ran for his life when I joked, "OK, but under protest, because I don't like the commercial where Peter Parker suggests one person cannot make a difference."

Another guy was excited when the fire alarm went off at a restaurant and quite mistakenly assumed I would be also, telling me, "We're already outside, so it is going to be so easy to skip out on the check."

Another one plucked a stray potato chip crumb off my chest at a party and told me he wanted to sell it on eBay.

Another asked if we could make a quick stop as we walked to the restaurant on our first date, then took me to his salon, where he complained to the receptionist that the hair gel they sold him was not up to standard. Apparently, it made his blond hair "fuzzy—kind of like a dandelion."

A guy I really liked but could never get out of the friend zone.

A guy who said he really liked me, then revealed his impression that deep down, all women want to be controlled.

There was the guy who showed up for our first date and offered to take me anywhere in Boston. He said he could get us in, and price was no object. "Anywhere?" I asked him. "Anywhere," he told me. Then I told him about a park near Fenway, where you could sit on a bench and hear the baseball crowd in the background while watching the best pickup basketball in the city. There was this incredible food cart where they sold brats and the cokes were the perfect temperature. Could we go there, and watch the sun set, and hear the baseball crowd, and see some great basketball while connecting over brats? He squirmed and said sure, and then was mortified when the guy at the food cart could not take a credit card, and more mortified when I offered to pay since I had our only cash, and then actually said "I can't do this" when the food cart guy saw how uncomfortable he was and announced our entire meal was on the house.

I found dating incredibly exhausting.

There were moments of fun. I met one guy on an airplane. I was flying back to Boston after Thanksgiving and had a ridiculous number of essays to grade. As I pulled them out of my bag in the overhead compartment, a pile of them slid onto a seatmate, prompting me to profusely apologize. Once it became clear that the mishap had gained the attention of everyone in rows 21 through 28, I turned to the group and asked them to listen up. We had a two-hour flight, one hundred essays on colonialism, and if we each took five, we'd be done well before landing. Everyone chuckled, and the guy closest to my age in the bunch actually approached me later at baggage claim and asked for my number. I had made him laugh. He wanted to return the favor. Could he take me to his favorite comedy club in the North End, then out for pasta and cannolis?

My dad called me after that date and asked how it had gone. "It was nice," I told him. "He was nice."

"Sound the death knell," my dad said.

"What are you talking about?" I asked him.

"Oh, Kristi," my father responded, "I know you. Nice is important to you. Really important. But if I hear 'nice' *twice* before I hear anything else about him, he's got an uphill battle to fight."

I became so frustrated that at one point I decided I was done. No more dating. I had met a ton of great guys. I thought maybe the one guy I was looking for didn't exist. That maybe the feeling of "*yes*" I felt when I stepped onto a basketball court or into a classroom wasn't going to happen when I stepped into a relationship.

I decided I could settle for any great guy who was a good enough fit.

I actually called some old boyfriends and tried to make it work. But we couldn't do it. They couldn't do it. I couldn't do it. And I reached a monumental milestone the day I decided I would be OK without all of it. No partner. Yes to friends, but otherwise alone.

～

Meanwhile, I had plenty to keep me busy.

There was so much to learn, and as my expected identities shattered, there were new ones to form.

By this time, I had graduated from HGSE and was teaching at South Boston High School. It was clear that I was not a doctor. Not an evangelical. Not currently living in the South. Not a wife. Not a mother. Not a Republican. And no longer color-blind.

Instead, I was a teacher. A religious pluralist on a mostly Christian path up a spiritual mountain that I admired for its diversity. A wanderer, currently navigating the North with a Southern accent. An independent with regard to both relationships and politics. The odd one in the family, who could never decide when to speak her mind and when to close her mouth. Introverted. But comfortable cracking jokes on a very crowded plane. Sometimes lonely. Often tired. An admirer of beauty who might have just given herself permission to enjoy life. And an activist who now recognized problems within herself and on an institutional level.

～

The role of teacher was the one that really consumed me.

There was so much going on at Southie. I was developing a new curriculum—and getting to know new students, new colleagues, and a new school district.

I recall one district-wide meeting where social studies teachers from all the Boston public schools gathered to hear a speaker discuss our pacing guide for the semester. When they asked if there were any questions about the document, I raised my hand. I had noticed the recommendation that we spend one class period reviewing the five major religions of the world, and I highlighted this as an example of several things on the document that seemed unrealistic.

The speaker asked me where I would be teaching. When I told him, he chuckled. "You can skip that day—and will probably have to skip several more. You're going to have your hands full with some other issues. Now for those of you teaching at—for example—Boston Latin . . . You should be able to cover the curriculum in full."

On another front, there was the Teacher's Union. It was there to protect me and my students. I had never been part of a union. Collective bargaining by public employees is actually illegal in North Carolina, a right-to-work state. I had seen what life was like without a union—without an organized way to voice concerns impacting teachers and students. So while working in Massachusetts, I was grateful for—and 100 percent invested in—the union. Until things got confusing. Until I was asked to join a work-to-rule strike that insisted I do only exactly what my job required of me, nothing extra. I understood the principle of the effort: We were not paid for the extras and refusing to do them drew attention to how much of our time and work was done without compensation. But it was hard to keep the big picture in mind when I had finally convinced students to show up before school for tutoring and now had to tell the kids I would not be there. Despite that, I stayed union-strong, canceling the student sessions and spending each morning with union reps in the parking lot instead, holding a pro-union sign.

Still, when those same reps told me not to write a student's college recommendation letter, I explained that I had to. There was a senior in my ninth-grade history class. He had failed the course years earlier and needed me to highlight that he was a different kid now, who had learned so many life—and history—lessons. He earned that letter, and I wrote it for him, which essentially meant crossing the line and breaking the strike. My reward for that action was having someone (I can only assume a colleague, due to the timing) key my car.

Or maybe it was keyed because I stated publicly that the union did not represent my view on one issue. I do not even recall the exact topic. I just remember the pit in my stomach when a school leader I admired came to my classroom and privately asked if I agreed with a particular union position. When I answered truthfully that I did not, I was told that if I could not state my honest opinion in a public forum, this leader would know they were alone in their advocacy and would leave the district. I put my opinion on the record—a public dissent I would have preferred to keep within union walls. But at what cost?

I would now like to put this on the record: I regret making that statement. While I do not recall the topic or words, if they caused issues for the union, I wish I had kept it internal. I am absolutely pro-union. I believe unions were and are vital, that teachers' unions represent the best interests of our students, and that the best interests of teachers and students are absolutely aligned. And I understand that short-term sacrifices must be made to ensure the long-term success of both our strikes and the kids in our classes. I know I made mistakes during that time. I just remember being so confused—so incredibly muddled while trying to make what felt like fraught and impossible decisions. I remember being laser-focused on the kids currently in my classroom. I recall being so extraordinarily tired.

Work sapped so much of my energy that one Friday, post–basketball season, I went home right after school and lay down for a nap before dinner. I was meeting several friends later for a meal and a night on the town. I woke up at 7:00 feeling rejuvenated and quickly got dressed for the evening—only to realize I had slept straight through it. There were voicemails from friends who assumed something must have come up. It was 7:00 *in the morning*. I had slept fourteen hours straight, in my work clothes, without stirring, after a tough week at school.

I was exhausted and confused. I was making mistakes and admitting them. I was learning—and becoming exhausted all over again.

But I was also happy.

I was teaching, and I loved those students—and my job.

~

I did not sleep through every social outing.

One Friday night, in February 2003, I was meeting my friend Liz M. to go salsa dancing at a club called Sophia's. Snow had canceled our plans the week before, so we were extra excited to be out. Liz, always insightful and fun, also proved to be an incredible dancer. She would spend the whole night tearing up the floor as a high-demand partner. I would give it a shot, but also spend some time engaged in one of my favorite activities: people-watching.

One person caught my eye: a tall guy enjoying the evening, dancing and laughing. When he headed toward a very crowded bar, I walked over, stood behind him as he ordered, and waited for him to turn. Eventually he spun, almost bumped into me, and apologized.

"Oh! I didn't realize there was someone waiting behind me. So sorry. I've been standing here blocking your path to the bar."

He hesitated briefly, then decided to continue.

"Let me make it up to you by buying your drink. What can I get you?"

This guy—Tim—was *fun*. Engaging, charming, and lively. He asked me to dance, and we had the best time, even though neither of us really knew the right steps for the salsa music. He asked me questions about my life and answered my questions about his. We connected during that very first conversation. When he told me he was in the process of a career change—that he had just spent a year abroad transitioning out of consulting because he didn't feel passionately enough about it, and he worried the schedule wouldn't be great for the family he wanted to have someday—my interest expanded. These were things I could appreciate. He wanted to shift into a field that was somehow connected to athletics. He had played tennis at Boston College—a Catholic University. Yes, he was Christian. And athletic. And a good listener.

And smooth.

When the club brightened at closing time, he stopped mid-sentence, took a breath, and then said quietly, "OK. The lights just came on. And I just realized the girl I've been talking to the last few hours is *beautiful*."

Liz M. had periodically checked in on me. He had bought her a drink, gotten to know her, and swapped funny banter with her as my cell phone rang after the bar had closed, wondering aloud why someone could be calling me so late. When I asked Liz what she thought of Tim, she said, "He seems amazing. Also, I'm pretty sure he said his name was *Jim*."

Tim was from New York, but he had traveled everywhere. He had a huge world map in his apartment (good for making a history teacher's heart flutter) that was attached to a bulletin board. Next to it was a sign that said, "Mark the places you've been with a pin! Ladies with green, gentlemen with orange." I studied the much larger number of green pins and said smugly, "Looks like the ladies are much more well-traveled." He studied me and replied, "Or I've just hosted a lot more ladies in this apartment than men."

Funny. And confident. I liked it.

I also liked that his map was an upside-down image of the world. This was a guy who acknowledged the nature of perspective and didn't mind flipping something on its head.

His unique angle and confidence came into play quickly, as he called me the day after we met. He said, "I know I should play it cool and wait a few days before calling, but I don't want to. I like you. Can I take you out on a real date sometime?"

"Yes," I told him.

I was dating other people (not exclusively, but Valentine's Day was coming up, and I had plans). Tim was in the same boat, as it turned out. In fact, I would later discover that the night we met, he had been expecting another girl to join him at the club. She had never showed because she had been involved in a fender bender on her way there. She was fine—no one injured. But for much of the evening, Tim wondered if his date was going to walk in at any moment.

We planned our second date for Saturday, February 15. I canceled; strep throat had landed me in the hospital the night before. (Tim would later joke it was the universe making sure my Valentine's date with the other guy didn't go well.) A week later, we met for a walk in the park. It was low-key, as I was on the tail end of my recovery. We chatted by the ice-skating rink, then on a bench near the duck boats, finally landing at a coffee shop. We had an amazing conversation, a funny moment when we realized neither of us drank coffee, and a sweet moment when we both said we would like to see each other again.

We put a date on the calendar, and I worried a bit when I realized that, once again, I was going to have to postpone it. I was healthy this time, but I was also on a city-league basketball team that had unexpectedly made the playoffs. We had just received our post-season tournament schedule, and game one was the same night as our date. I was so sorry, but could we pull out the calendars again? "We could," he told me, "or I could come cheer you on at the game." Hmm. This guy had taken it in stride—even made it fun. "That works, too," I told him. "I have to be there early, but if you want to drive over separately at game time, you won't have any trouble spotting me. I'll be the only girl in the gym."

Turns out he didn't have to find me. The early arrival didn't bother him, so he offered to drive me there. Once we had that arranged, I asked if he wanted to enjoy a pre-game bowl of spaghetti with me beforehand. He arrived at my apartment in time for pasta, with two wine glasses and a huge bottle of Gatorade in his hands.

I was hooked.

—

My sister, Ashley, came to visit around that time. She was a sophomore in college by then, looking for a weekend away. It was so good to see her. She was not the little girl I had grown up with, nor the teenager I had chauffeured around town. The elements were all still there—the wide-eyed kid in her loved Boston and the teenager who had supported my career journey wanted to see the school where I worked—but Ashley was grown.

She loved to write and was considering several summer internships. As she filled me in, she filled me up—with all the best parts of herself (sweet, sage, strong, and remarkably witty)—as well as with the best parts of home.

She met Tim and really liked him. It was impossible not to. But when I later asked her what she had told our family about him, she said, "Nothing. They've heard enough about great guys you've dated. So when they asked me about him, I told them about you. I have never seen *you* like this. You seem to really want this relationship. With that said, he is amazing."

He was nice to every waitress and cab driver and random person we encountered. He was involved with volunteering and mentoring a child. He supported my students, showing up to cheer them on as they completed their end-of-year action projects.

We had a fair amount in common, but there were differences, too. For example, there was a shared religious foundation (Christianity), but differences in both denomination (him Catholic, me Protestant) and practice (he was more relaxed about it). But there was no huge looming question of compatibility at the center of things, which was a relief.

He was extroverted. At the time, that was a relief also. Life was full, and he was happy to pick up the social baton whenever I wanted to pass it.

We had different career interests, but we both wanted careers we were passionate about, and we were willing to sacrifice and take risks to get them.

Another difference was that he never seemed burdened by the angst that so often weighed on me. He was thoughtful, but casual—caring deeply, but never getting bogged down. He had the ability to confront a question or a mistake and then move on. I recall one mistake he made at a Celtics game. He made a negative comment about a player who was having a terrible night, without realizing a kid who was decked out head to toe in that player's jersey and sneakers was within earshot. Though he had not seen the child prior to the statement, he saw him right after. The comment was relatively benign—something like "X can't do anything!" But the kid's eyes welled with tears, as his dad glared at us and pulled his child closer. Tim apologized immediately, owning the mistake, asking how he could make it up to the kid, and promising to do better. When the child left for the concession stand moments later (to get a treat funded by my date), Tim turned to the crowd that had witnessed the scene and announced, "He'll be back shortly—and for my next act I will bash both Santa and the Easter Bunny." The guy behind us chuckled at Tim's self-deprecating humor, then everyone laughed. Random strangers relaxed, and one said, "We've all been there, buddy. And while the kid's gone, can we just agree with you? It's been a terrible game."

An event that would have tortured me for weeks had been resolved within minutes, with everyone—including Tim—able to move on and enjoy the rest of the game. Because that's just him: kind, comfortable, resilient, able to own things, put others at ease, and land on his default setting of contagiously happy.

Exactly what I needed.

~

When we met, Tim had just left his consulting job and was trying to break into the field of college athletics. He needed experience in the field in order to become an attractive applicant to Master's in Sports Administration programs, and he was willing to cast a wide net to get it. There are a lot of universities in and near Boston, and Tim approached most of them with an offer to volunteer. Eventually, he approached MIT with the idea of an unpaid internship in their athletic department. He was offering to create the position.

As a former consultant, he was experienced in observing departments, identifying needs, and proposing solutions. If they would grant him access, he could figure out where they needed help, design a role to provide it, fill that role for the remainder of his time there, and leave them with a blueprint for other interns if they wanted to continue the program after he was gone. He was not asking for payment. If he did a good job, he hoped they would write him a letter of recommendation for graduate school programs.

It worked. MIT got an extraordinary worker for a year—one who left them well-positioned to recruit other interns in subsequent years if that seemed useful. Tim spent a year doing something he loved, confirming his career interest as well as gaining the year of experience and the recommendations he needed for admission to graduate school.

We met in February. We were engaged by August. He began the MIT internship shortly after and worked on graduate school applications throughout the year. The following spring, we were planning a July wedding when he received his graduate school acceptance letter from the University of North Carolina, his dream school. He was happy, and I was happy for him. And for us. The only twinge of sadness was that we would be leaving wonderful friends in Boston, as well as a job I loved at South Boston High School.

But we would stay in touch with our Bostonians. And we would make new friends elsewhere. And I would find another school I loved in North Carolina.

~

I discovered that one thing Tim and I have in common is being pretty deep thinkers, but we do this in different ways. For me to go deep, I have to carry a lot of weight. I end up getting bogged down quite a bit. Tim does it differently. He seems to be able to descend and then ascend again at will. He travels lighter.

He has lightened many moments for me. Most of the time, it's exactly what I need. Occasionally it's not. But it has filled our space with laughter from the beginning.

I recall one incident when we were dating. We were in Tim's kitchen—a rarity for both of us. Some joke about boiling water had turned into a contest. He was insistent that he could get a cup of water to boil on the stove faster than I could get it to boil in the microwave. Game on. He filled a saucepan and put the burner on high. I filled a glass and set the microwave for three minutes. It quickly became apparent that I was going to win.

Tim, teasing me, reached over to mess with the microwave. As he leaned, the white sweater he was wearing touched the hot burner. There were no flames, but we both grew wide-eyed as a spot began forming on his sweater. Small orange crackles were creating a black edge on a hole growing larger. I grabbed Tim's pan of still-cold water and doused it.

He was fine. He cracked a joke about it being a little humiliating that while my water was beginning to boil, his was still cold enough that I could throw it at him. I laughed and turned my attention to the sweater. "It's ruined," I told him. "I'm sorry."

"Kristi," he said, "I am never going to worry about material things. Let's not give a second thought to this sweater."

I was so impressed with that statement that I shared the story with Tim's best friend Chris and Chris's wife Rachel the next night at dinner. When I wrapped it up with a glowing review of Tim's incredible perspective— so beautifully illustrated by his statement about the white sweater—Chris nearly spit his beer across the table.

"Did you say a *white* sweater?"

"Yes," I replied, wondering why Tim had started laughing.

Chris put his elbows on the table and looked at his brother-like buddy. "Was that the white sweater that *I loaned you last week, Tim*?"

Tim leaned over the table and said, "You're missing the point of the story, Chris. The rest of us are focused on how we should never be tied to our material possessions."

Chris roared with laughter.

Chris was not worried about the sweater. And it never occurred to me that the box I mentally checked when Tim made his statement about material possessions (same viewpoint!) might need an asterisk. Tim is an incredible, generous, bighearted guy who invests deeply in his community. But he doesn't share the burn-it-all mentality that sometimes hits me. But that night, and for a very long time, it just didn't matter. We were too busy, all doubled over laughing.

That is the magic of Tim.

~

I met Tim's family that spring. They were wonderful. I learned where some of Tim's great qualities came from: his optimistic dad, his caring mother, his thoughtful sister, his engaged extended family. I loved hearing the childhood stories and learning how those events had shaped him. He had been a sweet, feisty kid—and a good teenager, even if he had to be redirected on occasion. One of those redirections made me appreciate his mother, who had responded to a teenage Tim's challenge by taking a stand that made a huge impact on him. Teenage Tim had been upset that a jersey he needed wasn't laundered, and in a rare negative moment, had implied his former-nurse-then-homemaker mother didn't do enough. She decided to stop doing anything for him for two weeks, to make sure she was never taken for granted again. For fourteen days, teenage Tim bought his own groceries, set his own table, fixed his own meals, washed his own dishes, arranged his own rides, laundered his own clothes, cleaned his own bathroom, and dealt with all the administrative elements of his own life. Three days into the scene, he appealed to his dad for help in reasoning with his mother. His dad, a former Navy guy, told him, "No way. She's still cooking for me. I know better than to get on your sinking ship."

Tim met the rest of my family when they invited him to join us on our family vacation at a dude ranch in Montana. Unbeknownst to me, Tim prepped for the vacation by taking a riding lesson. He laughed as he described it to my family later: learning to mount a horse while trying to keep his cool after realizing that, as an adult, he had mistakenly signed up for the class full of nine-year-old equestrian girls.

We were also able to see him keep his cool—and his sense of humor— during a few surprising vacation moments. First there was the moment my younger brother, Todd—who had flown in from a medical mission in the Amazon to be Tim's roommate on this trip—announced he might have picked up a parasitic worm in South America. "Sweet dreams!" we told Todd and a sour-faced Tim.

Then there was the moment a sibling selected the word "missionary" while playing charades and instead of pointing at Todd (just back from his mission trip), chose to mime the sexual "missionary" position. It is the only time I have ever seen Tim remove himself from a family competition. "I know lots of words for that, but I cannot shout them out in front of your parents," said Tim.

There was also the moment Tim botched the family photo we asked him to take. This was before digital cameras, so we only discovered how bad that picture was when the film was developed weeks later. It meant the only good photo—the one for the Christmas card—was the one with Tim in it. "Well played," my family would tell him. "I guess we're using the picture that includes Tim."

Finally, one of my favorite moments from the trip was when Tim first experienced the side of my mother I have inherited. Tim and I were on the shore of a lake, warming up for a game of beach volleyball when my mother walked over. She wanted to go sailing, but the rest of the family was not available. Did we want to come with her? We explained that we couldn't, as we had committed to the volleyball game that was about to begin.

Fifteen minutes later, Tim exclaimed, "Is that your mother?!"

Yes. It was my mother—by herself, sailing a small dingy out on a lake, and now wrestling with rigging. My husband was shocked at my mother. In response, I was shocked at him. She had just told us she wanted to go sailing. Why was he so surprised to see her out there?

"She doesn't know how to sail, and she wanted company, so I just assumed she would wait until someone could go with her," he told me.

I laughed. He clearly did not know my mother. She had felt inspired, so she literally waded right in.

It was a wonderful week, with him getting to know my family, and my family getting to know Tim.

~

Of course, there were small bumps along the way to the altar.

There was a lot of happy, then a proposal, then an engagement.

Then a moment of panic.

The panic was mine, and it was prompted by a discussion of where we would marry.

Ultimately, we married in the Catholic Church because Tim knew it was important to his family. That was fine with me; I was very flexible about where we held the wedding. However, I did not want to be spiritually pigeonholed after the ceremony, and it bothered me that the Catholic Church wanted Tim to sign a statement saying our future children would be reared as Catholics. He signed, but I wrote a letter (which Tim shared with his family and his childhood priest who officiated) saying I would not make that commitment. And that both of us would do in the future whatever we felt was best for our family *then*.

As we talked, I told Tim about my own parents' wedding and how my mom's father had chosen not to attend. To me, it felt like her dad had prioritized being ideologically steadfast over being loving. I had different priorities. (Tim's family did too—they would have attended our ceremony regardless, I am certain.) But having a Catholic service felt like a way I could love them and honor Tim's faith. At the same time, it felt important to convey my own perspective in that letter. Spiritually, I would not lock myself—or any future children—in.

I don't like being locked in. And now, many years into the marriage, we can joke about my aversion to spiritual stalls. We can both laugh when someone else tries to pin me down with theology, and Tim pulls out the popcorn to watch the show. But back then, it was angsty. And the whole process scared me.

I remember the night Tim and I talked to our friends Chris and Rachel about it. I admitted that the process had triggered me. I had been feeling good about things, but now I was worried. I was not afraid of committing to the relationship, but I was very worried about this relationship requiring me to commit to other things.

What if the spiritual search I had been on forever nudged me into places Tim didn't like? I currently felt good about living in the North End of Boston, but we wouldn't always be here. What if a future place that spoke to me made him uncomfortable? I wasn't one to live in the most typical environments. This current setting fit, but if I knew I might want something different in the future, was it fair to commit to Tim?

Our friends listened. And then Rachel laid some wisdom on me that felt so important, I had her words read at our wedding. That text is upcoming, but her basic message was this: We were *not* making a vow to never change; we were instead making a vow to be together through all sorts of changes—for life.

If we were the right partners for each other, we could continue to grow and change and talk to each other about nudges and options and exploration.

If we were the right partners for each other, we would support and celebrate each other's paths.

If we were the right partners, we could sometimes travel together (like we were currently doing) and sometimes cheer one another on from a distance while maintaining key moments of connection (like George and Denise had modeled as she hiked the Appalachian trail).

Were we the right partners for each other?

I think so.

~

I wrote a letter to everyone who attended our wedding, to be read during the ceremony at the church. This was the moment I amplified Rachel's words.

At the rehearsal, I told the assembly of our closest friends and family that I wanted them to pay special attention to that particular reading. It was special because it was written to them, from us. To write it, we had borrowed and commented on some of our close friends' very own words.

Everyone nodded until Tim spoke up, at which point they all began laughing. He said, "You might want to tune in to the other readings, too. I mean, our letter is pretty good, but the other ones were written by *God*."

Cue the laughter. And me burying my face in my hands. Until Tim pulled them away and kissed me.

My college friend Jim read our letter the next day, during the ceremony, shortly after Tim and I exchanged vows. Jim spoke its words aloud, saying:

Dear Friends and Family,

We want our first words as an official couple to be words of love and appreciation for one another and for all of you. We want everyone here to know how blessed we feel, not only because we have found each other, but because we have been taught how to truly love one another as friends—and as life partners—by such an amazing circle of people. We want to publicly thank all of you for the examples you have set. We hope to emulate the relationships you share, and we hope to honor you as we honor each other.

We also want to acknowledge that our bond to one another is one of many bonds being formed today. In the midst of celebrating our new marriage, we are also celebrating ties to new cousins, sisters, brothers, aunts, uncles, and friends. Everyone here has played a special role in our lives and will continue to be a special part of the family we are forming today. We want to thank all of you for your love, support, and guidance—and as a symbol of the respect we have for your friendship and counsel, we want to celebrate your words in this reading.

You have told us the following:

Work at your marriage.

Play at your marriage.

Hold hands as often as possible.

No matter how busy or crazy the day was, ask how the other's day went.

Listen to the answer.

Kiss each other good night.

Make decisions together.

Remember that marriage is never 50/50. Sometimes it's 70/30 one way and sometimes it's 40/60 the other. Never keep score.

Keep making each other laugh.

Always take the time to have a meal together. Turn off the TV, light a few candles, and enjoy the other's company. It's amazing how much you can learn from each other over a dinner conversation.

Remember that the act of getting married doesn't fix you permanently in time. You don't have to decide who you are now and never change. That's not the promise. Part of your vow, perhaps the scariest part, is vowing to be with each other through all the changes—and changing—in life.

Love, love, love each other.

(And start your kids' college fund tomorrow.)

We will love each other always—and will always love all of you.

Most sincerely,
Mr. & Mrs. Timothy Dillon Smith Jr.

MARRIAGE AND MOTHERHOOD

I need to convey the joy of family. I need to highlight how much I love, appreciate, and celebrate this unit—how lucky I am to have each person in my home.

As I write about our first few years as a family, I need lots of pages to detail the happy: how my husband and I moved to North Carolina the week of our wedding, how he enrolled in a graduate program he loved and I took a teaching job I loved, and how excited we were the day we found out we were expecting our first child. We embraced each other and then her and then each of her siblings. They are my greatest joy and so much of my world.

We celebrated when my husband's graduate school internship turned into a job in North Carolina. I enjoyed studying in the doctoral program at UNC's School of Education and mentoring new teachers online while my babies were young. And I was very grateful to be at home after I graduated. The faces of these children! Pure love.

~

A fear I have about writing this book is amplified in this section. My fear is that I will do exactly what I have been fighting against for much of my life: externally assigning identities. I want to state for the record that everyone mentioned in this book gets to say for themselves who they are. I have encountered a lot of people in my life. And—as I try to make some sense of my journey—I am doing my best to say how my perception (or misperception) of their words shaped me. My hope is that the friends and family I have talked about will be viewed in, and as, positive lights. Because they have illuminated my path. And when I pay attention, they illuminate me.

This attempt to describe moments and celebrate character without assigning identities is nuanced and difficult, and it has even higher stakes when my kids make appearances. They are young. I am their mother. I don't want to say something identifying that a child then internalizes. Kids, be who you are. And never let a description of who you were on a particular day define you. You get to tell your own stories. What you need to know about this part of my story is that while I kept searching for myself, I was also actively embracing each of you—in a home filled with playfulness, laughter, and love.

The second reason this section is tricky is that the goal here—of writing this book—is not entertainment, instruction, nor to create a family or personal record. The goal is for me to figure some things out. I tend to learn things the hard way, which means the hard moments are going to be disproportionately represented here. It's a risk without guarantee of reward, because I learn *while* writing, so I can only hope I will glean something helpful. The only thing I know for sure is that writing this section scares me.

The third reason this section is tricky is because I am a storyteller. I can make this dramatic and well written, and I can lace it with anecdotes and illustrations. But what I need is not an engaging segment; what I need is clarity. I need to figure out how to be everything that is required of a wife and a mother—and also be *me*.

~

Tim and I married in 2004. We were overjoyed to welcome our four children in fairly rapid succession: Ella in 2006, Sienna in 2008, Tyler in 2010, and Hudson in 2012.

In 2014 I turned forty years old, and Tim and I celebrated our tenth wedding anniversary.

I began our marriage with a strong sense of self. I was a teacher, an activist, and a (still somewhat scared) pluralist and Christian. I was politically liberal and over the years leaned even further left. I was aware of my skin color. I tried to be aware of my privilege and how it came at the expense of other people. I was no longer as wealthy, but I had an enormous safety net, a marketable education, and a spouse who was excited about his new line of work. I was keenly aware of those with less, but as my own income dwindled (particularly in those years when my husband and I were in graduate school), so did the ball of angst in my gut. I was a person who could live with little and show respect to everyone. I was also a woman who would demand respect—in the world and in my own home.

Initially, the newlywed me found that marriage bolstered these identities. If there was a stretch when teaching required more from me, I could work late while my partner covered things at home. If there was a political argument over dinner, I had an ally. There were two of us eating ramen noodles, and I loved the simplicity of it, as well as the camaraderie. My sense of feminine strength grew as I used my voice in conversations about contraceptives and when to remove them to try for children, and as I met my firstborn, a spirited hazel-eyed girl.

In addition to enhancing my current identities, those early years of marriage added several others. In addition to being a teacher, activist, liberal, ascetic-leaning storyteller, and feminist, I became a wife, homeowner, and mother of four. I considered these new arenas in which I could still express who I was, and I enjoyed discovering these new expressions. I read progressive parenting articles and bought environmentally friendly cloth diapers, and even though I stopped working as a teacher, I was still constantly in schools as a parent. In addition, I filled our house with diversity-rich library books and secondhand, eco-conscious educational toys.

And then—almost imperceptibly at first—things began shifting.

Some things faded (discretionary time, for example . . . there seemed to be none of it) while others emerged: disposable items, including diapers, and much greater commitments for my husband at work.

And, a trickle at a time, *every part of me that was not a wife and a mother seemed to disappear.*

Thirteen years later, I looked around and thought: *Wow. I really love these people. And these have been happy years. But where did the Kristi I knew go? How did I lose so many of the identities I fought to claim—lose so much of the person I fought to become? What happened to* me?

~

The quick answer is that I got completely lost in my primary roles—the roles of wife and mother. Looking back, I realize I allowed them to consume me because true conditions (and perhaps a lifetime of conditioning) kept my attention on three influential things.

The first was that when my kids were tiny, my family roles felt both important and extremely *urgent*. When a belly is hungry, and a diaper is exploding, and the toddler is injured, and the only other adult is out working (and I can *probably* write that essay later?) there is very little question of what takes priority. So, I focused ever-increasing amounts of time and energy on being a wife and a mother—things that felt like immediate needs.

The second was that I really *enjoyed* the roles of wife and mother. I still love these roles, and I do not take them for granted. I know people who struggle with infertility and isolation. I also know people who would love the chance to choose whether to work or be a stay-at-home parent. I considered both, and I did spend hours away working toward my doctorate when the kids were little. And I may get to the end of this book, or to a new line in our budget, and realize that working outside the home is the next step for me. But for a while back then, after I graduated and before the angst hit hard, I was privileged enough to have options and decided that home was where I wanted to be.

And finally, I got lost in the roles because the act of emptying myself into a task was something I had always done. It just so happened that this time the task I poured myself into was caring for my family.

This last influence is enormous—and not purely personal. Yes, there is something about me that feels compelled to give until it hurts, but I also think there is something about my cultural arenas and motherhood in general that feeds that compulsion. Motherhood is an arena where depleting yourself is unabashedly celebrated.

I was talking to my sister about this yesterday. Ashley is now the mother of three, and she also works full-time outside her home. As we talked, we admitted we were both so extraordinarily tired, and we wondered aloud what it was in our nature or rearing that propelled us to leave it all on the court, collapsing into bed each evening, exhausted.

I suggested the triple whammy of being Protestant (that Protestant work ethic), American (not known for a good work–life balance) and female (celebrated for nurturing others at the expense of ourselves).

Ashley replied, "And don't forget the pressure you feel to prove you're earning your keep as a stay-at-home mother. I wish you didn't feel that."

In my house, this pressure is self-imposed. My spouse would likely be thrilled if he walked in from work and found me reading a book. But if that happened, I would jump up as if I had been caught doing something inappropriate. He is working his ass off in a demanding job—I feel I should be working my ass off at home. Especially since it is not some pristine, pulled-together space that gives you the sense that everything is done, clearing me a bit of time to read. Everything is *not* done. Everything will *never* be done. If I want to take a moment, it will *never* be because "Whew! I'm finished!" It will be because I have looked at our world and—for a moment—prioritized *me*. And I will feel guilty about that.

~

Motherhood supplies many joys. I have celebrated those joys in both quiet and boisterous, private and public ways over the years, and I have certainly highlighted them for my children. To make sure my family does not forget that joy—to make sure they remember the smiling, snuggly mama who loved and loves her days with them, even as she writes about struggles in a book—I am going to speak directly to my husband and children here, saying: The photos in this section are for you. They capture the truth—a woman who deeply delights in *us*.

The first photo ever taken of the six of us, capturing one of the happiest moments of my life.

I don't want anyone—especially my family—to forget that delight as I expand the spotlight to include (or during much of this section, shift it completely to focus on) some difficult things: the physical and psychological demands of motherhood.

~

For almost ten years, I was pregnant, nursing, or both. Some kids kept me up much of the night. Others woke me early in the morning. My body was desperate for rest.

My husband was gone a lot for work: every weekday, many evenings, lots of weekends, and a number of holidays. Working hard to provide. That provision is an incredible gift, but it meant he was gone. A lot.

There was no real outsourcing. No family in town. No budget for regular sitters. No daycare. Not even grocery delivery (a service unavailable until many years later).

Our kids were all so little. By 2014 (the year of our tenth anniversary), they were ages eight, six, four, and two.

One of many fun birthday celebrations.

Those are precious ages, and I especially loved how quickly we could get everyone laughing or dancing or acting silly during those days. At the same time, life with littles is not easy. Nothing we did together was simple. A trip to the grocery store was exhausting. Dinnertime: exhausting. Bath time: exhausting. Bedtime routine: exhausting. Potty training. Doctors' appointments. Birthday parties. Nursing all night. Toddlers all day. Getting people into diapers. And out of diapers. Into car seats and out of car seats. Into shoes and out of shoes. All while grappling with a world that is suddenly full of danger. Yanking kids out of high chairs to perform the Heimlich maneuver. Lifting a dresser off a crushed child (the only piece in the room not bolted to the wall because it was "too low to tip"), terrified he was dead. Bike helmets, swimming lessons, vaccinations. All while scared I was missing moments. Because every day we survived, they were a day older. And I needed to snuggle them before they got too big. And also terrified because I was raising humans who needed to learn things. And amid all of this surviving, what was I teaching? Cue the chore charts and the devotional books and the learning games. And *the guilt*. Because one night, when my husband asked our three-year-old how she was, she sighed, put her head on the dinner table, and said "I'm ezzhausted." (Not because she was tired. She had pointedly told me she was *not tired* at least six times that day.) But because she heard her parents say it so often, she began to mimic it. So, in addition to putting on my big-girl panties and getting things done, I felt I needed to put on a mask in front of the children. How was I? "I'm *great!*" We actually went so far as to adopt a family mantra, which was "it's not going to be easy, so let's make it *fun*."

And there were moments when it really was fun. And there were moments when I really was great.

A random family dinner at Burger King, when we were so festive they mistook us for a birthday party and brought us crowns.

There were so many moments when I belly laughed at their latest antic, or my heart almost burst because it was so full of love for this unit, or I just felt happy to be right where I was.

But there were also moments when I was not great and could not fool myself into thinking I was because the stress and exhaustion of the whole "this is not easy, but I'll just work my ass off" approach were actually manifesting in physical symptoms.

Before I get to those physical symptoms, I want to dip into the psychological challenges of motherhood.

Being a mother feels like being the placeholder on a football team. The placeholder is the guy who receives the snap (catches the ball) so he can hold it for the kicker. Almost no one notices the placeholder unless he screws up.

As a mother, I can count on one hand the times I heard "thanks for getting up with the baby" or "thanks for feeding the fish" or "thanks for making sure the pantry is full of groceries or my schedule is full of fun activities or my closet is full of clean, well-fitting clothes." But the second you sleep in or skip the grocery run or neglect to wash the favorite outfit, it is noted.

To add insult to injury, if anyone else does these things—even once—you are expected to throw them a fricking parade. Unless the community has already done it for them. When my husband took all four kids to the grocery store, everyone told him he was *amazing*. They basically handed him a personal shopper for the hour. When I took them to the same store, I received glares. Could I not keep them under control?

What the hell?

There were also plenty of times when I worked my ass off and received negative feedback. The work it took to pull that dinner together, only to see my toddler spit it onto the table and declare it "yucky." The work it took to pack for a trip, only to have my husband frustrated because he wanted to leave an hour earlier. But the more common occurrence was that my work was never even noticed because it was undone so quickly. This was partly due to the nature of the tasks: laundry, dishes, rooms, and children got dirty again. Soap dispensers, toilet paper holders, refrigerators, and bellies got empty again. Nothing was ever crossed off the list. One mommy blogger bemoaned this when she wrote, "It has just occurred to me today that the only way the laundry will ever be completely done is if the whole family walks around naked while I do it."

I am tempted to offer a saucy retort about how most husbands would misread the whole "my wife as the naked laundress" situation, but instead I am going to redirect us to an educational study I heard described on the radio while I was sitting in a carpool line. The study talked about the impact on students when they were assigned a task that was immediately undone—when the structure they built was dismantled just after completion, right in front of them. Not surprisingly, the children became frustrated. When they were asked to do the task again, they were less invested, less motivated, and less creative. They cared less. And who could blame them?

There is a parallel here, friends.

But those tasks have to get done. And partners are dealing with the same things, right? I mean, how many times have I thanked my husband for going to work? Not enough.

And I am very lucky, because my husband comes home from work and pitches in. But even here—when partners are, well, partnering—it can be tricky. How are tasks divided? While figuring this out in my own home, I considered (not) thrilling my husband by pulling out a reading from my old HGSE Idealism 101 binder. In class, I had reviewed an excerpt from *The Second Shift* describing a study of workers' mental and physical health. The study revealed that the most hazardous tasks were those that combined "high demands and low control—lots of things to be done and little control over when to do them."[1] When the authors took this labor study into the home, they discovered that many of the traditionally "female" tasks—planning and preparing meals, buying the groceries, cleaning up after meals, house-cleaning, and doing laundry—were low in control. These tasks also share another feature: They tend to be everyday, repetitive, and endless kinds of work . . . In contrast, many of the "male" tasks—making repairs around the house, taking out the garbage, looking after the car, and caring for the yard—are jobs that permit a high degree of control. You don't have to do them every day, and when you do them is up to you.[2]

Is it a shock that women are at risk of becoming "stressed out, resentful or angry . . . and since one of the predictors of sexual frigidity in women is repressed anger, a couple's sex life can suffer as well"?[3]

I am guessing it is not a shock to a lot of women.

~

My husband—overwhelmed with work—tried to gift me breathers by suggesting assistance from others.

"Hire a sitter."

"I'll have the grandparents visit."

"I have an even better idea. I'll have grandparents come, and we'll *both* take a weekend away—together."

Cue the naked laundress—adult version. Or the guilt if I just cannot be needed in one more way.

~

I do need to celebrate my husband's intentions. I also need to honor these grandparents.

The kids, at a favorite vacation spot, where we meet grandparents and other extended family each year.

I enjoyed getting to know my parents as grandparents. I also enjoyed getting to know my in-laws in all sorts of ways. They are good folks who have done three priceless things for me: raising my husband, embracing me as a daughter, and loving my children.

They have also done amazing things for each other and the world. My mother-in-law is a nurse-turned-homemaker. She is sweet, patient, and caring, worrying over all of us and willing to drop anything to engage a child. My father-in-law is a veteran and was a director of student affairs before becoming a college tennis coach. He is a force of positivity—counseling, cheering, supporting, and playing with us all along the way.

If I called any of these grandparents and said, "I need you to be here," they would drop everything. I am so grateful for that. Still, that does not mean it is easy to get away.

~

It is *hard* to get away.

Physically and emotionally.

Cleaning up for any sitter, prepping the children, transitioning a screaming infant to someone else's arms, reassuring a toddler that I will come back, all while trying to remember where I wrote the list of instructions leaves me frazzled—a state from which I find it hard to recover during time away. And that screaming infant—that noise has triggered a milk drop that means my breasts will be uncomfortable and leaking the entire time I'm gone. Unless I take a breast pump. Into a public bathroom. Which I have done, on my two-hour "break."

And I'll take us into the realm of the ridiculous on the emotional impact. I'll skate right by the teary toddler and the child with separation anxiety who is trying to stow away in my car. I'll not dwell on our anniversary weekend, where I waited until my husband fell asleep, then spent two hours on the cold tile bathroom floor fighting bills and paperwork (because there had been no other time to do it, but I knew he would be disappointed if I asked for the time the next day to tackle everything. Much better to work until 2 a.m., then thrill him by sleeping in on our *so relaxing* trip the next day). Instead, I'll tell you about the evening that my sister and her husband were passing through town, and we decided to do a couples' dinner out with them. To maximize our time together, we decided to all ride in one car to the restaurant. And it hit me, twenty minutes before departure, that we would be in the same vehicle, and then the same restaurant, with my sister and her husband, the two people we had named as our children's guardians. We would all be out together while the kids were at home. My sleep-deprived brain kicked into mama overdrive. If disaster struck—if the four of us died in a car wreck or kitchen explosion—who would decide where the children lived? What if my children were separated from all of us—and then from each other? Fifteen minutes before departure, I decided to address this issue by quickly drafting a handwritten addendum to our will and placing it in an envelope on a pillow in the master bedroom. The envelope was labeled "Open if we don't return."

My husband found it ten minutes before departure and staged an intervention. "Kristi," he said. "*Really?*" When I explained my concerns and said that I had merely put into writing what we had planned on adding to our will when we found time, he said, in a too-calm tone (like he was talking to an unbalanced individual who might tip and crack at any moment if we could not locate the proper restraints), "Hmmm. Yes. I understand that. But the sitter is going to see this envelope and think we have abandoned the children. She is going to call the police, or maybe child services. You cannot leave a sitter in the house with an envelope ominously labeled '*Open if we don't return*'."

Oh. Right. Well, I know what to do. I'll just *explain what it is* to the sitter before our departure. And so I did. And we all had a good laugh. And then I left the addendum to our will right where I wanted it—propped up on our bed.

~

To be fair, I did receive a few breaks (once the sitters and the kids and the list of everything everyone might need during my absence was securely in place). Those breaks generally accomplished two goals: They made me feel human, and they helped me reconnect with my husband.

One of my favorite photos of us together.

Those are both huge, but also not enough. Yes, I am a human. Yes, I am a wife. But when do I get to be *me*? I would like a little time when no one—including my husband—needs my attention. And I want a break I don't have to prepare so much for, and then feel exhausted during. What I really want is twenty-four hours alone listening to see if there is a small voice inside me that says, "I'm still here" and then tells me what she wants next. And I don't want to spend that twenty-four hours completely exhausted from the preparations. I want to—just once—walk out the door and leave everyone safe and happy with their dad while I am able to write and recenter—for one day—alone. Just *me*.

On several occasions, over the course of several years, I told my husband I needed that experience. Just a low-key exit to a local hotel where I could sit and think and write for a day—maybe even a *weekend*. (Cue the angels singing!) We could pick whatever day worked for the family, but it could count as a birthday gift. Please? The gift of a quiet moment away.

But during those years, on each occasion, his response was the same. Confusion. Hurt. Disappointment. He said, "It bothers me that the gift you want is time away from us."

More guilt.

Too much, on top of all the other guilt.

So, eventually, I stopped asking.

~

He actually did gift me one night in a swanky space the week of my fortieth birthday. It was fancy. The venue was gorgeous, and I appreciated both the gesture and his desire to mark the occasion. I invited my sister to fly in for that evening (and for other celebrations happening that weekend), and he booked us connecting rooms on the concierge level. He also reserved us a table in the hotel's restaurant for a five-course dinner. To make sure he would not need my assistance during that one evening, he asked his parents to come down from New York to help him, and he rented two Red Box DVDs for the children to distract them from my absence. It was a production, me being gone for that one night. It was his attempt to show love.

I feel that love. I do. And I loved that time with my sister. But a production is not what I wanted.

What I wanted was quiet.

What I wanted was a momentary retreat to a silent space where—if my inner voice was whispering something—I could hear it. Maybe even write it down.

I also wanted my husband *home*.

He is a workhorse. I respect that. I relate to that. I benefit from that. But it was consuming. Nothing was sacred: birthdays, vacations, holidays. *Tons* of work travel. Tons of work in general. I missed my aunt's funeral (which was on a Sunday that also happened to be Valentine's Day and our daughter's birthday) on a day he was slated to work a UNC game and did not feel comfortable telling work he could not make it. That meant my choices were to skip the funeral or peel a tiny, teary girl off my leg for transfer to a sitter on her birthday so I could board a plane. I ended up sobbing an apology to my cousin on the phone.

I felt like I was alone all the time, without ever actually reaping the benefits of solitude.

Still, I had so many blessings to count. My husband was an amazing provider. He was patient as I placed crazy signs all over the house, reminding myself of the person I wanted to be. He was supportive of whatever project I decided to tackle. And he could play endless games with the children (while after an hour of Monopoly trades, my last thread of sanity is worn). Whenever we went to a pool, he would dip a toe in the water and if it was cold, would volunteer to swim with the kids while I sat in the hot tub. To me, *that* is love. He loved me well in so many ways, even when he didn't quite understand where I was coming from. I know I am lucky to have him.

I am lucky to have this whole crew.

There was just so much else going on.

And everything going on was absolutely consuming me.

~

As I struggled to find my footing in this new stage of life, I went through four personal phases.

First, I tried to be everything—at a reasonably high level. I mentored teachers online, finished my dissertation, volunteered, mothered my children, and supported my husband in his new job.

But I was *exhausted*. And after I graduated from my doctoral program, I decided to stop juggling all of those roles. If we made some financial sacrifices, our family would not need me to work—and it seemed my husband and children would benefit from my increased focus at home. I knew I was lucky to have options, and I tried to exercise this one joyfully.

So my second approach was to shelve those other identities and lean heavily into the role of homemaker.

I loved this for a while and tried a variety of approaches to homemaking. I kept it simple, then challenged myself to do more. I tried to be present in our cozy space, then took us out on an adventure. I didn't give anyone whiplash—we just went through seasons (often dictated by what stage of pregnancy or newborn-ness we were experiencing). But eventually, I was edgy. I had fought so long to discover *me*, only to then allow myself to be buried—to suffocate under piles of everyone's laundry and dishes and needs.

My third approach was to find expression within those piles. I could be an educator, volunteer, ascetic, storytelling philosopher, and activist at *home*. I hung words from Reverend Molly Shivers on a cabinet to remind me that "God honors the mother who is up in the night with her sick child(ren) as much as God honors the person who travels to Panama or Jamaica or Haiti to build schools and clinics." I printed out signs (using corporal works of mercy as a guide) and taped them around the house in an attempt to maintain this perspective. Our fridge had a note taped to the front that said, "Feed the Hungry." The faucet had a note that said, "Give Drink to the Thirsty." The washing machine said, "Clothe the Naked." I tried to remember the vital and absolute truth that my own home was a part of the world, and my work within it *mattered*.

It did matter, but it still wasn't psychologically easy.

During this stage of mothering, I was actually asked (randomly, by someone who did not even know I enjoyed writing) if I would pen an article for the church newsletter. The topic for the month was "Connecting Your Passion to God's Purpose." I agreed to write the essay, and I included a sentence that said, "I am haunted by those I have seen but am not actively assisting—and that causes me to stumble in my new attempts to serve."

Not exactly uplifting. But the truth was, I really did feel haunted. I was living in a nice suburban home, with several luxuries that I was being asked to appreciate but which actually made me very angsty. Not in a "look at me, I'm so woke" kind of way. But in a "my husband hired someone to clean the house and instead of saying thank you I made him feel crappy about our privilege and stole his joy and made this nice lady feel awkward by trying to work alongside her" moment.

I was struggling. The atypical environments that always drew me—and the underserved populations that always called me—seemed so incredibly far away. And the part of me that quickened—that felt alive—while engaged in those communities was getting no oxygen.

And that's the selfish perspective—how it impacted *me*. When I thought about others, it was worse. I knew firsthand that people were out there—kids quitting school, families struggling, people dying—while I planned our next trip to the pool.

There was no shortage of advice, and most of it involved being patient.

"Life is long," I heard.

"This is a season."

"Count your blessings."

Daily, I self-corrected, sternly admonishing my whirring brain to *Get over yourself. Honestly!*

I appreciated the advice of the little old ladies at the supermarket and never wanted to make the mistake of ignoring their wisdom. Time and again they told me, "Do not wish these years away."

~

I was not wishing any years away. I knew all too well how quickly our children were growing. I stopped to savor moments every day. Multiple times a day.

But I also stopped being fully me.

And I felt guilty all the time.

Guilty that I couldn't just enjoy the moment while I had my family close by me.

Then guilty that I was enjoying the moment while others in need were struggling.

~

I met my friend Melanie in Boston before I met Tim. One night, my college friend Priya came through town and organized a group outing. Priya invited me, Kevin (her buddy from medical school), and Melanie (Kevin's fiancée). We all had dinner, then joined my HGSE classmates for karaoke night at a club called the Purple Shamrock. I often joke that I latched onto Melanie because I knew she would see me through anything after she stuck with me through my horrific rendition of the Dixie Chicks' song "Goodbye Earl."

Melanie and I took alternate routes, but we both landed in North Carolina. By then we were both married and working toward doctorates in different fields while home with very young children. For years we took turns watching each other's kids so we could each attend our classes. Then we both graduated and shifted into being full-time at home.

One evening, Melanie and I both attended a preschool parent meeting that unexpectedly wrapped up early. We were both exhausted, but we both had childcare (a rarity) for another hour. Huzzah! We decided to grab a drink at a place nearby. As we sipped our beverages, we talked about this crazy stage of life. Our husbands were drowning at work. We were drowning at home. We decided, together, that if this period of time had a motherhood mantra, it would be "Don't let it die."

Landing on that phrase opened the conversational floodgates.

Melanie and I spent that hour talking about everything that we worried might die: Our children. Our marriages. Our careers. Our interests. Our friendships. Our various identities.

We acknowledged there was not enough time or oxygen to keep everything thriving.

But, we wondered, was there enough oxygen to keep most things alive? Not thriving, but not dead, either. Dormant. On life support. Able to be revived later—if we were lucky—when we had more energy and time.

~

So far, marriage and motherhood had taken me through three phases.

I had tried to be everything at a reasonably high level, but it was too much.

I had tried completely immersing myself in the roles of wife and mother, but eventually I began suffocating under everyone else's piles.

I had tried to see my home as a microcosm of the world and express my identities within its walls, but not engaging with communities I cared about left me edgy.

Finally, after my conversation with Melanie, I had a new approach: Figure out what matters. Acknowledge it might not flourish. But don't let it die.

~

I selected a few identities that mattered to me and took them outside the house to air. I pulled them out from underneath the suffocating piles that had accumulated in my inbox, sink, and laundry room and gave them external oxygen. The wife in me took an anniversary weekend in Charleston. The volunteer in me began monthly food collections for an organization named PORCH (People Offering Relief for Chapel Hill–Carrboro Homes). The teacher, activist, and environmentalist in me helped our children form a family nonprofit, Kids Coloring For a Cause, that focused on inspiring their classmates to create sponsored artwork to raise funds for endangered animals. The writer in me started a family blog. The get-up-and-go part of me actually took the kids to Washington, DC for a mini, personal protest the day after Trump imposed a gag order on the EPA, and Greenpeace called on us to resist.

The point is that every effort was small. Some didn't last long. Most were still connected somehow to nourishing the children—my natural instinct as an educator and mother, but also a very effective strategy for sustainability (since if something benefitted the kids, I knew I would keep it going, and those shared infusions of oxygen benefitted us all). Regardless, each endeavor kept a portion of me alive for later. And when frustration seeped in about not doing enough, Melanie was there with words of encouragement. She reminded me of the New Testament parable of the loaves and fishes. She said it illustrated how God could multiply small portions if we were willing to give them. I loved that idea. It relieved some of the pressure. My meager offerings could grow.

~

My journey through these four phases was not a logical progression, and I was not driven by thought. There was a lot of flailing and backtracking. I was emotional.

Looking back now, I can see the path and the patterns. But back then, even as I projected external aptitude, I was an internal mess. The children got my best; everyone else got a portion. My husband got a wife who was trying—and was capable—but was also mentally taut. And exhausted. And lost. And full of so much angst.

In addition, putting everything down on paper makes it seem like I devoted a lot of time to developing strategies—I didn't. If you are picturing me thoughtfully contemplating anything back then, please stop. The day after I called Reverend Shivers to ask if I could have a copy of her full quote, I had to email an apology for the complete chaos happening at my house during our conversation. In that note, I specifically referenced "one crying baby, one 3-year-old who got a boo boo and a 7-year-old holding up a sign that said, 'Can I play on the computer?'" Clearly it was no deep meditative session. Like everything else, it was a lifeline grabbed amid churning waves as I tried to stay afloat.

~

One of my first physical symptoms was headaches. Dull, constant, just-power-through-them headaches. I actually went to the doctor once, with three of the kids. The baby was strapped to my chest. The toddler was screaming until I took him out of the double stroller. The four-year-old crawled out of the stroller front, into the low back space designed for the toddler, causing the stroller to flip. Within minutes, everyone was cry-ing—all while the doctor looked at his chart and said, "I see you are here to discover the source of your headaches. Hmmm. This is not going to be difficult to diagnose—the volume level in here is quite something—but it might be tricky to address . . ."

The next was grinding my teeth while I slept—something I did not even realize I was doing until my dentist pointed out the damage. I left that cleaning (which I completed with a newborn on my lap while two toddlers dueled using sample electric toothbrushes: "Nooo! Get that *out* of your mouth!") with instructions to come back next week and pick up a mouthguard. It might help with the headaches but would definitely help with my oral health.

The third symptom was a panic attack, which I absolutely disregarded. It happened while we were caring for our child who had asthma. She was only eight, but we had been managing her asthma for years and were well-versed in using the inhaler. But for several days, something about her symptoms seemed different. The episodes were more frequent—and more frightening—and for some reason, only happening at night while she was sleeping. I had taken her to the doctor twice, received more intensive meds (a nebulizer in addition to an inhaler), and reviewed the caregiving instructions. Still, one evening—while my husband was working late—her lips had actually turned blue, full-on *blue*, before she caught her breath. She was shockingly calm about it. She trusted me, and she trusted her medicine, but I was terrified. My husband arrived home shortly after, and we debated taking her to the hospital. But she had seen the doctor that morning, the inhaler had worked, and now she was sleeping. Did we really need to wake her up, only to hear again what the doctor had told us twelve hours ago? Wasn't it better to trust the advice and let her rest? I already had a bunk set up in her room, so I went in to watch her breathing. I recall crying, then sobbing, then feeling my heart literally clench in my chest. Pain began shooting down my left arm, and I could not catch my breath. I woke up my husband (asleep after a late night at work and preparing for an early work morning—work that paid for our child's health insurance) and told him something was wrong. Was I having a heart attack?

"We need to get you to the hospital," he told me.

Hell no. I only woke him because if I was incapacitated, someone else needed to monitor our child's breathing. Because let me tell you what is *never* going to happen: You are never going to see me decide *my child* is OK being managed at home, right before checking *myself* into the hospital. I'd rather be dead.

Besides, the episode—which I now know was a panic attack—was very quickly forgotten. Because the next day, I took my daughter back to the asthma doctor, who ordered a chest X-ray at a nearby radiology clinic. The technician at the clinic agreed to break protocol and let me and then my husband into the room with our daughter, but we could not bring the siblings. I texted three mom friends and said I needed childcare for twenty minutes, starting ASAP. Was anyone available? There was a pizza place next door to the clinic where I could get them a table and buy pizzas for everyone if they could keep an eye on the kids. My amazing friends showed up. And one (the amazing Melanie) called her husband, an ER doctor (the amazing Kevin), who reviewed my daughter's case and called in a favor with a specialist who revealed we were not dealing with asthma. My daughter's vocal cords were collapsing, cutting off her airway. If these were laryngeal spasms, there was a protocol we could follow. If the cords were otherwise damaged, we had to act immediately because that could be fatal. How quickly could we get her to him so he could check?

The relief I felt when that specialist told us she had laryngeal spasms—and that he knew what to do, and that her life was not in danger—was immeasurable. Still, the next few weeks, before her new medicine took full effect, were brutal. Our child stopped breathing twelve times, always at home during the night, while I watched her sleeping. But we knew what to do and knew it would not ultimately be fatal—and she made it. Within a month we had our rested, bouncy, breathing easy, let's play, giggling gal back.

Then the weirdness, when one evening—right after our follow-up appointment that revealed our precious girl was completely cured—I began to itch. And itch. And itch. Everywhere. All over my body. What the hell? And now spots. Hives. Everywhere. Including on my face. And in my *mouth*, which frightened me. What if my throat started to swell? This time I did head to the ER. On the way, my husband called Kevin again, who met me en route and listened as I described what was happening. Kevin, that wonderful friend and doctor who had closely tracked our daughter's development these last four weeks, diagnosed me immediately. "You finally believe your daughter's going to be fine. Your mind has given your body permission to react to the psychological trauma," he told me. "And it is reacting. Take this medicine for the itching and hives. And carry this EpiPen in case you have a more extreme reaction to the stress."

I was so grateful for his insight and assistance. In fact, I was so relieved that it never even occurred to me that I had now gone from headaches to carrying an EpiPen in case my body had a potentially fatal reaction to stress.

No, it did not occur to me that things were operating at too crazy a pitch until two and a half years later, when I flew off the handle at my husband right as he was leaving on a work trip, and then—while he was on that trip—I received a phone call telling me I had cancer.

~

Friends, please hear me. If you are operating in an unsustainable way, your body will let you know. Softly at first. Then slightly louder. Then by screaming. And ultimately by breaking. Pay attention to the whisper if you want to avoid the big hit.

~

Also—as a daughter who once blamed herself for her father's ulcers—I need my children to hear this: Caring for you did *not* make me sick.

I *love* caring for you. My greatest joy comes from being in caring relationships with you. I would walk across glass—and then through fire—*without hesitating* to keep those connections with you. And—this part is even more important—if I had a free day to spend with any companions in the world, I would choose *you.*

Me with my favorite buddies, happily covered in cake frosting and snow.

The part of me that rebelled had nothing to do with you.

That portion of me that is just me—pure *me*—that weird, eccentric, eclectic core . . .

That core told me she needed more oxygen, and I chose to ignore her. And instead of withering and dying, she stood up and *insisted.*

And honestly, I love that about her.

~

I think part of my mistake was only allowing my volume to match hers at any given point.

I whispered needs along the way.

Well, there is no way to whisper the words, "I have cancer." Even when (after the echo of that word dies down, taking part of you with it) the next sentence contains the words "stage zero." Even when you tell everyone,

"The nurse said it was going to ruin the summer and involve some very hard choices, but I'm not going to die."

Those words come out at full volume no matter how softly you try to say them.

In my case, they came out loudly enough to match the volume of a different conversation—one my husband and I had shared a week earlier.

~

It was May 2017. I was forty-three years old, had been married almost thirteen years, and my four children were ages ten, nine, six, and four. There was no indication I had cancer. There were headaches. Teeth grinding. One panic attack. A dusty EpiPen. Exhaustion. But I convinced myself those were normal for a busy and angsty mom. We had no idea the big diagnosis was coming. Instead, I was trying to get through the month of May.

May. What a month. Every year.

Each May, my husband was out of town almost the entire month for work.

In May, every activity the kids were involved in had its grand finale. My evenings were double-booked with recitals, playoff games, and curtain calls, all while the school emails told me everyone needed to have a good dinner and long rest so they could do well on their end-of-year exams.

During May, there was almost no alone time for this introvert to recharge. I went to school with everyone for field day or the end-of-year assembly or the class party. College students left for the semester (goodbye, occasional sitter). Preschool ended a month before elementary school dismissed (goodbye, two mornings a week that allowed me to race home to manage the checkbook, calendar, inbox, and appointments for everyone without my toddler's help). And in May, I could not just let things pile up and await my attention because shortly after the month ended, school ended. I loved summers with the kids, but very little paperwork got done.

The environmental nonprofit we created worked best if we followed a school year rhythm. This meant our annual grand finale (which involved planning an event for, and giving a presentation to, our primary sponsor) happened in May.

Each May, I marked the anniversary of my dad's death. He had passed away on May 19, 2009, from a GI bleed I could not stop thinking about—one that proved fatal because of the blood thinners he had to take for his heart. Was the bleed connected to those ulcers that developed when I asked him to swallow those words in high school? Back then—before my sister (and later, my mother, who earnestly apologized for the insinuation) convinced me otherwise—I suspected I was at fault. And I was so incredibly sorry. I missed him. I missed his laugh. His sarcastic drawl. His hands—a surgeon's hands—that were always applauding. I felt his absence, and the experience of that was at its most potent in May.

In May, I also celebrated my own birthday. This should have been a positive thing, but for the last few years, it had been a trigger: a hot spot in the cold war of my midlife crisis. This cold war was a standoff between my current self (who knew she should be at peace with her efforts) and the voice of my younger self (who told me I wasn't doing enough). Normally, these selves considered one another. But in May, they judged each other more harshly.

May also brought Mother's Day. This was the day to which I was clinging. My husband made plans to be in town for a few days that covered both Mother's Day and my birthday. When his parents heard this was the only time he would be home before they took their trip to Ireland, they asked if they could stay with us for the week. I told my husband to please have them pick *any* other time—not this month, and not during the only stretch he was home. I needed those few days to be the eye of the hurricane. Simple. Easy. Calm. With him helping me juggle. And selfishly, I didn't want to plan a nice Mother's Day for someone else. I needed one day that didn't require forethought. A day people expected me to take it a bit easier. A day we could just let unfold.

But his folks are wonderful. And it was nice that they wanted to see us before they left for Europe. And so we said yes, and they came, and true to their generous natures, offered to watch the kids one afternoon so I could get a few things done. I thanked them—and scheduled my annual mammogram during those two hours alone.

~

Over the course of that month of May 2017 several small things happened that represented big issues for me—incidents that, one at a time, made me wonder how my life had gotten so far offtrack.

First, my friends asked if they could edit their will to list us as guardians for their children. This was an easy yes for me, but a no for my husband. This was not an impasse. Instead, it was a no because something like that *has* to be a unanimous decision. I understood my husband's perspective. We were drowning already, and we needed to be realistic and honest. He was trying to protect his wife, who was clearly hanging by a thread. Still, I was incredibly frustrated. We had been asked if we would take in orphans—in the event that was needed—and we had said no? What kind of people were we? Also, *I was not drowning in busyness; I was drowning in angst.* And the angst only became more consuming when someone asked me for help, and I turned them down.

Next, as the chaos of May engulfed me, my husband suggested we figure out a way to take something off my plate. "Maybe it's time to let go of the nonprofit," he suggested. I remember thinking, *He has no idea what fills my bucket and what drains it. Letting go of that nonprofit means another part of* me *is being surrendered. After looking at everything on my plate,* that *is what you think should be abandoned?*

Then there was the Sunday, two days before my birthday, that was Mother's Day. It was also graduation day for local universities, and my in-laws were in town. The men wanted to take us out to eat—it was our day, after all—but we were a party of eight with no dinner reservation. My husband and his parents drove to a restaurant intending to wait for a table. They would call me and the children when it was ready.

But then they discovered that the wait was over two hours.

No problem; they had a plan. We could eat at a country club. There would be no wait at the exclusive establishment. My husband had a work membership, and my in-laws had enjoyed meals there during previous visits. But I disliked the space—how it made me feel and its exclusivity—and my husband knew it. Yet he called me, with his parents in the car, on Mother's Day, as I wrangled four children at home, when my only choices were to either go or shoot their best plan down. I shot it down, then felt crappy. And then angry. And then I tried to fix it. I called back and suggested that we all skip town. We could grab takeout, hop in the car, and spend the night at a hotel near a small kid-themed amusement park that would make tomorrow so fun and festive and different. My husband told me, "My parents and I are traveling almost every other day this month. None of us have any interest in leaving town."

And finally, I talked to my husband about an idea I had for a children's book. I was excited enough about it that I made sure the kids were occupied and invited him into a quiet room, where I told him everything. He listened, expressed enthusiasm for the project, and then said (I'll keep this G-rated), "Smart is *so* sexy."

There is nothing wrong with that particular statement. I'm *glad* he thinks smart is sexy. There are plenty of guys out there who think it is intimidating or threatening or just plain unnecessary (since they plan to do all the thinking). Those guys are the assholes. My husband is great.

But even though I tried to respond positively in that moment, my real feelings surfaced not long after. I did not feel celebrated. What I felt was *rage*.

I had been telling him about an idea I had. A good idea. An idea that centered on my mind and something it could create. A process that could help me forge a connection with communities I was missing and the most neglected parts of the authentic me. And instead of exploring my new thought, he had shifted attention away from it onto my body. It felt like yet another moment when I was on the brink of something new and bright, and the nearest man had seen the glow, been drawn to it, and then made it about something else.

I know that is not fair to my husband. I was already irritated about other things, and the way he intended the gesture is not the way it was received. I am acknowledging here that part of the problem was *me*.

But still, all of these moments—and the years that preceded them—congealed into a message that thrummed in my brain. That message was, *You are not living the life you were called to—the life of a good person—and maybe that's partially* his *fault.*

~

The dust settled on all of these moments. And a few weeks later, on a day that had no connection to a book idea or a country-club invitation or an endangered nonprofit or potential orphans—on a day where I was simply back to being what everyone in the immediate vicinity needed—I confronted my husband. I accused him. I told him how good I could have been with his encouragement and support. Instead, I was living in a suburb with a spouse who hired housekeepers and yard guys and wanted dinner at a fancy country club. *None* of that was me. Why weren't we living in an impoverished community? Why weren't we willing to take in orphans? How could he suggest I stop doing the nonprofit work, while I was pushing for us to do more of those things?

And speaking of more, why weren't we giving away more of our money? More of everything? Didn't he see it? Didn't he feel it? Didn't he recognize that we were not doing enough?

The peak of the critique came when I glared at him and said I was tired. Specifically, I was tired of being the only one who was pushing us to live *better* lives.

~

It was a horrifying moment for him—and a moment of instant realization for me. As soon as the words came out of my mouth, I looked at my husband and immediately understood two very big things.

The first was that I had shocked my spouse.

And that was absolutely not the reaction I had expected to see.

I had just accused him of failing to live into—of failing to encourage—The Vision (that ascetic life full of radical generosity and meaning). He should have looked chastened. He should have looked guilty. But he didn't. He looked shocked and baffled, and those particular expressions on the face of the man I loved powered a light-bulb moment for me.

He had never wanted *any* of the things I had just listed. He was never drawn toward adoption or asceticism or an off-the-grid, somehow-atypical lifestyle. I had accused him of not answering the call, but those things had never called him. They had only called me.

That new awareness led to my second realization, which was that I had just metaphorically whacked my spouse with an external measuring stick.

I hated external measures. For so much of my childhood, adolescence, and twenties, I had been subjected to them. I didn't measure up professionally: *whack*. Or spiritually: *whack*. Or personally: *whack*. I had finally burned all of those external measuring sticks and crafted personalized ones, just for me. But after creating my own measuring sticks, I had held them up next to my husband. I had done the very thing I hated others doing to me.

My husband is an individual, with his own vision. And he uses it to enact all types of kindness, including ones I struggle to embrace. The most frequent example is him wanting to open our holiday dinner table to strangers. It is a generosity my introverted nature resists. I could take in four more children and live as a family of ten in a tenement building, no problem. But small talk with strangers in my own home over Christmas dinner? I need a minute to get there, because my reflex reaction is no.

What I realized in that moment—as my husband sat there with that shocked expression on his face—was that my core, and the nudges it gave me, were my own. He did not feel them. He felt other things, which I needed to respect.

This was a very important awareness, but it left me with two significant questions: First, how do I apologize for whacking him with my personally crafted measuring stick? And second, what does it mean for a marriage and children when you realize you and your spouse don't share identical visions?

~

It turns out that, as apologies go, saying, "I am so sorry. I have just realized that I was being unfair, and judgmental, and wrong" is a good start. Also, the fact that we discovered I had cancer shortly after this conversation had an impact. Anger softened. Perspective peeked through. That summer, he said some things he now regrets also, which was almost a relief, since it somehow made us more even. We could both be forgiving.

And we could just kick a lot of those other cans down the road.

~

After that conversation with my husband, my awareness altered in two separate stages.

The first stage was realizing that I had unfairly judged my husband. That alteration, and the apology for it, happened almost immediately.

The second stage was recognizing that I needed to reevaluate how I was assessing my own life. Maybe, just maybe, I was also unfairly judging myself. Considering this has taken longer—and working through it is part of what motivates me to write.

THE BEAUTY

I have focused—disproportionately—on the hard. Let's look at the beauty.

I have not really introduced my boys, the two youngest members of my immediate family. As I write, they are ages eight and ten. They are individuals with unique interests, personalities, and aspirations—but they are also quite a team.

For several years, when they were very small, they were a team of super-heroes. We went through a phase where, in addition to approaching every policeman and fireman we saw (often crossing paths at the library, where first responders held a few meetings), my tiny caped crusaders approached every moment in life as an opportunity to assist.

I would have my hand on the counter, and five-year-old Tyler would snap to attention. "Mom! Your hand is *stuck*! Let me help you!" As we exited the house to meet the girls' school bus, Hudson would remind us, "Someone might need help! We have to all wear our capes!" Our jack-o-lantern was at the ready year-round because its glow looked like the Bat Signal. One year, I asked each child to pick something special he or she wanted to have at Thanksgiving dinner. I was thinking my youngest might pick something like donuts. Instead, Hudson said, "What I want at dinner is *everyone* in *costumes*." Well, why not? We *all* heroed up. Tim carved the turkey while dressed as Captain America.

We took the kids to Universal Studios once, a theme park that stages an afternoon drama involving actors paid to play villains. It also involves actors paid to play superheroes, but do you really need those? Maybe not, because Hudson—only age three—was wearing his Superman costume. And after he sprinted away from his parents toward the show's villains, he began actively kicking a bad guy in the shin.

Superheroes, dressed for—and living—the part. And I got to live (and have Thanksgiving dinner and vacation) with them.

~

Tyler (my oldest son, currently age ten) is an active kid with a large array of interests—some social and rambunctious, others measured and quiet. He loves sports (mainly basketball) as well as construction, computer coding, and movies with friends. Tyler also loves words. I now wake up early every morning to write in my office, and occasionally I find Tyler has beaten me there with his own paper and pen. He once wrote a haiku about heroes that remains one of my favorite poems of all time. It reads:

Heroes around me.
Heroes are nice, kind, helpful.
Can be everyone.

I have seen Tyler use words to enact kindness on several occasions, writing a note or consoling a toddler. I have also seen him use them to connect. He once asked me if we could host a party because a classmate had not been included in someone else's event the previous weekend. His friend was upset. So Tyler planned a party. The whole group came—none of them knowing the entire event was inspired by Tyler wanting to extend an enthusiastically worded invitation to this kid.

Words can hurt. They can also delight. Tyler has learned this lesson early. I appreciate that. And I appreciate how he shares that delight with me. I remember once, during virtual learning, when Tyler ditched a class because he could not wait to tell me about a pun his teacher had made during the lesson. "Mom! We're learning geometry today, and guess what? The teacher said as far as this topic goes, we're in great *shape*. Ha! Do you get it? The *geometry* class is in great *shape*. Ha! I just had to tell you. Now I'm going back in."

Oh, how I loved the sparkle in his eyes during that moment. Oh, the joy of him wanting to share it with me—and letting me share it with him.

I also recall another shared moment with Tyler. He was only six years old. The whole family was sitting around our kitchen table. I had just told the kids I had cancer. My husband and I were offering reassurance. Comfort. Details about what life would look like. Information about who would take care of them at various points. I realized, twenty minutes into the conversation, that everyone had spoken except Tyler. "Tyler," I said, "do you have any questions?"

"Yes," he responded quietly. "How are you feeling? I mean, *is it hurting you?*"

With that one line of inquiry, Tyler shifted the entire conversation away from managing the moment to feeling it. He transformed me from mama-the-caregiver to mama-the-person. While I prattled on about how everything at home would be okay while I was gone, his thoughts were elsewhere. He wanted to know if I was in pain. There is quite a heart inside this kid.

~

Hudson (currently age eight) has quite a heart also. You can usually find it on his sleeve. He is expressive, engaged, and a self-proclaimed extrovert. I once asked him to make a list of friends he would like to invite to his birthday party. He returned it with one word written at the top: everyone.

"*Everyone?*" I asked him.

"Everyone," he told me. "Even people I don't know. I want a huge crowd. Bring *everyone* in."

He gets that from my husband, who would also love to celebrate everything with everyone. I am willing to do this only because I feel like maybe if everyone comes, they can entertain each other. Maybe if the crowd gets big enough, no one will even notice I've left and that for the last half-hour I have actually been in my bedroom, with my feet tucked under the covers and my nose in a book contentedly reading while listening to the distant but happy din.

Hudson would not sit behind the door. He wants to be where the action is. If that is not allowed for some reason, he will create action right where he is standing.

When Hudson was three years old, he announced that afternoon quiet time was "all done!" by exiting his room, ripping a baby gate off the top stair (hello, hole in the drywall), toddling to the bottom of the stairs, ripping the next gate off that level (hello, broken staircase spindle), and announcing "I'm here!" Never mind that quiet time wasn't that long—or that quiet, really. To illustrate: During a previous quiet time, we had a rare North Carolina earthquake. The entire house was shaking. Did I evacuate the children? Did we hide under a solid table or protective doorframe? No. I stood at the bottom of the stairs and yelled, "What's going on up there? Are you all in one room together? Do we need to start the quiet time clock over again?"

Hudson will also insist that others take action.

Once, four-year-old Hudson was on the back of my bike when we had to ride off the beach onto a path. The route took us through a thirty-foot stretch of much softer sand. It was a short enough segment that I kept Hudson in the bike's child seat while moving us through the quagmire. Getting him out would have required removing his helmet, then his five-point harness, and then Hudson himself—only to then have to convince my child to get back in the seat, harness, and helmet all over again. So Hudson begrudgingly sat while I pushed the bike, with its unmoving wheels and thirty-five-pound child, through the sand. As he sat and I pushed, two people walked by us, one after another. Both of them separately commented on what a difficult thing it was to get a bike through that stretch of sand. Hudson listened to this and squirmed in his seat, and when a third man walked by and made a final remark about how hard it looked, Hudson yelled at him, "How about less talking and more helping!"

"Right!" this guy responded—and then offered assistance. "Ma'am. Young sir. May I please give you two a hand?"

Hudson is full of life. Energy. Drive. And crowd-centric connections. But he is still little, and he does have a soft streak. When he gets tired, he wants to snuggle one-on-one while I read him a story. And although Tyler occasionally beats him to it, Hudson is typically the first to pad down the hallway each morning, open my office door, and peek in. I love starting my days that way: Hearing him. Seeing him. Fixing breakfast together. Or fixing breakfast and then realizing that my beautiful bundle of extroverted energy is suspiciously quiet, which either means he has gone back upstairs to wake everyone up ("Hudson, wait! Seriously! It's *Saturday!*") or what I thought was a fuzzy pile of warm blankets on the couch is actually a fuzzy pile of warm blankets on top of Hudson, who is still young enough to curl up on a loveseat and fall back to sleep.

I love this family, with its beautiful members and moments. I am so lucky to spend my life with them.

CANCER

My dad died in 2009 of a GI bleed.

I was home with my daughters when I received a phone call from my sister, Ashley, telling me to pray—Dad was in trouble. He was in an ambulance, barely hanging on, currently unconscious. My mom and sister were two hours away from him, in my mother's car, racing toward our hometown hospital.

I immediately followed my sister's directive: "Pray Dad makes it. And pray for Mom, who is currently speeding down the interstate." She was trying to get to her husband while he was still alive. Praying and driving, while my sister made these phone calls from the passenger seat.

It was a Tuesday afternoon: Tim was working, and I was home with the kids. We only had the two girls back then. Ella was almost three, and Sienna was fifteen months old. Both girls crawled over and padded around me as I knelt and prayed. I welcomed the undespairing energy of these littles.

Fifteen minutes after that initial call, the phone rang again.

Dad was gone.

~

In my dad's obituary we requested that in lieu of flowers, donations be made to Habitat for Humanity in honor of the loving home he created for our family.

I spoke at his funeral and said the following words:

> There have been a couple of times during the last fifteen years when we were worried about my dad—before a surgery, for example—and I tried at those times to make sure that I said everything I needed to say to him, thinking that if we ever got to this point, I wanted to know that, at the very least, I had communicated what he meant to me.
>
> What I didn't know is that sometimes there are things that you only realize you want to say—need to say—after a person is gone. After I got the call that he had passed, I felt his absence in emotional spaces that I didn't even realize he had filled for me. So today, I want to thank him for filling those spaces.

Here, I turned away from the congregation and—through tears— spoke directly to my father in his coffin.

> Dad, I miss you. I am grateful for so many things. I tried to express that gratitude to you while you were here. But I don't know if I ever specifically thanked you for loving me so unconditionally—as a little girl, before you knew who I was, and as an adult after you knew who I was, and at all those times in between when I was trying to figure out who I was.

I turned back to the congregation and put my one-page paper of notes down, interrupting my own prepared words. I told the crowd, "When I practiced reading this earlier—to my younger brother, Todd—he told me, 'You are so right about the unconditional love part. The only time anyone ever felt rejection from Dad was when they tried to shoot over him on the basketball court.'" The congregation chuckled as I glanced at my brother, who smiled at me as we both remembered, then I turned my attention back to my dad and told him,

> I love you, and I know that you always loved me. I am so grateful for that. I will do that for my children. Thank you for teaching me how.

~

My dad loved me. Every expectation he had was an attempt to move me toward happiness. He never once rejected me (aside from those blocked shots my brother mentioned). And there were a number of occasions where he was the one who intervened when he felt someone was being too hard on me—or that I was being too hard on myself.

I miss him the most when I'm using the phone. It might seem weird, but every time I have ever called someone other than my parents, my socially anxious self has always paused first and thought, *Will this phone call be intrusive? Maybe this is too [early/late/often] to call. Maybe I'll just email* . . .

But with my mom and dad, it was different. They were (are, in the case of my mother) *always* happy to hear from me. Even if it was early, or late, or I really had nothing to say. I never had to think prior to dialing. If I had a moment, I could call home. There were so many moments in the years after my dad's death when I caught myself dialing his number without thinking.

I also think of him whenever the number 51 pops up. It was his basketball jersey number at The University. It became our number when I chose it for my varsity high school and then college jerseys. My kids eventually claimed it on several jerseys as well. Now every single time I see the number 51—whether it is on a receipt or in the red dot indicating the count of my unread text messages—I think of my dad.

Around the time of the funeral, some friends in Boston asked me what they could do. Send a meal? Flowers? Some sort of comfort?

I told them that what I really wanted was for them to take their own kids out for an inappropriately timed ice-cream cone in honor of my dad.

I explained that there were so many stories about my dad prioritizing his children. One of the most outlandish (but completely true) tales is about him stopping to get my older brother a milkshake on the way to a wedding—his sister's wedding. A wedding to which he was running late and during which he was supposed to walk the bride down the aisle. The wedding coordinator (whom my family absolutely considers the villain of this story) insisted the ceremony start on time. My dad missed it. "It was unfortunate," my dad always said at the end of the telling, "but kids *do* need ice cream. I mean, they are only little for such a short time."

Oh, how I loved the response card I received in the mail from my friend about a month later. She described the scene at her dinner table as she sat with her husband and two young children, just beginning a well-balanced meal. She described hearing the ice-cream truck—I can just imagine the tune it played, nightmarishly interrupting her insistence on vegetables—and then she thought to herself, *This is the perfect moment to honor Kristi's dad.*

In her note, she detailed the shock on her kids' faces when she put down her fork, stood up, and said, "Who wants to ruin their dinner with some ice cream?"

She said her kids squealed with delight as the entire family rushed to enjoy a treat—and create a memory—outside.

~

I received the phone call telling me I had cancer on a Thursday afternoon. June 1, 2017. My husband was out of town. I was home with the kids (then ages ten, nine, six, and four), who were playing in the living room. The nurse on the phone said, "I have your biopsy results. There is some bad news. You have ductal carcinoma in situ. It is an early form of cancer. It is not going to kill you, but it is going to ruin your summer and involve some very hard choices."

I remember the nurse telling me she was so very sorry. I remember her asking if the kids she heard in the background were mine. And I remember her saying that I needed to meet with the oncologist tomorrow at 1 p.m. if that would be possible. Was there any way I could make that time?

Yes. Absolutely. Making the time. Even though getting a sitter on short notice for a Friday afternoon in June—after all the college kids had gone home for the summer—would be nearly impossible. I would scramble if needed.

I remember exactly where I was when the phone call ended. I had not wanted the kids to overhear my questions, so I had eventually moved out of earshot into the garage. As I stood there, surrounded by the gardening tools we once used to help the kids grow a single, but well-earned and much enjoyed carrot and the extension cord we always used to position the way-too-many Christmas lights, I could hear my kids looking for me inside. Tiny feet padding up and down the hallway. Tiny voices calling for me. Tiny people who needed their mama. And whom their mama needed. Always. But especially right in that moment.

I opened the door from the garage to the house, surveyed the chaos that had unfolded during my ten-minute absence, and said, "OK kids. I have one question for all of you: *Who wants to ruin their dinner with some ice cream?*"

They squealed, and we pulled out every container we had in the freezer. And we had a messy, sticky, fantastic picnic where the only culinary option was ice cream—eaten with giant spoons and whatever toppings they wanted.

～

The cancer phone call shocked me. My mammogram had revealed a particularly dense area to be biopsied, but I was so overwhelmed by May chaos that I viewed that follow-up procedure as a break. It seems ridiculous now, but I was so exhausted (and unconcerned) that I actually fell asleep while on the biopsy table. When a nurse woke me—first explaining she could not risk the needle jolting me awake and then expressing her surprise that I was more tired than anxious—I quipped, "That nap is the closest I've gotten to a day off in years!"

In response, the nurse gave me a half-smile before saying, "If that's true, then I want you to tell your family this procedure took all afternoon. Please, go do something relaxing." I didn't, but after they bandaged the bleeding spot on my breast, I did gift myself twenty minutes to write, sitting in the middle row of our minivan with my laptop, quietly typing on level three of the hospital's parking deck.

～

Once I recovered from the shock, I realized I was lucky to have discovered cancer at an early enough stage that I could decide how to approach it. When faced with a decision, I did not have to wonder which option was more likely to keep me alive.

Still, there were lots of decisions to make, and I had to figure out how to make them. Ultimately, I determined that, at every juncture, I would ask the following questions: Which option made cancer less of a factor in my day-to-day life going forward? Which option was ultimately going to give cancer less of my mental energy and time?

I remember thinking, *I have so few moments to myself, and this cancer is going to consume all of them. Every sitter I get will be for an appointment. Every quiet hour will be spent researching options.* I quickly decided I was going to choose the path that demanded less of my time and attention—and added less mental stress—even if that path required a literal pound of flesh.

I did not want a lot of follow-up appointments—exams to monitor potential spread—on my calendar. That meant amputating my infected right breast.

I did not want to deal with being extremely high risk for cancer in my left breast—a status that would mean taking medicine every day for the next five years (with unavoidable side effects) and constantly monitoring that tissue through more frequent examinations. This meant opting for a preventive mastectomy on my left side.

I considered forgoing reconstruction altogether. Sometimes I still wish I had chosen this option. But just like I had never wanted attention for my breasts before, I did not want attention for the absence of them now. I elected for reconstructive implants. I went against the doctor's advice (silicone would look and feel more natural) and opted for saline. I chose this because if one ever ruptured, dealing with the aftermath would require less attention and time.

I just wanted to get everything over with and get back to my life.

~

It did occur to me, shortly after my diagnosis, that I could use cancer to make my life look different. That the disease would in some ways provide me with some leeway and freedom.

I do not know why it took something like cancer to convince me that I could say no to serving on committees without feeling guilty. Or that I could breathe deeply and say, "Seriously. I am going to need a slower pace and more time."

I do know that amid some very tough moments post-op, as I mourned the loss of emotional and physical familiarities, I actually celebrated that liberating aspect of confronting mortality.

Part of it was a shift in me, but part of it was a shift in others. True—I was able to speak more freely. But it is also true that when I did, others seemed to really listen. Recruiters for tasks understand (or at least remain silent) when you want to reprioritize post-cancer. I am grateful for the folks who do the thankless and vital job of community committee work, but I seized onto the exit ramp cancer provided. The disease was an opportunity to stop everything for a while, and then only resume what I really wanted to take on.

Cancer was a big part of my identity for a short time—as well as a card I played as I made several exits. But I never wanted it to define me.

~

My husband was there for me. On that Thursday of the unforgettable phone call, after I put the kids to bed, I called him. I actually debated whether to bother him. We had just had a rough month, and then a rough week, for which I was largely to blame. And now he was hosting the biggest work event of the year—a four-day fundraiser, which I never interrupted. Still, I had an appointment with an oncologist tomorrow, and I assumed the doctors would tell me I needed surgery ASAP. Wasn't that how cancer worked? And I had to get our family's medical history from my mother. I couldn't call her—or anyone else, including the friends I was going to ask to watch the kids during the next day's appointment—until I let my husband know. I left him a message to call me back. He did. And when we connected, I was not overly emotional. I had not had time for that. I was numb, and I told him I would be fine during the appointment and throughout the weekend. I was sorry to dump something so heavy on him, but I didn't want to start lining things up without letting him know.

He was stunned. And worried.

And the next morning he told me was going to leave the huge event he had spent six months organizing and was in the process of hosting and come home.

My people were there for me, too. Friends who had been on similar paths carved out hours to share their experiences and offer advice. My mother dropped everything and stayed with me, taking on the task that I struggled with the most (physically and psychologically): emptying my post-surgical drains. Family came into town during and post-surgery to care for the kids. On the morning of my double mastectomy, while Tim and I were at the hospital, two friends (Katie and Melanie) surprised my children and their grandparents with donuts and distraction. They brought their own kids—two of whom were dressed in those enormous, padded sumo-wrestling outfits—and offered breakfast and antics. Sometimes love is sugarcoated and silly and there right when you need it.

I also learned that the breast cancer community is fantastic. I experienced a "you do you; how can I help" mentality (aside from one person who told me my cancer didn't count because it was stage zero). Aside from that one person, every member of the village I encountered respected and supported one another's journeys from start to finish. They even respected my choice not to take up cancer as my dominant cause after the fact. These fearless warriors who choose to devote their time to breast cancer awareness and research and support have saved and improved so many lives, including mine. Due to their public messages about the importance of early detection (and some genetic luck), I had choices about how big a deal this was going to be for me. I chose to keep its impact on my post-surgical life as small as possible, opting to take quick invasive action and then move on, focusing future energy elsewhere.

~

My husband went with me to every appointment, including an appointment with a psychiatrist who specialized in helping families cope with cancer. My oncologist had recommended him when we asked her for advice on sharing the news with the kids. He gave excellent recommendations on that front, but that is not why I am sharing the story.

I am sharing the story because it connects to all the other parts of this memoir and because I think it has power.

So much power that I actually sent Melanie the following email a few days after the appointment. That email read:

> Melanie,
>
> I just came across a quote I thought you might like. Backstory first:
>
> Last week, when we met with the child psychiatrist to get tips on talking to the kids about my diagnosis, he asked how I was doing. I told him I was truly fine and gave a few examples of how normal life had gone on. He laughed and said, "No great existential crisis then?" And I told him, "Not related to cancer anyway! I prefer to have my existential crises at other times. I just had one earlier this spring when I told Tim I wasn't sure why we weren't living in a developing country with all our foster children." So the psychiatrist tells us about a lady he met who had fostered sixty-five children, one of whom had cancer. And Tim said, "Stop! Don't tell her that! We cannot revisit the existential crisis this summer." And the psychiatrist said,

"Right. I can absolutely tell you that you need to take saving the world off your summer to-do list."

So I was thinking about all of that, and about all the conversations you and I have had in which we try to figure out what is next for ourselves, and what we "should be" doing, and what we *are* doing, and what makes us stop, go, commit, and decline. And then this morning I read a quote that I thought was quite powerful, so I thought I would share. It was written by Anna Whiston-Donaldson, a wonderful woman who sadly lost her son in a freak accident when he was twelve. And now his friends were graduating from high school, and she wrote them all a graduation letter. In that letter she apologized for how their childhood had shifted so abruptly when their friend died but hoped that one "fruit" to come out of it was that at an extraordinarily young age they had learned "how important each person, each life, is to this world." She said that as they began making post-graduation choices and taking next steps, she wanted them to "Remember that you don't get your value from what you do, but from who you are, and whose you are."[1]

Wise words, I think.

Which I still take with a grain of salt, because unfortunately we still have to figure out what we're going to do at various points. But it was super nice to have someone with such a hard-won perspective state so clearly that what we decide on or skip doesn't determine our value.

Also, on the heels of a quote that highlights who and whose we are, I want you to know that I think who you are is amazingly awesome.

Existential crisis avoided, until next time.

XO,
Kristi

~

That email to Melanie was not the only one I sent after that appointment. In fact, after we spoke to and reassured the kids, I sent emails to our community, including this one to a group of recipients that included my old friend Denise.

> Friends,
>
> Apologies for the group email, but we've kept some news very close until we talked to the kids about it this weekend, and now that they have heard it from us, we want to loop a few family and friends in.
>
> The bad news is that I have been diagnosed with breast cancer. The good news is that we caught it amazingly early—stage zero. Assuming that diagnosis holds, there will be no radiation and no chemo. I will need surgery sometime in July or August—not yet sure exactly when. And I will be absolutely fine; the plan is to be cancer-free by the end of summer.
>
> I know this lovely group of folks will ask what we need, and the honest answer is nothing tangible at the moment. If that changes, we will absolutely reach out, and I will update once I know what weeks I'll be out of commission. In the meantime, we would be so grateful if you would help us keep the normal playdate, camp, and carpool routines going. And we'd be extra grateful if you'd keep our kids on your radar, especially if they are nearby during caring conversations. Our crew knows the truth—that there are all types of cancer, some more scary than others, and that Mom is super blessed to have the "stage-zero kind." They have been watching us closely this weekend to see if we are worried, and we are grateful that we really aren't. We know they will be watching our community as well,

so when the kids are around, if there's any way to lean toward the "I know you've got this . . ." (i.e., going to beat it) in lieu of the "So sorry you've got this . . ." I think it would help them a ton (which helps us at least four tons by extension).

Thank you so much for being a part of our village. We are extraordinarily grateful!

Kristi & Tim

And here is the reply I received from Denise:

Hi Kristi,

Thank you for still including me in your village: the community of people who love you and root for you. Because I do. Even though we haven't seen each other since my sister moved out of Chapel Hill, and even though I'm spotty with my Christmas cards, I'm glad you still count me as part of your universe. You are part of my universe as well, and it makes me happy to know that you're still out there, rooting for me, and sending me good thoughts—even though our paths haven't crossed recently.

Thought number one: You got this! All signs say "good." Good that you discovered it early (I've never heard of a stage-zero case!), good that you're in medical care, good that you've got an eye on your kids' mental health, good that you have Tim to lean on if your confidence ever wavers, good that you're surrounded by a community of people that will run carpool and show up with casseroles. (Know that that would be me as well, if we lived in the same state!) Good that you've lived a life that builds this support—because not everyone has—and now is the time that you get to draw on some of the interest you've accrued, over this lifetime of building it.

Thought number two: I need to stop blowing off rescheduling the mammogram I missed over spring break.

Thought number three: If I've ever met a badass warrior princess, it's you, Kristi. It's commendable that you're actively seeking to shield your kids from the pain of a cancer diagnosis, but badassery is a heritable trait, and I'm certain that they've inherited this from you. They will want to be part of this (sucky) journey because they are part of your family, and because they love you, and because it's not just *your* cancer, it's theirs, too. Let them know honest truths when there are truths to be shared. Badass warriors strengthen when they're tested . . . in fact, it's literally the *only* way they are strengthened. Let them support you; they'll want to.

So much love sent to you and your band of warriors. You got this! Thanks for keeping me in your village.

xoxo, Denise, George, Callahan, and Witt
(badasses-in-training)

〜

That email from Denise not only shifted my perspective, it altered our entire family's experience. She was lovely, encouraging, kind, supportive—and absolutely right about me wanting to shield the kids. She was also absolutely right about what we would *all* lose if we shielded them entirely. Because of Denise's email, Tim and I measured out age-appropriate cancer weight and asked our children to carry it.

I eventually wrote Denise another note thanking her. Within that email I revealed that:

My initial mass communication did what we needed on one level: shielded our kids from constant cancer conversations at the park, grocery, pool, and even at their own birthday parties. But you got me thinking about what sort of exposures they did need, and I am so grateful for that. We were able to provide this summer as an example of how families pull together; we shared lots of moments with them—including the down ones—and admired what they had to offer our family in those moments. They supported me, which was pretty amazing. It was good for me, for them, and for us. Thank you.

And then I told Denise a story about one of those down moments—and how leaning into it together lifted us up in a way we never expected.

~

It was August of 2017, only a few days before my surgery. We were at the beach with some extended family, soaking up sunshine and time together. But it was not fully relaxing. Between nice moments, there were a lot of last-minute surgical stressors—to the point that Tim and I eventually left the beach for one brutal day midweek to see a new doctor (driving twelve hours round trip) while his parents watched the kids. The day after that visit, I was feeling overwhelmed and truly down.

I went for a walk by myself, crying in private. And then I thought of Denise's email and turned around. The kids were still little, but this was something they could handle. More than that, this was something with which my budding badasses could help. I went back to our rented condo, briefed Tim, and together we gathered the children. I told my family, through tears, that I was sad I had to have surgery, but the beach had always made me feel better and I wondered if they would walk there with me and collect some shells that I could take with me to the hospital. Of course, they were worried. Mom was upset. But there was something she needed, and they could help.

I cannot overstate the power of that moment: watching their fear turn to determination, seeing them grab their buckets and head out. And then, as we arrived on the beach, seeing something incredible that stunned all of us.

The kids know my special number is 51—the jersey number I shared with my father. They also know my favorite color is purple (I have even painted a wall in my office bright purple, and it was—at that time—the only colored wall in our house).

So you can imagine our surprise when we walked out to the beach and saw a huge number 51 surrounded by purple on a parasail right above us.

"Mom!"

"Look!"

"That's your number!"

"That's your color!"

There it was: The most wonderful thing I could never have imagined. Would not have even known to ask for. It felt like a sign of reassurance—to my family from my dad.

Later, as my kids collected shells, I approached the parasailer, who revealed that he had not been planning to go out that afternoon until he just felt like he had to. He also figured out that if we had arrived twenty minutes earlier or later, we would not have seen the number 51. He would have been turned the other way, and we would have seen the actual number on his equipment: the number 12. We only saw a 51 because we were viewing it from the wrong side. The inside. The underbelly.

If that is not a reminder that timing (and perspective and trial) matter, I don't know what is.

A few days later, I had my surgery. There were bumps and tears, and I didn't like my new boobs, and I wondered if I made the right choices. But I do believe cancer gifted me a few things.

Perspective. Vulnerability. Time with family. A position from which I felt comfortable asking several people for grace. An opportunity to nurture badassery in my children. And ultimately, a new photo of a parasail for my office, near a jar of really special shells collected by my kids, for me.

Uprooting

OXYGEN

I still craved twenty-four hours alone in a hotel to write—nothing that required a huge amount of prep or coordination or management, just twenty-four hours to breathe and attempt to type away my angst.

I used cancer as an excuse to take that.

I had read an article called "Stages of Grief After Losing a Breast." Stage 4 was detachment, and the article said women in this stage often need to "go off quietly by ourselves and sit with our loss."[1] I sent the article to my husband and told him I needed a weekend away.

And he helped me take it.

~

There have been several occasions when I have truly mourned my physical loss. But that weekend was not one of them.

Yes, I had lost my breasts, but I thought I knew why: It was because I had lost myself, and the angst of that had made me sick. I needed to find myself before I lost anything else.

Fortunately, I knew how to do that. The idea that I had to sit quietly and write this out thrummed in me, clear and insistent. I had not prioritized this practice before, and I had not communicated it well to my husband. Cancer gave me an opportunity to do both in a nonthreatening way.

I spent that weekend thinking about the difference between who I had aspired to be in my twenties and who I actually was now in my forties—beyond the roles of wife and mother.

In my twenties, I thought my life would be atypical in some way—not better, just different. I come alive when I'm a bit off the main road.

My life now felt very normal—meaning what many would expect it to look like, given my background—and that bothered me. I felt like I had done the grand tour of possible settings, only to end up very close to where I started. It is a tried-and-true plotline—coming full circle with a new perspective—but it was not what I wanted.

I was not sitting comfortably in my old space with my new perspectives. Ghosts from my journey were haunting me. That weekend, I finally sat and asked the ghosts to speak to me. And, to my surprise, I did not hear them saying "come back." I did not feel drawn back into teaching, or back into the village, clinic, or city. But remembering felt right.

~

That weekend, I examined my old ideals in several arenas. One of those arenas was financial. Money had been one point of contention during the May marital argument—and an enormous source of angst for my entire life—and I needed some degree of resolution.

My husband is very generous, but some of my ideas about money seemed crazy to him. In fact, our very first disagreement was about money. The year we met was a year of professional transition for him. He left a job, took an unpaid internship, and paid bills on a credit card. Unbeknownst to me, he was chipping away at the payments when we married. So when I approached him a few months into our marriage to decide together where our first tithe would go, he was shocked. "You are planning to give over $6,000 dollars away?" he asked, disbelieving. "You have over $17,000 in credit card debt?" I asked, equally incredulous. Clearly, we had neglected to have even the most basic of financial conversations.

The tithe was tabled for many years. We gave as much as we could at the end of each month, but to me, it felt backward. And it exponentially increased my angst.

It had taken me a while to realize that, for me, setting aside 10 percent up-front was incredibly liberating. During my twenties, every extraneous purchase made me feel guilty—until I completely committed to a tithe. That commitment meant there was always a pool of funds available, and that pool enabled me to say yes to others without thinking. Someone needs this: yes. A group needs that: yes. The money had already been designated. There was no "let me check the budget," or deciding what I could live without. The decision of what would be sacrificed had already been made; the 10 percent was there to give. The remainder could be used for expenses and possibly a few luxuries (travel!) that I could finally enjoy without angst.

When we stopped setting aside a full 10 percent, my angst came back. Why were we getting takeout? We could cook for less and give the difference to charity. Why were we getting *anything*? It came up on small purchases (movie tickets vs. renting a video) and big ones (apartment or house?). And it definitely came up in the realm of services. My husband was working a lot and wanted his time at home to be positive and focused on family. Hiring someone to clean would eliminate a source of frustration. He sees grime I don't even notice. He doesn't have time to deal with it, and certainly does not want to point it out to an overwhelmed wife. Hiring someone to take care of it is a solution that relaxes him. But he cannot relax and appreciate it because anytime we utilize those services, I become a very tense spouse. I am uncomfortable. I don't know whether to accept my discomfort (cancel the service, knowing it will hurt a local business, irritate my husband, and not actually inspire any progress on the family chore charts I struggle to monitor) or try to get comfortable with the idea (keeping the service, while worrying about how my kids perceive it and squirming within my own privilege). Yes, it is a first-world, ultra-privileged marital problem, but it is also something we can't quite figure out.

I also refused to acknowledge—for a long time—the financial responsibility he feels. He did not have a magical experience in college when he asked the universe, "What if I give it all away?" and loads of provisions were instantly laid upon him. I have never received a call from HR telling me insurance costs were going up—or that pay was being cut across the board—and then had to share that news with dependents. All of those moments leave residue that has to be weighed.

I spent time weighing them on my own that weekend. My husband and I have spent time weighing them together since. We try to remember that we feel different degrees of pressure regarding provision (what most would perceive to be a blanket of security feels to me like a crushing weight). We also have different triggers (the state of the house for him; outsourcing its care for me). We are different people. But we can still figure it out together, and we have big things in common, including within this arena. We both recognize that we are privileged, and we try to do the right thing with that awareness. And we both want to keep talking to each other. Eventually those conversations, and the care we try to show within them, have resulted in a balance (and a house and a budget, and now a tithe) that work (most days) for everyone. It was not easy. Things come up, and it's still not easy. But it is worth it to us to keep working on it *together*.

~

So that first part of that weekend away was spent considering who I had been, and who we could be, with regard to provisions. But there were other arenas that were begging the same question: Who had I been? Who was I now? And was I OK with the transformation, or did I need to do something differently? As I journaled about all of it during those days, three major themes emerged: *plotlines*, *remembering*, and *ghosts*. Before connecting them, I had to understand them individually, starting with plotlines.

~

I like movies and TV but am usually a few years behind the trends. My husband loves both and has taken it upon himself to educate me. He is wonderful about revisiting what he considers the classics so I can enjoy them. Ten years into our marriage, he was appalled to discover I had only seen a few episodes of *Friends*. "You'll love it," he said. "There's some drama and plot twists, but it's not really about that. It's a character-driven show."

The phrase "character-driven" made such an impression on me that I remember exactly when and where I was sitting when he said it. It was the week of my fortieth birthday. We were in Chapel Hill at a restaurant on Franklin Street, enjoying a bottle of wine. I had tried to set aside my midlife crisis for the celebration, but the question of where my life was going hovered around me. My personal plotline seemed *meh,* and it bothered me. I knew I should be counting my blessings. I knew I should be finding joy in the ordinary. But at heart, I was a storyteller. I was crafting my life story as I went, and I lacked a sense of engagement in my own plot.

At that table for two, with a bottle of wine between us, my husband had just given me a new way to view stories—maybe even my own story. Apparently, plot wasn't the end-all-be-all for every narrative. What if I stopped focusing on my personal plotline? What if I recognized that mine was primarily a character-driven life?

The idea grabbed me immediately. It took some of the pressure off the question of what was next or what I was doing (or not doing) and refocused me on "Who's here?" It felt like a new lens on everything. Was my time in Africa really a plot twist? From one angle, perhaps. But from what felt like a more significant vantage point, it was simply the place I had met Luke—and a woman who made it rain with a prayer. It was a place full of people where the character of others shaped my own character (and possibly vice versa).

And the world was full of characters. I saw them everywhere, including right here. I just had to pull my head out of my own ass—or off my own road map—and pay attention.

The day after that celebration, we took the kids out to an ice-cream shop for more family friendly festivities. Near the register, there were five bowls with different colored spoons: purple, blue, green, yellow, and pink. I had been to this shop dozens of times and always grabbed a purple spoon without thinking. But on this day, after I grabbed my spoon, the woman behind me in line asked the store manager a question. She said, "I'm curious. What color spoon is the most popular?" I stopped, turned, and listened. I heard an absolutely fascinating reply that touched on seasonal shifts and local sports teams and concluded with the manager's confusion over why no one ever seemed to want yellow. In fact, she was considering offering only yellow spoons for a while to get rid of a tower of yellow-spoon boxes in her back room. I was intrigued with the yellow-spoon aversion, but even more intrigued with the woman who had asked the question. I knew nothing about her, but I loved that she had noticed something right in front of me—something I had missed, something that inspired her to wonder and inquire and listen with such fascination. I had encountered a character right there from whom I could learn. I watched in awe as she selected her newly chosen yellow spoon and used it to salute the manager.

I am surrounded by characters and character; we all are. And in recognizing that life could be character driven, I realized I could let go of some plot planning and simply pay attention.

The realization reminded me of a moment when Luke and I were backpacking around Europe. We were on a crowded Italian bus trying to figure out which stop would get us closest to the Vatican. When Luke pushed down the large map I was holding—so he could peer over it—I scowled at him. But I had to swallow that scowl when I heard him say, "I know you could eventually figure this out with that map, but I thought it was worth advising you to look around for a moment. Because we're trying to get as close to the Pope as possible, and an entire flock of nuns is now leaving the bus. Maybe we should just follow them."

In addition, this whole idea of prioritizing character over plot reminded me that I still had my old copy of *The Portrait of a Lady*. I pulled it out and reread the preface. This time I did not hurry through it, trying to get to the "real" story. Instead, I slowed down, and I soaked in Henry James's thoughts on how plot and setting can influence the development of character—or not.

Finally, it reminded me of my friend Kevin's birthday dinner. This is the same Kevin who married my friend Melanie and saved my daughter and prescribed me my very first EpiPen. This is the brilliant ER doctor who has plenty of drama at work—and no small degree of it in his past. His story is not mine to tell, but it is inspiring. His life has had plenty of plot. Still, at his own birthday celebration, he looked at the group of us assembled around the table of his favorite cheeseburger joint and said, "As I get older, I think about how I will measure my life. I don't have a full answer yet. But sitting here tonight, it has occurred to me that if the company I keep is a worthy measure, I'm at peace with how I'm doing. Thanks for being here, tonight and always. It means a lot."

A character-driven life. Both in terms of those around us (characters) and what they mean for developments within us (character). A focus on our people instead of our plot.

It is at least worth considering.

~

Remembering. Its formal Latin etymology includes "re" (again) and "memorari" (be mindful of). So it means to be mindful of again, to recall, or (in the time of Middle English) to "give an account, narrate." But there is a folk etymology also, which has less to do with the mind and more to do with the body. *Remember.* The opposite of *dismember.*

According to the breast cancer article, I needed a weekend to accept that I could not physically re-member my body. Part of me had literally been dis-membered and was gone.

But there were other parts of me I had a choice about. I could think back, mentally revisit people and places and ideas and then choose what I attempted to graft back onto my life. What I would recall. What I would try to re-member.

Maybe that's what a midlife crisis is, at its heart: remembering who you were and what you aspired to, and recognizing you are at the point where you either need to live the dream or let it go. (I do know it is not like this for everyone, particularly those who find comfort or hope in dormant dreams.) But for me—in that moment—I knew I had too many dreams on life support. I needed to make choices about what to revive and what to mourn because having them all lie there untended was not good for me.

That weekend, I sifted through my old dreams. I decided which ones to live and which ones to let go.

It was an emotionally driven process, but it makes sense logically, too. My most recent stage of identity sustainment was the "don't let it die" stage. This was the next step. The stage of "revive it or let it go."

I let go of the idea of raising my kids in an atypical environment.

I let go of the idea of fostering or adopting a child.

I let go of the idea of teaching full-time.

These things still called to me, but not enough to act on. So I took them off my bucket list. I mourned them. I looked at the impulses behind them and created new visions that fit into my actual and chosen life. For example, my family was never going to live as nomads. But we could carve out a few months to wander. And maybe with a new mindset, I could celebrate the excursion instead of thinking the whole time, *This should be my life.*

Saying goodbye to some old dreams was difficult. But there was a silver lining: I could shift more focus onto what I wanted to thrive.

~

As I journaled that weekend, I realized that letting go is a two-way street. Yes, there were once-future dreams I could let go of, but there were also a few ghosts-of-past-acts that would not let go of me.

That weekend, I really looked at my ghosts. And I discovered that I am most often haunted by the witnesses to my shame.

I still see the little girl playing in the cold, while my old, pink coat hangs in my closet.

I still see that teenage boy, escorted away from our classroom after I notified the office.

I still see communities that I fit within, loved, and enjoyed—those places that embraced, taught, and exchanged good for good with me. I still see those communities facing incredible challenges while my distraction, and my angst at only visiting, keeps me away.

I am haunted.

~

To move forward, I was going to have to do more than choose which aspirations to abandon and which ones to nurture. I was going to have to do more than appreciate any characters or character-building encounters. What I was going to have to do, in addition to all of those things, was pull my head out of my angst. So that weekend, I asked my ghosts a direct question: *What do I have to do to make peace?*

I actually sat down in that hotel room with my hands on the keyboard of my laptop—like it was some kind of Ouija board from a teenage sleepover movie—and waited to see what my fingers would say.

And eventually I typed out the following answer:

I have to figure out what I learned from each ghost that haunts me.

If I cannot revive or release my ghosts, then I will need to embody the spirit of each lesson.

I would *honor* these individuals. I would begin doing that by writing down what I had learned from our original encounters. And then I would hold onto precious hope that the things I had learned could inspire something positive.

Maybe if I could remember my ghosts, it would help me stop focusing on plot and reorient me toward the wonderful cast of characters I had encountered. Maybe if I could remember their lessons, it would help develop my own character.

I left that weekend knowing one thing: I needed to remember. And for me, the way to remember was to *write*.

NOT WAVING
BUT DROWNING

Unfortunately, it would be almost two years before I took another weekend away.

During those two years I tried to squeeze in moments to write at home, but it was difficult. Life was demanding, and I was responsive. At the beginning of this period, I had a cancer-filled summer of things to catch up on, four young children (one of whom was not of school age), and I was still in the feel-guilty, ask-others-for-permission space. Also, all of this was happening while I was post-operative, dealing with all sorts of physical and emotional challenges that popped up at unexpected moments.

In other words, it took me two years to learn this significant lesson: There is a big difference between *deciding* to do something and *planning* for it. I had decided to write—but I had no plan for when to do it. I never put it on the calendar, so it never happened.

Here's what happened instead: Life picked back up. I tried to return to my regular pace. I ignored my own intentions. And I got sick again.

~

It was temporary, but it scared me.

My poor husband had patiently waited until three months after my surgery to take his first overnight work trip. On his very first night away, he called me only to discover I had become violently ill. It was late. The kids were all asleep, and he patched in a nurse from his work's new tele-health number. I told her I was experiencing a sharp stomach pain and could not stop vomiting. I didn't know if it was appendicitis (meaning I would require immediate surgery) or something contagious (meaning I could not leave exposed kids with my neighbors), but over the course of several hours, things became progressively worse.

I finally woke the kids at 1 a.m. and, between horrible stomach epi-sodes, loaded their wagon (for sleeping) and lovies (for comfort) and toys (for distraction) into the minivan and drove all of us to the ER, where a nurse explained to the children why Mama needed to be wheeled off to X-ray. We eventually discovered I was dealing with kidney stones. Painful, but a huge relief in terms of no long-term impact. Still, it was a scary night spent with four kids tucked around my hospital room watch-ing the Disney channel while I hid (and hurt, and hurled) in the hallway, hooked up to an IV to fight dehydration.

I waited until 5 a.m.—when I finally knew we were not contagious and thought someone might be awake—to text friends to see if anyone could come get the children. My friend Katie walked in forty-five minutes later and validated everything I was feeling by saying, "Oh, *hell* no" in response to our sick and shocking state before collecting both herself and the children.

It felt like my insides were trying to get my attention again. And I knew I had to start listening because I feared my body had already used most of the loud-but-curable ailments she had at her disposal. If I refused to listen at this volume, I was convinced I would face something really awful and incurable next.

It hit me, in that moment—three months after my cancer surgery and one day after my ER visit—that I had to protect myself.

I did not make any sweeping changes of circumstance.

But mentally, I hardened.

I was done feeling vulnerable. And I was done waiting for something to change. *I* would change. I decided I was done asking for alterations that would reduce stress. I was done requesting time for self-discovery that would reduce angst. I was frequently the only adult in the room. There were advantages to that; I had a tremendous amount of control—and I was going to exercise it.

On some levels, the timing of this hardening absolutely sucked. I decided I was going to protect myself right around the time my husband really heard what I needed. But the locus of my trust had shifted, and I liked the new status quo better. I felt powerful and in control. I was going to carve out my own space.

～

Over the course of the next three and a half years, my independence grew. It happened in stages.

Right after that fear-filled night of sickness in the hospital, I hardened emotionally. I let go of the idea that my husband should help me out of deep water. I learned to swim, and I built my own boats. When I needed a break, I took it. Until this phase, I had never independently picked up takeout when my husband traveled; I had always viewed it as a date-night thing. But guess what? There are servings for one.

Furthermore, when we traveled together and work limited his time away, I decided to be sympathetic from a distance. We would miss him, but the kids and I did not want to go home. We began extending our trips. I embraced adventures with the children, far away from our normal. We enjoyed calling Dad to swap stories and appreciated his supportive encouragement, instead of fielding thoughtful calls from him when something kept him late at work while all of us were at home.

Happily hiking with the kids in Yosemite National Park
(carrying Hudson and a can of bear spray).

Two years into this phase, I was a new level of happy. I felt like me again. I was exploring. Teaching our children. Learning from them and with them, in all sorts of places. Visiting some of my old haunts (including Kensington)—and certainly my old nature—as we roamed. In addition, as I made decisions about how we would experience these spaces, I discovered that I liked making these adult choices alone.

Finally, after two years, I put writing on my calendar. I took two weekends away to jump-start the process. There was tension as I planned the first weekend. My husband's parents were available. Would I rather make it a date weekend, he asked me. The answer was no.

I needed to be alone in a room with my inner voice and a blank page.

~

There were several parallels between my self-discovery (in my twenties) and that time of rediscovery (in my forties). One is that during both periods, I had to step off my paved path with only the *hope* I would find something valuable off-road. I strained relationships, with no guarantees. Each era had an unsettling moment when I stood at the starting line of a new dream, already exhausted from the effort of getting there, and then wondered if the dream was going to pan out.

I had that moment in the fall of 2019, as I sat in a hotel room with my laptop. I took a deep breath, and thought, *I am finally here; I have claimed time to write*. And then I realized, *I don't know how to do this*. What was I supposed to type on that page?

I needed to revisit my history. I needed to study my story. My primary goal was to figure out *me*. But I had this squirmy sense that my ghosts wanted a larger audience—that I might need to write this in a way others could read.

But how?

Not in a way that could hurt anyone in my family.

Also—since I was still in my "selfless is good" era—*not* in a way that centered me. The task felt impossible.

That first day in the hotel room, I struggled. I soon realized it was hard to start with nothing and began opening old files on my laptop. Over the years, in small, stolen moments, I had tried to start whatever this was going to be. Due to interruptions (life) and the aforementioned impossibility (how to search for self while seeking to remain selfless), I had always stalled on the preface—the part that would explain why writing and sharing this was important to me.

As I sat there that day, with those old files open, my frustration grew. These files were false starts, leading me nowhere. I decided to alter my strategy, closing the documents and opening an internet browser. Maybe I could find an essay that described how writers did this.

That very evening, the internet delivered in the form of an article. And by the next day, I had drafted a new preface entitled "Who am I?" Over the course of writing this book, the segment expanded and relocated here, but it still tells the story of that first night. It also explains how—after reading that article—I gave myself permission to go on a written and spiritual journey, with the purpose of rediscovering *me*.

That night, I wrote the following:

WHO AM I?

This book will be a collection of memories: things I experienced or learned as I stumbled around life. I have been trying to write them down for over a decade but have had trouble getting started. Even when I can find time to write, I always stall on the preface—the part that will explain why I want to write and to share.

Today, in a fit of frustration, I went back and read every version of a preface I had ever crafted. There were several, each representing a different moment when I sat down (again) to write. A decade ago, I tried to make this a letter to my young children. After that, a testament to my midlife crisis. Still later, a piece of immortality as I faced cancer. Underlying each of these prefaces was the sense that I needed to justify this work. It had to be for my kids, my younger self, or a placeholder for when I was gone.

While taking a break from perusing my own collection of beginnings-turned-dead ends—while needing to be reminded that writing was something people could actually do—I came across an article about Elizabeth Gilbert. The article's author interviewed Gilbert and asked her to reflect on the process of creating *Eat, Pray, Love*. Gilbert's response revealed that when looking back at her own writing, she was "struck by how much shame there was in that book, and how apologetic I was as a narrator, about myself, and how embarrassed I was by the fact that I wanted to go on a spiritual journey."[1]

Today, I have realized that my former prefaces have the same undertone. Within them, I apologize for taking time to write—for attempting to bring my thoughts together in one place and create some sort of meaning. The truth is

I am desperate for some sort of meaning and—for years—something in my gut has been telling me the only way to find it is by writing my story. In this midlife moment, I feel lost. More precisely, I feel like I have lost something valuable. I feel like I have lost me.

Who am I?

I worked really hard for many years—mainly in my teens and twenties—to answer that question. The journey upset my family and required me to buck expectations. My road introduced me to an eclectic mix of company (homeless men, rebellious students, ascetic activists, distinguished professors, and one absolutely kick-ass exterminator) and took me into an array of unexpected places (inner-city halfway houses, African villages, Ivy League institutions, rural middle schools, and the most confusing corners of my own psyche).

Along the way . . .

I carved out new identities.

I discovered myself.

I chose my life.

And then—somehow (over the course of the last fifteen years)—I have let that life consume *me*.

To the point that I am lost again. Buried. Under piles of laundry and emails and guilt. Guilt that I cannot be content with my chosen path and my family. Guilt that I am not doing enough for and with the people I met and left along my journey. Guilt over the privilege I possess. And then guilt that I am now centering myself—a middle-aged White woman—as I confront and decide what to do about that privilege.

I am slowly suffocating underneath an avalanche of angst-ridden questions. Decades ago, I carved a new path. At the time, it seemed BIG and monumental and risky.

But now? Well . . . that authentic life I fought to embrace is not as *different* as I expected it to be. I have a different job, a different belief system, a different perspective on politics, gender, sexuality and . . . well, just about everything. But the physical spot where I landed? It doesn't feel that far from where everyone expected me to be.

Is it OK to measure my life by how and what I learned instead of where I am now? To measure my personal revolution by its ideals instead of its outcome? Do the discoveries I made back then matter, if they don't make today any different? I don't know. And all of this guilt—and all of these questions—are crushing me.

I need to get out from underneath all of it.

I need to change something. But what? The world? My personal trajectory? Or just my tired, angst-ridden, midlife crisis attitude?

I am not sure. But I have the sense that writing these words will help me figure it out.

This is my story.

I am writing it because I have to remember myself.

I am sharing it for a few reasons:

First, I am rediscovering who I am—and one of the things I am is a storyteller.

Second, I have hope that sharing what I learned from some of my most meaningful encounters will honor those moments in a way my current life does not.

And third, I want to be seen. Not looked at, or looked over, or overlooked—but *seen*. And I want to share how my fight to be seen makes me realize what a horrible disservice I do so many others when I fail to see and celebrate them. I am so sorry. This book will be part confession, part progression, and hopefully part of a larger conversation from which I am still learning—this time as a much-humbled ally.

I want to share this story for all of those reasons. Still, it feels important to say that I am not sharing my story because I believe it is particularly valuable.

I am sharing it because I have learned, over the course of my life, that ALL stories are incredibly valuable—and this is the one I am able to give.

~

I left that weekend exhausted, but also—on some levels—exhumed. No longer buried. I sensed that the next time I sat at my laptop, it would be without shame. I could take time and go on a spiritual journey. I could write about my experiences for no other reason than I felt like I needed to. I could take a turn—claim a moment. I could use that moment to explore the philosophical and physical pivots—those turns of thought or trail—that felt significant to me.

I was ready. So several months later, during my next weekend away, I began writing my story. At that point, the pressure release was immediate and cathartic. And the timing seemed good. It was February 23, 2020. The kids were finally all in school. I had finally caught up on a decade of paperwork (actually sending a thank-you note that began with the words, "I realize this is seven years late"). And I finally made this commitment to myself: I would set aside other tasks: all the work that kept the house running, the meals prepared, the budget sustainable, the appointments booked, the schoolwork supported, the occasions marked, the extracurriculars (and their carpools) coordinated, and the family nonprofit managed (which involved research and teaching, as well as creating content for handouts and web pages while also engaging young artists, their sponsors, our environmental partners and quite a few volunteers). I would set it all aside for at least an hour each day, and I would write my story while no one was home.

I made that decision. Time to write was on my calendar. It was there—in glorious ink—for exactly fourteen school/workdays before coronavirus closures brought my entire family home.

But I was determined. And as we mapped out our new family rhythm, I made a rule: Unless there was an emergency, the hours from 5 a.m. to 7 a.m. would be my own. I would set an alarm and, for those two hours, when everyone in my house was asleep (or could simply take care of themselves for a few minutes), I would write.

I would do other things during other hours. It was 2020. There was much to be done; I would do it. And then I would write about it the next morning.

~

Journal Entry, Spring 2020:

Hospital beds are overflowing. First responders are exhausted. Small businesses are crumbling. People are dying. Hearts are breaking. The lonely are becoming even more isolated.

My family is among the lucky. It touches us, but we are not hit as hard as most. We miss marking milestones—a child's middle-school graduation, a cousin's wedding. My uncle dies, and the funeral is back in Alabama, and I can only pay my respects via phone. I cannot be there as my mother tries to determine whether the chairs have been set on top of my father's grave site (they had not) and as she visits the plot she has already purchased next to my father's. She tells me, during the call, that it is strange standing on top of a grave you know will someday be your own.

We are disconnected.

It matters.

My husband's pay is cut as part of department-wide COVID cost savings. We need to make some adjustments. But we see lives lost and families devastated, and our hearts break for people in far worse situations than our own.

We try to do our part: We stay home. If we have to go out, we wear masks. We cannot visit the retirement community that receives artwork from our nonprofit, so we connect with them virtually.

We donate where we can. We recruit more families for our neighborhood food drives. We fund a space for a child at a virtual learning center. We prepare for the upcoming presidential election. And when George Floyd is killed, we decide to send a message. So far, we have stayed *in* for our community. To make the point that Black Lives Matter, we put on our masks and walk *out*. We begin attending marches. One speaker says the main thing White allies can do to help is talk to our families.

I call my mother, then more family. We all grow.

~

It is 2020, a year of many things. It is also a year that I realize something about my writing.

I realize I am not writing only to remember and honor characters I have encountered.

I realize I am not writing only to figure out who I want to be right now.

I realize that I am also writing because right now, *this is me*.

Right now, I am a writer.

~

In the film *Three Kings*, Mark Wahlberg plays a soldier named Troy who is shot and develops a tension pneumothorax. This is a condition during which air fills the pleural space just outside the lung, leaving the actual lung no room to inflate. Victims suffocate. The only way to save them is to get air out of the pleural space, so they can breathe air into their lungs.

Troy's life is saved when that pleural space pressure is removed by inserting a tube that allows the air to escape. The immediate pressure release is dramatic; it even makes a *whoosh* sound. Troy can breathe again.

But it is not enough to release that air and pressure once. If Troy wants to continue breathing, he must intermittently open the valve on that tube—to release any new pressure before it suffocates him.

In other words, this is Troy's survival sequence: one massive lifting of pressure that saves him, followed by occasional but consistent releases that are equally vital.

In the film, Troy does well with the initial pressure lift. And he does well with several of the follow-up (life-sustaining) pressure releases. But then he is handcuffed and can no longer reach the valve.

I felt like Troy as I began writing. There was a massive release of pressure when I wrote the first words on February 23, 2020. There was vital follow-up as I let myself breathe and write during those next two weeks. And then COVID threatened to handcuff me.

No.

I knew COVID would take many things that year, but it would not take this new source of oxygen from me.

I could still write. I just had to create a new space on my calendar. I could set my alarm for 5 a.m. every darn morning—and learn from each ghost while my family slept.

~

This new me—the one who lived and wrote at my desk from 5 a.m. to 7 a.m.—was simultaneously strong and incredibly fragile. The 2020 part of me was tough, able to defend that time and space to create. But there was a new me emerging, and she felt undeveloped and vulnerable. I had to write her out—and could not yet out her writing. So I kept the whole process private. My husband and children knew mom liked to journal, but that was it. I worried if I said anything more, the magic I felt at my desk would disappear, taking the writer in me with it.

My sister was the only person on earth who had a vague sense of what I was doing. I told her that if I got hit by a bus, I wanted her to find this file on my laptop and read it so that I could rest in peace knowing that by, at least one person, I had been *seen*.

~

But during those days, I did not exist in a vacuum: It was 2020 and our family quarters were closer than ever. My husband—who was now working from home and had canceled tons of work travel due to COVID—realized there was something *different* going on with me.

He wanted to be supportive.

So he was trusting and patient when I told him, "I journal in the mornings, but I don't want to talk about it. I have learned that I need something that belongs only to me."

And he listened when I said, "Give it time. I am working on myself at the moment. We have reached a sustainable equilibrium. Just let it be."

It was not easy terrain to navigate.

Sometimes, as I wrote our history, I was angry. I felt like I had fought for a tiny sliver of time—and against a whole mountain of angst—for over a decade, and during that period he didn't *listen* to me. What was I supposed to do with that anger?

Sometimes, when I left my desk, I was afraid. I didn't know how to be vulnerable with my spouse and protect this more fragile me. What was I supposed to do with that fear?

And sometimes, when I saw the stranger parts of myself on those pages, I felt at peace. I felt authentically acknowledged. There I was. But then I started to worry. Was I—once again—in a home where I was loved by someone who would not like those parts of me?

But in spite of all that, I was mostly just happy—in a different way than I had been before. I was less adept at some of my roles, because I didn't allow them to consume all my time, but I felt more like *me*.

~

As I carved out more personal space—my own little separate, safe, emotional sphere—our marital dynamic shifted into an equilibrium that he found unsettling. He was patient and understanding and supportive, but I was not as emotionally available as he wanted me to be. I was there for the kids. I was here, in these (still private) pages. But my priority had shifted from connecting with him to protecting this fragile new version of me.

Which probably didn't make me the best partner.

I can see things from my husband's perspective. He had spent over a decade working hard to support our family. He worked extra so his wife could stay home, just like she wanted. He sacrificed, missing a number of birthdays, holidays, vacations, and dinners. His time away was for work, which he would want me to acknowledge as personal (to honor the friends and meaning he found there), but not an escape. When he came home to the family he loved and supported there was a lot of happy, but also piles of dishes and laundry and angst. He offered help: being there when work allowed and encouraging his wife to outsource when it didn't. He prioritized family over personal and social interests, and he turned down professional opportunities in other places because the kids liked it here in North Carolina. He did carve out time—driving elementary-aged kids to school most mornings, putting all their activities on his calendar, and taking two weeks off every summer. His children adored him, and he connected with them beautifully. He loved his wife and did not understand why—during his infrequent time off—she would rather be alone. When she got sick, he hit the pause button professionally and cared for her. Things were good for a while, but after that last trip to the ER, she seemed tougher. More distant. Angry about things that happened a decade ago.

Still, he remained optimistic. Maybe this pandemic would offer a silver lining—more time together at home. It did, but the connection had limits. She went to bed early every night so she could spend mornings alone with her laptop. And when he asked what she was writing, she revealed a bit, then said, "I don't want to talk more about it." He wondered how she could accuse him of not listening, and then when he made the effort, decide she wouldn't talk to him.

His perspective was *valid.*

But my perspective was valid too. I was hurt. And I was afraid to be emotionally vulnerable again.

There is a Stevie Smith poem that details what I remembered feeling—and was afraid of fully experiencing. It describes a person going under—a struggling swimmer who flailed, then failed—as no one realized this was "not waving but drowning." As no one realized a struggling spirit's words and motions were significant—the calls of someone starting to sink.

I needed to be *heard* and *seen.* For years, when I complained about headaches. When I said I needed a day away. When I put in my mouth guard every night to protect my teeth from the grinding. When the headaches became such a constant that I rarely mentioned them—and when I did, they no longer elicited sympathy. When the panic attack hit. When the hives started. When I purchased an extra EpiPen for the glove compartment of the car. When my husband ultimately asked me to go back to the doctor because "we really need you to have more energy," and I wondered—as I drowned—if his main concern was that I would not have the strength to keep everyone else afloat. I needed him to see me. To worry less about me the wife and mom and more about me the person.

The person who is now a strange mix of strong and fragile—who knows she can do a much better job of seeing his perspective but wants to make sure that she, too, is seen.

~

So, after those two weekends away—and during daily 5 a.m. sessions at my desk—I was a writer (even if no one knew it yet) and a wife (who probably needed to talk to her husband).

But I was still—more than anything else—a mother.

I truly love being a wife and mother. I hope discussing the demands of marriage and motherhood—acknowledging that I lost myself in those roles—does not diminish the power of that testimony. I especially love— and also like—being at home with the kids. In fact, the only thing I like more than being home with the kids is exploring the world with them, especially if we can adventure in a rented RV.

My experience during the pandemic affirmed that. I feel guilty writing it, because I know it reeks of privilege. We have enough money that I don't have to work. We have enough extra that I can occasionally rent an RV. Even though I tell myself that I would live in that RV to do it, that I would give up everything to do it, I know it is still privileged. To have a spouse whose job offers health insurance for the whole family. To have the option of taking it as an adventure instead of committing to it as a permanent thing. To have the option of working full-time, or part-time, or volunteering. To be able to choose what balance works best for us.

I know it is the ultimate privilege to be able to say—especially during that crazy time when COVID crushed so many—that the extra time with the kids, with so many things canceled and schooling from home, was precious.

But it was.

Yes, things were nutty. Everyone needed a different thing at the same time (five minutes ago). And there was so little privacy—and so many opinions on how to share space—that I once dreamed the family was in the bathroom rearranging my tampon boxes while I begged them to get out because I needed to pee.

But we were together. We played cards and took walks and hung twinkle lights. We read all the Harry Potter books and watched every movie. We got takeout from struggling restaurants and lingered over it. And if anyone in the house was struggling, they didn't have to do it alone. As a mother, that meant everything to me.

I was going to include one last photo for my family in this section—a fun one to remind them of those adventures in the RV—but I decided it was more important to include an image of the words I always posted on that RV dashboard. For me, they served (and still serve) as both a reminder and a truth.

LITMUS TESTS

Back in February of 2020—two weeks before COVID upended everything in North Carolina—I was in a hotel room writing and experiencing that first *whoosh* of pressure release.

I was excited to breathe. I was prepared to write. But I was also terrified. I was wading into old, stagnant waters that I knew were full of ghosts, hoping a lightning bolt of realization would strike me. I remember what it felt like that weekend, not knowing what I would notice when I looked in my rearview mirror—and also not knowing where anything would lead.

There was no map—just a blank page and me.

~

Journal Entry, Winter 2020:

It is February 24, 2020. I am in a hotel room by myself, writing. It feels more like fighting, actually. I have unpacked boxes of old journals and letters and am trying to figure out who I was. I have made a special trip to Walmart to purchase a particular type of surface-safe tape—God forbid we damage walls during our spiritual journeys—and I use that tape to post index cards that show a timeline of my thoughts. It is a timeline of my midlife crisis, but it begins in my teens. The root of my current struggle seems to be that I am not who I thought I would be, despite fighting so incredibly hard to become.

As I look through the boxes and add to the line of cards snaking across the wall, I am particularly jarred by the contents of one box full of artifacts from my twenties: old letters from family, friends, and ex-boyfriends. It is clear I have hurt a lot of people along my path.

I need a break, so I flip on the TV and scroll through the channels. An episode of *The Bachelor* is playing. I have not watched it at all this season, but I soon discover that the bachelor has already narrowed it down to three women. One is from Alabama, and her religious beliefs are a focus. She won't sleep with anyone before marriage, and she won't accept a proposal from someone who has made sex part of this discovery process. There are so many tears, and it all looks so familiar. I mentally note that this episode falls somewhere along index card number 17 in my own life.

As she cries and leaves, and comes back, and explains again that this is just who she is—that she won't sacrifice integrity for love—I find myself having an odd reaction.

I fight that reaction initially. In fact, I try to turn off the TV. But the remote that functioned perfectly just moments ago has stopped working: Nothing when I push the power button, and nothing when I try to change the channel. Nothing when I set the remote down and push buttons on the base of the TV. I actually call the front desk and ask them to send someone up to my hotel room because I do *not* want to watch this. When the maintenance guy finally arrives (and solves the issue by unplugging the TV, a simple solution I never considered), I am sitting on the bed, having watched the entire episode. And this twenty-something girl, who reminds me of myself, has not elicited the reaction I would have anticipated from me.

I do not want her to stand her ground and find her path and blaze her trail unfettered.

I want her to *relax*.

I am startled by this thought.

What do I want her to relax about, exactly?

Who she is? No. Who she will partner with? No.

I mean, I am sitting here surrounded by evidence that twenty-five years later I am still not able to relax about spiritual and relational choices. I am also surrounded by evidence that my process hurt people. Paraphrasing from an ex-boyfriend's letter that I read just before turning on the TV:

> Kristi . . . What are we doing? We say we care about each other, but then pick each other apart. This whole thing has left me sad and confused.

I read that. I see her. I look at the wall, where I have removed two framed photos of peaceful waterway scenes to make room for my snaking index cards. And I am left with the feeling of . . . enough. Enough pain in others' hearts, in my past, and in this reality TV drama.

Enough.

~

As I sat there, staring at the newly unplugged TV, I could not comprehend my own reaction. What had made me say "enough"? What did I want her to "relax" about?

I didn't know, so—in what could be considered the opposite of relaxing—I proceeded to ruminate on that hotel-room moment for months. Finally, I reached two conclusions: First, I did not want her to relax about anything. I was talking to myself, while using a woman I knew nothing about as my proxy. Second, what I wanted to say "enough" about was *litmus tests*.

~

In the scientific sense, a litmus test measures pH to categorize a substance as an acid or a base. In the figurative sense, according to *Webster's*, it is "a test in which a single factor (such as an attitude, event, or fact) is decisive."

I don't like litmus tests. I don't like it when I measure up. I don't like it when I fail. It's not the outcome; it's the process. Enough.

My whole childhood, it felt like I was preparing to take a litmus test in each arena.

Professional litmus test: Are you a doctor? If not, it's a *fail*.

Spiritual litmus test: Are you an Evangelical Christian? If not, it's a *fail*.

Political litmus test: Are you a Republican? If not, it's a *fail*.

Racial litmus test: Can you accept that things are fine, and that mixing too much just causes problems? If not, it's a *fail*.

Gender litmus test: Are you heterosexual, gender normative, in a Biblically submissive marriage, and also quiet about any "boys will be boys" moments? If not, it's a *fail*.

Clearly, I am a failure across the board. I suppose a test facilitator might want to award me points for being in a heterosexual marriage, but being single so long and eventually becoming a full-fledged ally of the LGBTQIA+ community makes my results on that subset somewhat inconclusive, and there is no room for sliding scales on a litmus test. *Fail.*

Enough.

I reject your litmus tests.

Stop measuring *me* by *your* standards. Stop measuring me altogether. And don't do me any favors by loving me "no matter what" or "even though."

~

But there was another problem that had been highlighted by that episode of *The Bachelor*: In addition to submitting to a lifetime of litmus tests, I had been applying litmus tests to those around me. That hotel room was littered with artifacts of the destruction they wrought.

Yet there I sat, in front of that hotel TV, marveling at the amount of energy the drama consumed and thinking about how real love could get lost in the weeds.

~

For the record, I do think a distinction has to be made between litmus tests (which involve objective standards and are largely unaffected by conversation and context) and compatibility checks (which involve knowing yourself, getting to know whatever is external, and assessing whether cores must be broken in order to fit). I don't mind compatibility checks when they are done with respect by folks who are making decisions together: Want to get married? Start a joint business? Relocate? Let's respectfully look at our cores and see if they fit in these new spaces—and if these new spaces allow room for acceptance, adjustment, and growth.

A litmus test is different. Administrators are less flexible. They don't offer much compromise. They do, however, sometimes attempt to cushion the blow of failure by offering a consolation prize. For example, when I failed family litmus tests, I received the consolation prize of being loved "even though." I recognize that this consequence is nothing relative to those others suffer, where being true to oneself leads to being abused or disowned. Still, it is hard to be loved by someone who doesn't like you, or really even try to get to know you. It hurts to hear, "I don't need to know you. I already know you're not that and I can't convince you to be, so let's just have a relationship that ignores those pieces." It feels like a rejection. Having to place certain parts of me in the coat check because there's no place for them at the dinner table feels like a rejection. Those parts of me are not welcome—or at least cannot be there in emotional safety.

Finally, motives matter, but not as much as you think. If you reject part of me (or encourage me to reject part of myself) because you love me and want to save me pain down the road, you have become a more personal version of the problem you were trying to prevent. Your rejection hurts more than having my credit card rejected (because I've chosen a career that pays less) or my relationship rejected (because society won't accept it) or my values rejected (by a God you're convinced is standing there ready to administer litmus tests).

~

Since I projected myself into that episode of *The Bachelor*, I will clarify that my reaction actually had nothing to do with that couple. I was simply wishing I could tell the younger, Alabama-accented version of me three things: that her spiritual road would be long, that any marriage would require work beyond what it took to get to the altar, and that—if she wanted to survive—she would have to *relax* about a few things.

The same three messages the middle-aged me still needed to hear.

~

Meanwhile, as all of this was muddling my mind, my children were growing, and my oldest was thirteen.

Thirteen!

Was this really the year I should *relax*?

As I considered the question, real life pressed in on me—and on my daughter.

~

It was now March of 2020. Things in the United States were beginning to shut down due to COVID. My thirteen-year-old would not see her friends for months. She had been learning to navigate her ever-increasing independence, but now this pandemic had clipped and dismantled her wings. Everything had been canceled or transformed into a virtual experience, including her coursework, middle-school graduation, eighth-grade dance, club volleyball, and confirmation classes at church.

At age thirteen, kids are invited to join these confirmation classes. At the end of the course, they are given an opportunity to confirm and publicly profess their beliefs.

My husband is Catholic. Our kids have marked many milestones in the Catholic Church. But for over a decade, they have most regularly attended spiritual services at University United Methodist of Chapel Hill (UUMC), a liberal community that keeps a literal rainbow of doors on the front lawn announcing "God's Doors Are Open To All" and "Black Lives Matter." We gave my daughter a choice: She could attend confirmation classes at either institution. She chose UUMC.

I really liked the way UUMC conducted the classes. They divided the kids into "houses" (à la Hogwarts) to make it more fun. They focused on community service. They asked all the kids involved to *think*. On the very first day—one of the only days parents attended with their children—they had all the parents say in unison (while reading off a printed pamphlet) that decisions about whether to be confirmed at UUMC would be up to the teens. No parental pressure.

Teens could call bullshit on that last part, of course. All of us parents had raised them in this church, driven them here this morning, asked them to listen, and placed them in a peer group whose families leaned a certain way. What were the chances that one kid would stand up and say, "No thanks"? Still, the spoken (perhaps token) gesture is better than nothing, right?

I talked to my daughter about it when we got home from that first meeting. I told her I truly did not care whether she confirmed. I said that at her age, asking the questions was much more important than deciding on an answer. There were so many possible answers, and she was free to explore them. I was happy to help her or put her in touch with people who didn't have my leanings.

But, I told her, these questions about what we believe and why we are here, were *important*.

Naturally, my brilliant teenage daughter gave the only response that could have truly shocked me. She said, "Mom, I've looked at all these questions. And I really appreciate your flexibility about how people answer them. But here's the truth: These questions about religion are important to *you*, but I am not sure they're important to *me*."

Wait. What?

I had been prepared for any answer, but I was not prepared for her to dismiss the *questions*.

Holy moly, I really love teens.

~

I have always loved teens.

When I worked full-time, people used to ask me why on earth I chose to teach eighth and ninth graders.

I told them it was because I really appreciate and relate to teenagers. Most adolescents I have met are actively engaged in self-discovery and rebellion—two things I find incredibly valuable and that I feel are often abandoned way too early in life.

Also, I do not know many teenagers who are apathetic about who they will be. They want to express themselves, and they do it through a variety of means: commitments, causes, fashion, music, friend groups, food choices, room décor, course selection, interests, extracurriculars, the words they choose, how they speak them, and more.

Teenagers have spirit. Sometimes it gets crushed under anxiety or warped under pressure or ignored until it withers or explodes. Those are hard situations for anyone, especially teens. But amazing things happen when teenage spirits have room to breathe.

My questions felt narrow to my daughter. She was not interested in offering her opinion on my church's religious creed.

But she was very interested in discussing her spirit.

~

It took me over a month to realize I needed to relax about Ella's confirmation. In the interim, several things happened: First, I read Glennon Doyle's book *Untamed*. Then, I wrote a long letter to my daughter (before I realized I was talking and writing too much and started listening). Finally, I called my sister to thank her for sending me the book and to ask for her perspective on everything.

Below is a version of the letter I read to my daughter. I was afraid to give her a copy, as I knew my thoughts were still (and will always be) evolving, but after I read it aloud, we talked.

> Ella,
> You are 13, and the church we regularly attend has asked all 13-year-olds to consider whether or not they would like to be confirmed. You are thinking about that, and it has made you think about your beliefs.
>
> As you know, you have been introduced to Christianity while immersed in a friendship pool that encompasses a variety of beliefs and nonbelievers.

Some of the basic spiritual skills and concepts I have tried to introduce in this setting are as follows: the power of reflection; the possibilities of meditation and prayer; the value of story and example; the validity of faith in things not seen; the idea that we are part of something bigger; the concept that each life is valuable and that none of us are the sole center of the universe; the idea that our lives can include both individual growth and connection with others; the idea that our lives have meaning; and the concept of a Creator who deserves our attention and admiration.

I have also tried to introduce the Jesus that emphasized love: love of God, love of neighbor, love of the poor and persecuted and downtrodden. The Jesus who railed against those who used religious rules as a weapon and who managed to defy societal—and alter spiritual—expectations.

Through Christianity, I have tried to convey the understanding that things are not always what they seem on the surface. In fact, they are often the opposite: life through death, strength through weakness, gaining through giving, and so many counterintuitive principles that ring true for me.

As a young child, you were introduced to these ideas through Bible stories. Recently, you have begun to question them. One example is questioning the creation story. You and I talked about that—covering lots of different perspectives.

But the point I'll make here is that the heart of your upbringing is not creation stories—or any other specifics. It is the basic spiritual skills and concepts listed above. We have given you roots (or a foundation, or a launching pad—whatever you decide it is, ultimately), but you are not tethered. Where you go or grow is up to you, and you will be loved and celebrated always.

You are valued. And so are your questions. In fact, your recent questions have made me shift the types of devotionals I do with our family. I decided to put the religious storybooks away in favor of books that simply inspire *wonder*. I did that because I wanted you—and your siblings—to realize that life is full of small miracles, and it is worth wondering what that is all about and seeing where that wondering takes you. It is also worth noting the small (and big) miracles that happen in your own life and deciding what you attribute them to.

I also want you to note the small nudges that come from inside you—and trust them.

I was never told to do that as a child. Instead, I was raised to believe that human nature is evil, and that we need to fight our instincts at every turn.

But I now *absolutely reject* the idea that my core is bad and that those nudges are something to fight against. In fact, over the course of almost five decades, I have come to believe that each of us is an incredibly unique creation and that part of our job on earth is to follow those nudges and figure out who we were created to be.

All of this has led me to believe that this year, we have asked you the wrong question. The question should not be: Are you a Christian? The question should be: Who are you?

If any part of your answer identifies a core that believes in a Creator, then some follow-up questions might include: What do you believe about that Creator? and What are the implications of those beliefs?

It takes a lifetime to answer those questions. For me, it has been a worthwhile pursuit. I actually banged into many brick walls and hurt quite a few innocent (and not-so-innocent) bystanders because I failed to ask myself the

first one. So, I am asking you—and will continue to ask—
Who are you?

I will also encourage you to remember two related
things.

First, that tiny voice and nudge get louder when you
learn to listen to it. And if you ignore or squash it, it can
become difficult to hear.

Second, there is a difference between a nudge and an
impulse, just as there is a difference between our spiritual
core and other parts of our psyche (including our ego).

I do think all of us—at times—have impulses that go
against the core of who we are. There have been times I
have wanted to smack someone—or to give up on something I valued—just because people and things can be
difficult. But those have been impulses and when I looked
deeper, I realized that they were not coming from the tru-
est core of me. This is where I think things were missed in
my childhood, as there was no distinction made between
my core and any negative impulses. I was taught to dis-
trust all of it and look to an external standard against
which to measure my leanings. In retrospect, this makes
no sense to me. Are there things outside of us that are
worthy of belief? Yes. But we have to know who we are to
recognize them. *Who are you? Who am I?* has to be asked
early and often. Or, if you reach a point that you accept a
Creator, the question, Who have you/I been created to be?

This also brings up a question I have had to confront
recently: whether or not selflessness is an ideal. I was raised
to believe it was, but I have recently been challenged to
reject that teaching.

Glennon Doyle writes that we have been taught that
"the best way for a woman to love her partner, family,

and community was to lose herself in service to them." She lived that way for years and almost lost herself completely. Glennon argues—and I agree with her—that losing oneself is a tragedy. She insists that "what we need are women who are *full of themselves*"—people who have "detoxed themselves" from the "world's expectations" and know and trust themselves "enough to say and do what must be done."[1]

I agree.

I now—after a lot of reflection—believe that selflessness is *not* an ideal. Maybe generosity of self is? I am still thinking about that, because it's a question that's important to me. That doesn't mean you have to ask it, or any other question. I will encourage you to instead do one very important thing: Be *you*. Let us know *you*. And when you discover who *you* are, consider sharing the real you with the world. Or—if you are not comfortable with that—please know I want to be a safe space, if you're willing to share the real you with me.

Despite too many words that might indicate the contrary, I want you to know that I am backing off any questions about your confirmation.

If you want to do it, great. If not, great. But know this: You were right.

My questions were way too narrow.

Thank you for helping me broaden my perspective.

Know that I am here as a resource and a celebrant as you come to know more about who *you* are and what *you* think.

I love you—the real you—whoever *you* discover that to be.

Love,
Mom

Back when I had that ninth-grade class that was becoming less engaged, I had two choices: I could either crack down or relax all the rules (including the one that said "teach!") and work on knowing my students.

Well, I really want to know my own kid.

So I am going to relax. And reframe. And retreat. And let her *grow*.

~

During that same 2020 spring, I called my sister (who is also Ella's godmother) and told her I thought I might be doing this all wrong.

"I encouraged her to think about all of this," I told Ashley. "But *why*? I have been thinking about this for decades, and it has brought me closer to misery than it has to meaning." I told her I knew plenty of people who thought and questioned less and had much happier lives.

My wonderful, wise sister replied, "I don't know if asking your questions has made you any happier. But it has made you more *you*. It's just who you are."

She was right. This is how I engage the world—always. It is simply who I am on a core level, and that is an important identity acknowledgment.

I question.

Maybe if I can accept that, I can also accept that I will never fully find answers. Maybe one answer to the big question of *Who am I?* is *Someone who asks questions all the time.*

Some answers resonate with me. Some don't. But whether or not I find a piece of myself in the answers, I now recognize that the search is—for me—an authentic and identifying expression. That's something.

And it's not something I'll impose on my kid. I will encourage her to discover and express herself. I thought I was doing that when I said, "Ask! I'll accept any answer you find!" But I need to back away even further.

If she doesn't have the same questions I do, that is genuinely wonderful. I am a little bit jealous, honestly. And I am lucky to be a part of whatever approach she decides to take to *her* life.

~

Speaking of the *Who are you?* question, Melanie and I were enjoying a glass of wine one evening when she announced, "I am a cactus."

Hmmm, I thought to myself. *That's interesting. I would not have guessed that because Melanie is not at all prickly. Still, she can sustain harsh conditions—like a cactus. And she does have incredible reserves—like a cactus. She's beautiful and can flower, but knows how to protect herself—like a cactus. I guess she* is *a cactus.*

But I did not impose my wheels-spinning, mind-sparked interpretation on Melanie. Instead, I said, "Tell me what you mean when you say, 'I am a cactus.'"

Melanie looked at me quizzically and said, "I mean the wine charm on my glass is a cactus. I mean: Do not drink out of this glass! It's mine."

Melanie is brilliant. Thoughtful. Considered. Unbelievably generous. And—perhaps most significantly—manages to be all of that while also carving out space to relax and enjoy life. In other words, she is willing—on occasion—to allow a cactus to simply be a cactus, living its best life on her wine stem.

This is something with which I struggle immensely, and something I envy. The struggle reminds me of a passage in *Eat, Pray, Love*, by Elizabeth Gilbert, where she describes her difficulty quieting her mind. She reveals that she once prayed to God, "Look—I understand that an unexamined life is not worth living, but do you think I could someday have an unexamined *lunch?*"[2]

Elizabeth, I *relate*.

And the compulsion to examine exhausts me.

Recently, I was out on a walk, and I encountered a friend. When I removed my headphones to exchange greetings, she asked if she was interrupting a podcast. "No," I confessed, explaining that I can only listen to podcasts at my desk now because hearing things I want to remember but cannot take notes on (while walking or driving) makes me anxious.

"That's unfortunate," she responded.

It *is* unfortunate. Why can I not simply enjoy listening, instead of treating every episode like a homework assignment?

And I did not even tell her that my podcast problem was just the tip of the iceberg. I also skip e-books (I need to put pencil to margin). And I cannot sleep without a pen (because when thoughts jolt me awake, I have to write them down to get them out of my mind—and ready for review tomorrow—before I can fall back to sleep).

And those are my breaks—when I am on a stroll, selecting a book, or dozing. While actually working, I am even more compulsive.

So like Elizabeth, I am hungry for an unexamined lunch.

I would also love a casual walk, a light read, a good night's rest, and the ability to enjoy something sweet without always analyzing its charm.

REFLECTIONS

S ince I have mentioned *Eat, Pray, Love*, I want to talk about one other thing Gilbert discusses: the "word."

The idea of the word comes up in a conversation with her friend Guilio. Guilio has heard Elizabeth say she does not really fit in the city of Rome, and he has suggested that perhaps she and Rome "just have different words." He believes that every city has a word—a "single word that defines it," and that "if your personal word does not match the word of the city, then you don't really belong there."[1]

He reveals that Rome's word is "sex." She reveals that New York City's word is "achieve." Then Guilio asks Elizabeth the million-dollar question: "What's your word?"[2]

Elizabeth isn't sure, and she wonders if her year of travel and exploration is about finding her word.

Well, I love words. And I have been on whatever this journey is for over a year now. So what's *my* word?

~

It might be "reflect."

"Reflect" has two meanings. The first, according to the *OED*, is to bend or "throw back (heat, light, or sound) without absorbing it." The second is to "think deeply or carefully about."

Both types of reflection come naturally to me—whether I want them to or not. Throughout my childhood I learned to reflect, as in mirror. I could mirror—but could not fully absorb (or be absorbed by)—my surroundings. As an expert in presentation, I was a puzzle piece that could look like a perfect fit in almost every situation, but never fully went in. This continued in later life. I have moved through different environments, able to bend and reflect my surroundings. But there has always been a barrier, no absorption in either direction. Not fully taken in, nor fully taking in.

But I am always thinking, reflecting. Deeply and carefully. To the point that I have driven myself—and lots of people around me—nuts.

But choosing "reflect" as my word means deviating from Guilio's idea that my personal word should match the word of my community. The first kind of reflector (a mirror) doesn't want to be around other mirrors. You end up with an infinite hallway of nothing. As that type of reflector, I want to be around light.

But the other part of my reflective nature—the thinker—does not want to be around light. It wants to step off the well-lit path onto an unfamiliar road, where there will be something new to see and experience and think about. Something that hasn't been spotlighted before. I want to discover new people and hear about their lives. And then I want to sit alone in a room lit only by the glow of my laptop and think and process. And discern layer upon layer of meaning.

This part of me wants to discern meaning in everything. When I got married, my mother insisted we have a bag of goodies awaiting out-of-town guests. She offered to pull them together quickly and place them in rooms, but I told her I would take care of it. I added seven items that were useful (snacks, water, etc.) but also included a letter that explained the significance of every addition. A bottle of water was not just a bottle of water. The chips were not just chips. Much like a cactus was not just a cactus.

My mom looked at me and said, not for the first or last time, "Being you must be exhausting."

She was right. And as I realize this, it is important for me to own it. At various points, I have tried to blame others for my fatigue. But that's a mistake. I am tired because I am wired to dig deep until I slam into solid rock, and then to consider what sort of sense (if any) the impact might have knocked into me, and then to find a new excavation site and start digging deeply again.

There are several ideas I could dig into here, but I only want to summarize three. The first is that I like playing with different words. Doing that has made me wonder how much of a stretch it would be to shift my word from "reflect" to "thoughtful." There is certainly overlap in the definitions, and I like the idea that I could shift from reflecting light to thoughtfully lightening someone else's load.

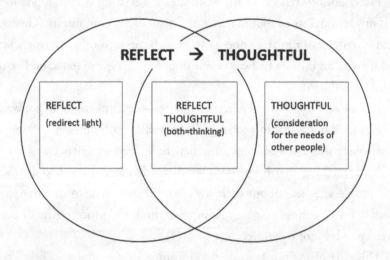

Or, I could pick a new word entirely. For example, I really like the word "wonder." It can mean "doubt" or "curious" or in "awe," three familiar states of being for me. I also like that wonder is only one letter away from wander. That appeals to the so-close-yet-so-far-from-fully-expressed nomad in me.

~

My second thought extends naturally from the reference to nomads. I would like to think the nomad in me is inspired by adventure and enabled by a tendency to pack light (with regard to material things). But the truth is my itch to discover and experience is not the only reason I regularly leave professions, communities, and relationships. I am not always moving toward something; sometimes I am moving away from connections. Away from intimacy. Away from expectations. Away from the pressure of the logical next step.

Would you like to know the quickest way to guarantee I will never show up again? Tell me you cannot wait to see what I am going to bring to the table next. My anxiety goes through the roof. It is too much pressure. Do not count on me. Do not pin me down. I like space, control, and introspection. Maybe I am so introspective that I have trouble connecting. Maybe I am so introverted that I don't need that many connections outside my immediate family. Perhaps, despite all this emotional weight I am carrying, I am flighty. Always itching to go. And the connections I do have? Sometimes the folks on the other end have no idea how connected I feel. I think about friends—and their words and their inspiration and their spirits and their awesomeness—way more than I talk *to* them.

My friend Susan lives twenty minutes away. I see her about once a year. I have spoken to her on the phone one time ever. We have swapped about ten text messages in the last twelve months. But one of the texts I sent said, "I think you are my spirit sister." We have no expectations of each other, but there is just something *there*. It was Susan I texted after my first meeting with an oncologist friend who was headed out of the country on a boat trip, but generously offered to review my cancer case amid her pre-trip chaos. It was Susan I texted because I knew she was the only one who would appreciate the mix of horror and humor I felt when, after the meeting, I accidentally typed the oncologist a message thanking her and wishing her a "non voyage" instead of a "bon voyage." I texted Susan because she loves words, because I feel a creative connection with her, and because she would not find it at all weird that I was texting her out of the blue, not with a medical update but with something about a *word*. And because Susan would not think it meant I wanted to follow up with a lunch date. Instead, she immediately replied with a text that said, "Non Voyage! I think you just named my boat!"

I didn't even know Susan *had* a boat. She told me it stays docked and needs repairs but is important because it represents possibility. My spirit sister—someone who loves space, control, introspection, words, her family, and her maybe-seaworthy boat. Someone who realizes that the non voyage can be as humorous and as meaningful as the bon voyage. Or something like that anyway.

~

Finally, my third (ironic) thought is that I am thinking too much. Digging too deep. Exploring too many excavation sites. I am tense, and I am tired. I need to *relax*. Unfortunately, "relax" will never be my word. In yet another ironic insight, I have discovered that relaxing is not easy for me.

RELAX

I am tense: "stretched tight."

I used to be tense because I felt stretched between two things: improving versus enjoying the world. With the help of Ecclesiastes and Elaine Scarry and several cardboard boxes that moved me away from spaces where I felt obligated into spaces where I felt *good* (in both senses of the word), that tension resolved.

Now I am tense because I feel stretched between worlds. I live in a nice place, but I am more comfortable in communities that have less. I live here, but constantly feel pulled.

But I am not moving in the foreseeable future; I have made that choice. My current community has embraced my family—and vice versa—and my husband and I have reached an equilibrium that works. I realize that doesn't sound romantic, but it's a foundation upon which a wonderful life full of light and connection and joyful giving and receiving can occur. Also, I really love my neighbors. They make me laugh. They make me think. They make me s'mores. They love my children. They make this intense introvert OK walking out her front door into the world.

So I visit communities that have less and ask to be accepted as a transient. I worry this makes me appear to have a white-knight mentality. I promise, I don't. Yes, I hope I have something to offer, but I also really respect and need something from these spaces. When I am there, something in me unfurls. I meet new people with new chisels that shape me in ways for which I am so incredibly grateful.

I am stretched between other worlds also. I speak both Conservative and Liberal. Both Christian and Pluralist. Both Southern and Northern. Both Afternoon Tea and Tractor Pull. Both accommodating Belle and Bellona, the patron of war. I recognize that being able to pass in all these spheres is a gift, but it also requires constant navigation and interpretation and some code-switching that blurs the border between being flexible and being authentic, which then threatens my peace of mind. It saddles me with a sense of responsibility, like I should somehow be able to connect worlds. And as I stretch, there is tension.

~

I have tried to reduce my own tension in a variety of ways, and it has left me wondering if there are certain separated spheres

that we have tried connecting (and found ourselves too strained),

tried moving closer to one another (and found them too rooted),

○ ○

and I wonder if the only option we have left is to abandon one (hard when there are loved ones there—and when you value diversity).

○

Or if it's ever possible to somehow encourage the polar-opposite spheres to grow and expand until it's either a shorter reach across the chasm (less stretching and tension required to connect),

or there is overlap (common ground).

As someone who has traveled between spheres quite a bit, I can tell you they are often anchored. Planted. Requiring me to leave one to enter the other—and always through a very narrow door. Sometimes guarded by a troll with a question or litmus test.

What if we encouraged everyone to expand their thinking and their circles a bit? And to lose the litmus tests? Imagine what that would do within the realms of politics, religion, and family.

An example: I know plenty of people who would be considered liberal on almost every issue except for one: They are pro-life. As a result of this, they vote Republican, every time. They are applying a litmus test to candidates. It does not matter if the pro-choice candidate offers a world of good things. It does not matter if the pro-life candidate promises horrors. That one issue will determine who they follow. My own mother takes this approach. After Trump had put three justices on the Supreme Court and was running for reelection, I said, "You got what you wanted. Now can you vote with other issues in mind?" She told me no, that she truly believed God would greet her at the gates of heaven and judge her based on how she voted around this one issue. Litmus tests. Applied by voters. And apparently (according to my mom's view) applied by God. Also applied by political parties, even when they are desperate for votes. Am I welcome at your rallies if I think differently on this issue? Even if we agree on everything else? How narrow is the door?

Same with religion: so many yes or no questions, but where is the open-essay section? And families, rejecting people they love over one identification. Individuals, self-loathing over an identification they could celebrate. And on an entirely different note, individuals who have made a mistake at some point, self-loathing instead of realizing that one mistake does not define who you are.

It is all tearing, and keeping, people apart. To the point that no one can learn from anyone.

Enough with the litmus tests!

Enough with the ridiculously narrow doors.

~

Wait.

Darn it!

I have to stop.

I have to back up.

I have to rewind, because my goal in this section was to pose this sphere-expansion idea as a question, not as a position—partially because it is fraught, since we quickly lose anyone or any community that is holding a litmus test. But mostly—and this is a much bigger deal to me—it oozes with privilege.

Imagine for a moment that one of those spheres I talked about is a community with innate characteristics: a group of people who share a particular race or ethnicity or gender or orientation. A group that feels threatened—or is worried about elements being appropriated or diluted. I am fortunate to have been welcomed into these arenas for moments, and though I would never claim to speak the language, I have tried my best to listen to those who patiently communicate. And I have heard enough to know that it is the ultimate privilege to feel like we should all connect more often. I would not want to do that if my kids, or my livelihood, or my community, or my cultural continuity were in danger.

If I value your kids and your livelihood and your community and your culture, I need to respect what you choose to do with your doors.

So I promise that, even though I got carried away for a moment, I am not taking a position. I am just thinking about the tension and wondering what to do about it—not just in my own life, but out in the world.

Since my spheres tend to be privileged, I personally am going to work hard to open my eyes and open my mind and—as best I can—open doors to the privileged spheres I navigate. I want to invite people in and to the table. I want to offer to help move or restructure or replace the table. I am going to try to acknowledge my privilege and my bias. I am also going to try to recognize that it is that privilege and that bias that will try to make me feel tense at points along the way. And if that tension temps me to constrict my sphere, I am going to fight that temptation. Instead of tensing and constricting, I am going to put my effort into staying open and relaxed.

~

"Relax" does not only mean "to reduce tension." It also means "to rest." While working hard is good, I also need to prioritize rest, or I am not going to make it.

One of my kids has trouble putting on weight. This has both innate and experiential causes. He is naturally skinny. He also contracted a horrific stomach bug a while back, which led to ongoing issues with reflux that made eating unpleasant. It took about a year—and trips to the pediatrician and the hospital and the GI specialist and the nutritionist—to get that under control. His doctors also speculated that he may be one of those kids who simply does not experience hunger cues as acutely as others: He will simply forget to eat. We have set alarms to remind him to snack each afternoon. The doctors have moved past "eat healthy" into the realm of "eat *anything*." We are constantly making him milkshakes and buying him donuts and offering anything we can get him to consume.

Some people who are aware of this tell him how lucky he is to have this prescription. They say things like, "I'm so jealous! How I wish the doctor would tell *me* to enjoy as many milkshakes as possible!"

While the human in me understands, the mama bear in me wants to smack them. They are trivializing something that impacts my child. He wants to exit the school bus and head to the neighborhood playground, but he can't. He has to come home and eat first because his belly will not rumble a reminder in thirty minutes that his body needs fuel. Instead, if we do not take preemptive steps, his cue to eat will be that his body has almost stopped working. He will remember that he should have eaten when he is so faint he can barely drag himself home.

The alarms we set for him are disruptive. They are not organic or natural. They do not ramp up slowly like hunger. Instead, they boldly interrupt his day and pull him away from activities. So he stops and he sits and he eats—while thinking about what he would rather be doing.

The way he feels about eating is the way I feel about relaxation.

I enjoy it when it's the focus for everyone. I recognize it as necessary fuel.

But I don't experience the cues as acutely as others. My son realizes he is hungry when he begins to feel faint. I realize I need to relax when I am so torn up or burned out that I have become physically ill.

Assisting my son should have prepared me to navigate retreats more graciously. I have taught him to shrug it off when others comment about his menu. He is never in danger of overeating. He will never take more than his fair share of food. He is wired in a way that makes those nonissues. So when someone says, "Ice cream at this time of day? *Must be nice*," there is no reason for him to engage them. His job is to ignore them and take another bite.

Now imagine it is not him at the metaphorical table; it is me. I am doing something relaxing: reading a novel, seeking the ocean, heading out on a hike. I know I am never in danger of retreating too long. I am never in danger of taking more than my fair share of time. I am wired in a way that makes those nonissues. But when someone sees or hears about those activities, I feel embarrassed. I make excuses. I explain why I need to be reading this book or out on this hike. I feel like crap when someone says, "Oh yes. Well, good for you. *I wish I had the time.*"

Why do I care?

It is not because I care what they think. I know they won't think much about it past this moment.

It is because they are giving voice to that part of me that feels guilty. That part that says, *With everything going on,* this *is how you're spending your time?*

~

Yes. Yes, it is.

I wondered, when I began writing, what themes would consistently surface. What did I feel or hear or think time and time again over the years?

The one that has surprised me the most is "relax."

When I look back over my life, I realize that I have been told by many teachers, coaches, doctors, and friends that something about my approach was not sustainable. That I had to pace myself.

I am sure this popped up during my childhood—perhaps from the doctor who evaluated me when I was on hour thirty-six of my oatmeal hunger strike, or from the aunt who watched me shred my knees in my determination to exit the pool in an unorthodox way, or from the teacher who watched me check my long-division test answers again, even though it meant I was the only kid inside, missing recess.

But the first time I remember hearing it directly was in high school. I was running the final leg of the 4x400-meter relay. We were in last place when I took the baton, and I recall sprinting even though I knew I could not run an entire lap at full speed. I passed a competitor, passed the first straightaway, passed that final curve, and then—twenty meters from the finish line—simply passed out. Unconscious. Face-planted into the pavement. My mother, in what everyone agreed was the most athletic moment of the meet, hiked up her calf-length dress and hurdled over a fence onto the track. She ran to me, rolled me over and discovered—as I came to—that her relief was matched by my upset. My first words were, "Did we win? I can still finish. Or did I drop the baton?"

"It's over," she told me. "Just relax."

I heard it from my mentor during Teach For America, and then again at HGSE. It was prescribed by doctors. It was offered as wise counsel (along with hugs and playdates) by very close friends. My sister saved me with it the time I suggested it was my fault our dad died—that my teen years had given him the ulcers that must have paved the way for that fatal GI bleed. She said, "If dad were here right now, he would dismiss that idea as ludicrous. He would laugh at its absurdity. And then he would say, 'Kristi, *relax*. Because you don't have that much power. And you certainly never had that much power over *me*.'"

Melanie once told me to relax when I came to her in tears during a hard motherhood moment: I had just given birth to my third child. The house was in turmoil. And I was upset because I had just discovered that no matter how hard I worked, I could not get all my children everything they needed right when they needed it.

"Why would you want to give your children everything they need right when they need it?" she asked me. "Are you *trying* to create nightmarish narcissists? *Relax*. Waiting is good for them. And having their mama this upset is not good for anybody."

The idea that I needed to relax was insisted upon at increasing volume by my own body. My brain screamed it at my young proxy on *The Bachelor*, when I watched her and thought, *Oh. Bless her heart. She should relax.*

The very deepest part of my soul spoke it when I was guiding my thirteen-year-old through confirmation questions. The same questions that had plagued me for years were now being asked of my daughter. She wanted space to consider. That meant I was either going to have to push or relax. The answer was unbelievably obvious: I was going to relax.

I did not give that long letter to my daughter. I did not give it to her because I felt myself changing—relaxing about everything—and I worried it would soon be misrepresentative.

Instead, I apologized to her and read parts of it with her, and we talked.

I apologized for bringing an agenda into a spiritual process. Going forward, I would have only one goal: to help her get to know herself. I would listen. I would assist. I would support. I would celebrate. And I would relax.

The best part of realizing I could relax about this aspect of parenting was that it freed up so much time and energy to simply love and celebrate—and also discover more about—my oldest child.

Ella is a smart, competitive, fun, feisty, caring young lady. It is tempting to write pages about her.

I could tell you about the time five-year-old Ella stood up to someone who intimidated her—a kid who threatened to punish Ella unless she hit a younger child. Ella protected the child, putting herself at risk.

I could tell you about the time seven-year-old Ella taught the adults in the room about setting boundaries. A member of our group had hired a photographer. The photographer became frustrated with Ella's five-year-old friend, who had an ear condition and could not always hear where the photographer wanted her to sit. At one point, this grown man said to this young friend, "If you don't pay attention, look this way, and smile for the picture, this whole group is going to *hate* you." The adults gasped but ultimately just tried to get through it. It was Ella who drew a line. When we told her it was time for individual photos, she absolutely refused to sit. "No," she responded. "He was mean to my friend. I will *not* smile at him."

I could tell you about the times Ella's sweetness shined through. About how she read Mo Willems books to her younger siblings and let them dismantle her old Lego sets to see how they were built and how she explained to me why there was a "NO CLOWNS ALLOWED" sign on her brother's door in Ella's handwriting.

"He found my copy of *It*—the Stephen King book," she told me. "The one with that scary clown drawing on the cover. I'm sorry I left it out. But I think I fixed it. I told him clowns were like vampires: that they could only enter a space when they were invited. The sign on his door makes it clear they aren't welcome. I helped him make it and hang it and he's been happy in there ever since." It was a solution I would *never* have thought of.

Ella often sees solutions I don't. She has great perspective. I could tell you so many good stories about this sharp, sweet, incredible kid. But I want to focus largely on one event, which took place in an ice rink.

In elementary and middle school, Ella loved ice-skating. She took lessons and entered a few competitions. She worked hard and did well.

We quickly learned that figure skating competitions run on a very tight schedule. When they say, "Group A will have from 8:31 to 8:34 to warm up on the ice," they mean it. There is a huge clock on the wall of each rink marking the time. You have exactly three minutes to warm those muscles and practice that jump and then you exit the ice until it is time for your routine to be performed for the judges. If you ever want to see focus, go watch a group of skaters during those three minutes. It is intense.

During one of those three-minute warm-ups, at an event many had driven a long way to attend, one of Ella's competitors fell and didn't get up. She sat on the ice cradling her ankle, obviously in pain and in tears. Her parents and coach could not get to her because they didn't have on skates. Where the hell were the skates? Were there any adults around who were wearing skates and could get to this kid?

As the scrambled search unfolded on the sidelines, most of the Group-A skaters did exactly as they had been instructed: "Focus. You have only three minutes. Use it to get ready. You have to practice that jump at the end. "

Everyone in Group A was in competition with one another, and they continued their warm-ups around this fallen girl.

Except for Ella.

Ella stopped. Skated over. Crouched on the ice next to the girl, then offered herself as a crutch for this kid. Ella slowly navigated her through spinning, jumping colleagues to the exit ramp, where the injured skater was collected and tended to by her coach and her parents. Before Ella could even turn back to the ice, the alarm sounded. Warm-up was over, and the competition would begin.

One of the other coaches on the sideline approached Ella and said, "I've been doing this for years, and I have seen plenty of falls during warm-ups. Never once have I seen someone stop to check on a competitor. I wish they would give you another three minutes to warm up. They won't. So I want you to hear me say that I appreciate what you did."

Ella simply shrugged and said, "Thank you, but really, it's no big deal."

No big deal. She had trained for this competition for months. Worked on these skills for years. She had perfected a routine and awakened at dawn for this chance to perform it.

I was so proud of her in that moment for deciding that stopping and tending to someone was important. For shrugging off something that had been worth all of that effort but had become—in an instant—no big deal.

~

I had that moment in the spring of 2020. I looked at my daughter—at this wonderful growing girl—and suddenly the vast majority of the spiritual details I had obsessed over for decades simply became no big deal.

There was a person in front of me.

My whole life I had tried to learn about God in institutions and through organizations and books. Tried to figure out what I should be—what people should be. I tried to figure it out so I could mold myself after that model.

But if I really believed God had created me—that God had molded me—shouldn't I stop trying to alter my shape? Wouldn't the ultimate sign of respect for a Creator be to celebrate the way that Creator made me?

And to celebrate my daughter. For whoever she decides to be, and for exactly who she is.

A Garden

WHO AM I?

Who am I? It is amazing how long it took me to sit down and really try to answer that question. And now, after almost five decades of dancing around it, I am finally at my desk confronting it directly. Not surprisingly, I initially want to tackle it by making a list of words—specifically, words that describe my "core."

For years, "core" was the term I used to refer to the most authentic part of me. Thinking about my core focused me on what was solid and central about my true identity. As a child, I was taught not to trust my core. I was taught that human nature is evil and must be resisted. But for years now, I have rejected that teaching. And accepting and trusting my core has been both life altering and spirit saving for me.

Naturally, once I realized my core could be trusted, I wanted to know it better. So during my midlife crisis, I got bogged down trying to figure out which parts of me were innate (my original, authentic core) and which were long-term baggage (things picked up so early that they seemed a part of me). For example, I worked for years attempting to figure out whether my ascetic impulses were simply me—or if they were born of shame during the pink-coat incident. My first breakthrough came when I decided that, for me and with regard to that particular issue, it just didn't matter. I had been feeling something for decades, which meant it was significant. Maybe I was born with those impulses. Or maybe the pink-coat experience was a seed that found fertile soil in me. Either way, there was something in my nature that existed or responded.

As I thought about that, the word "nature" kept calling to me. Ultimately, it inspired a second big breakthrough. I was sitting at my desk, trying to type out that list of my core elements, but the page just didn't feel like *me*. So I closed my laptop, and I picked up a pencil.

And I began drawing my *nature*, in the form of a garden.

~

This image of my central self as a garden was incredibly helpful. All of a sudden, there were spaces for different parts of me: native plants, latent seeds, new growths that I could decide whether to nurture or weed.

Gardens evolve, and factors in that evolution include exposure and choice.

I have control over some exposures: selecting an environment, book, or experience that could provide seeds or tools. I do not have control over others, but I can exercise choice by trying to limit or nurture their growth. As I make these choices, I can ask myself, *What choice feels authentic and liberating? And what choice feels like an attempt to bury a natural part of me?*

I am not sure why it took so long for me to consider the idea of my "self" as a garden. When I look back at my words over the years, it is clear that I worry about parts of my core dying and refer to different parts needing oxygen in order to grow. I spoke of it as a living thing with elements that could flourish or shrivel, but never grasped the full implication. Maybe it was the word "core" that threw me off, bringing to mind a hard, round center. But that visual limited me, so I decided to create a new one. I was no longer trying to put my core elements into a list; instead, I was trying to describe my nature as a garden.

I am including a version of the image so I can highlight how adding elements to it was both enlightening and cathartic for me.

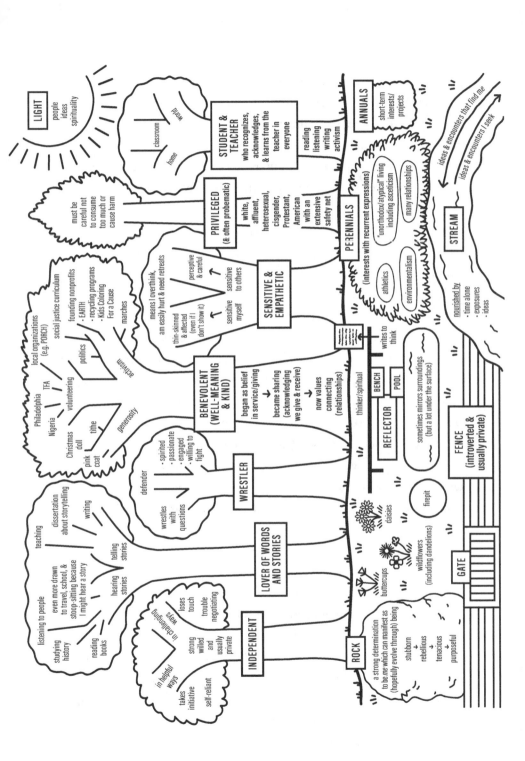

As depicted here, my nature is organized. There is a fence around the plot. I love boundless wildflowers—I have them scattered throughout my "identity garden" because I admire and appreciate them (and I will take a cabin in an open meadow over a castle with an English garden any day). But on some level—inside my cabin, residence, or nature—I need order.

There are seven main trees: things that are deeply rooted and represent elements of my nature. These are not the trees of my childhood, which were affiliations (religious, political, etc.). They are simply things I am: independent, sensitive, empathetic, lover of words and stories, wrestler, benevolent, student, and teacher.

It was a light-bulb moment for me when I realized I wanted some of these big-tree words to be *adjectives*. For years I was caught up in what my nouns would be (teacher, for example), and those are still things I value. But many of my most significant and consistent elements are not nouns. People are not only their nouns. If I meet someone, I am happy to honor their work as a father or lawyer or hairdresser. I also really want to honor the ways they are compassionate or adventurous or kind.

In my first draft of these identifier trees, there were only six. Then I realized something was missing. The fact that I was able to choose my identifiers—and the fact that I initially felt comfortable leaving so many common identifiers unacknowledged—was the ultimate privilege. In an attempt to address this, I added a tree that acknowledged my social location as a privileged, White, educated, American, Protestant woman with an extensive safety net. Later, after reading *White Fragility* by Robin DiAngelo[1]—I went back and added "and often problematic" to this tree. I am privileged. And I am often problematic. Yes, I have been socialized into a system of racism, and yes, I do exhibit White fragility: defensive moves that keep that system going. Personally, I am especially adept at the defensive moves of guilt, silence, and valuing intent over impact. This "I am privileged—and often problematic" tree contains a branch that reminds me I want to do better—and highlights that this is one arena in which I must be more vigilant instead of more relaxed.

These seven trees are large parts of me. And each of these seven trees has branches, indicating how different elements of my nature found expression at various points in my life.

But my identity garden does not consist of only trees.

There is a rock in my garden that represents a slightly evolving but always hard element of my nature: my childhood stubbornness that became rebellion, then tenacity. Still today, I am attempting to transform this part of my nature from a stubborn, rebellious, tenacious woman to a purposeful one (without becoming resolute or immutable).

There is a pool next to a bench that represents my identity as both types of a "reflector": someone who can mirror their surroundings (for good or bad), but also someone who is going to sit and think.

The sun represents the things that have enlightened me: people, ideas, spirituality. The stream represents things that have nourished me (some of those same exposures as well as time alone). I have decided that this stream has the potential to flow in either direction. Exposures can be things that find me—or things I discover and seek.

I have grouped my interests into the categories of "annuals" and "perennials." Annuals bloom for a season. Perennials come back again and again. In the category of perennials, I have included athletics, environmentalism, and many relationships I value. These are things that—for decades—have been my priorities. They are not always front and center, but they are important and bloom in different ways at different times.

There is a patch of buttercups drawn because they are the flowers my parents always planted around the yard of my childhood home. There is a patch of Gerbera daisies as a nod to my husband's most frequent gift when we dated. Those spots of beauty—and that history—mean a lot to me.

～

Creating this image of my nature has helped me in several ways:

First, I feel seen. I can see myself, right there on paper.

In addition, it takes the pressure off me to be everything all the time. The visual reminder that being a student (or a teacher or benevolent or a lover of words) can take on so many forms (branch or bloom in so many ways) is a good one for me. Just because I am not working every day in a traditional classroom does not mean I am not learning or teaching.

Also, embracing the image of a garden has allowed me to stop whittling away elements in some search for an immutable core. There have been seeds planted along my journey—that's a good thing. And this garden acknowledges them, along with my own potential for evolution and change.

And finally, this visual has provided a new way for me to explore some very hard-to-understand elements of my identity.

One of those difficult elements is the part of me that wants to live an unorthodox or atypical life. I don't really know what to do with this part of myself. It is this part of me that wonders whether I balked when I left Colorado. It is this part that wonders if I should ask my family to move to a different part of the world or sell everything and live in an RV. There have been many moments when this part of me manifested as an interest in asceticism—wanting to give up most of my material possessions and live differently. This was the teenage me who talked about living with the Amish or as a nun, the college student who loved that African village, and the twenty-something who found peace in inner-city Philadelphia and rural North Carolina. It is now the adult me who is not fully comfortable in her current suburban setting.

It's hard to talk about because it is my alternate life. My what-if?

It's also hard to figure out whether this draw comes from my authentic nature or some deep-rooted baggage.

If this aspect of my identity was a gift at birth, it was a good one. My aversion to some of the trappings of modern life could enable me to be happy in places others might avoid. That could be useful.

But if it's baggage, it's heavy—regardless of how long it's been there. Maybe it's a part of me that was birthed through shame at age five, when a child shivered without my donated coat. Or maybe it emerged when I became fixated on my own plot, at the expense of paying attention to character(s). Or maybe my wanting to live an unexpected life was not me at all, but a rebellion against expectations in general.

I don't know—and my point here is that I am no longer convinced it matters. If I was born with these inclinations, then they've always been a part of my nature. If I wasn't—if these were actually seeds planted or picked up along the way—they found extraordinarily friendly soil in me. There is something about me that embraced that exposure.

I have considered the possibility that the source of this inclination was one or more external seeds that grew because they came covered in fertilizer, surrounded by the shit of shame and guilt, which I internalized deeply. But I have done my best to excavate them. To remove the shit. To transplant the seeds. They find friendly soil regardless. There is something about the unorthodox and atypical—and maybe ascetic—life that appeals to me.

It has helped me to realize that this piece of me doesn't have to be the entire garden. It doesn't even have to be a tree. I experienced relief when I realized it could be a perennial: something that has a long-standing history as a priority but is not always front and center. It can bloom in different ways at different times. Shifting it to that seasonal part of the garden doesn't mean negating key aspects of my identity. I am still benevolent. I am still sensitive. I can still be me.

I will always struggle with this on some level. I will read accounts of people living unorthodox lives and feel wistful, maybe jealous. But I will also remember that I traveled many roads before choosing this one, and none of them felt 100 percent right to me. And I will remember that there will be seasons when that part of me will bloom.

In other words, I can find some peace by accepting that the impulse— no matter how it got there—is a part of my nature I want to embrace.

And I can recognize that there is more than one way I can embrace and express it.

At the moment, that drawing represents my nature. I am many other things also: a mother, a wife, a daughter. I love those roles, have given them attention, and will continue to value and prioritize them—but I needed this to be something separate: the other parts of me.

~

There is one patch of drama in my nature: a firepit that is typically contained.

It is not a firepit people gather around to roast s'mores, or a firepit that keeps you warm. It is more like a firepit you sleep near while camped in a clearing surrounded by a beautiful but dangerous jungle. The kind of firepit you might use to light a torch and fend off a tiger.

It has taken me a long time to understand this element.

I am not someone who enjoys external drama. I do not like conflict. I find any sort of tug-of-war exhausting. There are some folks who enjoy a healthy debate, who like fleshing things out even if they are not invested in the topic, who simply enjoy the back-and-forth.

I am *not* one of those people. If we disagree on any level, the first thing I am going to wonder is, *Does it matter?* Getting all riled up for the sake of getting all riled up—emotion for the sake of emotion—is something I avoid.

At the same time, I am all about the dramatic gesture. I am not afraid to—and often prefer to—make a point by whipping out a fiery flame. It doesn't seem to fit with my reflective, connective, conflict-avoidant, slowly warm process at all. But there it is.

After a lot of thought, I came to understand that there are several factors in this fire-wielding part of me, each of which has manifested in a different dramatic gesture in my life.

It was my stubbornness that made exiting medicine more dramatic. I could not quit until I had truly slammed into a brick wall made of "THIS

IS NOT YOU." For some people it is a quiet exit between rotations. (Or at least between classes. Most people don't stand up as the professor is calling everyone to attention and announce they are out.) But that stubborn part of me forged ahead, refusing to quit until that brick-wall collision—after which I had just enough strength to stand up and walk away from the rubble.

It was my tendency to second-guess or overthink everything—and to get sucked back into roles based on guilt—that made burning bridges feel necessary. If I leave a group or a class, I try to be kind, but I am also honest about why this is not my thing. This is not always the best strategy, but I simply cannot handle the stress of quarterly emails inviting me back or the strain of pretending I have consistent scheduling conflicts. Even if it generates a bit of drama, I need to say when I am done.

A third trait that has led to a bit of drama is that I am efficient—to a fault. Time is precious, and I don't want to take one hundred moments to convey something that can be communicated in one. For example, several years back I needed to communicate something important to my children. They were all very young, and their bickering in the backseat of our car was constant. After many trips full of reprimand and redirection and mild repercussions, I decided it was enough. So the next time a big car quarrel happened, we pulled over and I explained again that it was dangerous for me to be distracted by arguments while I was driving. And I announced that, from then on, every time it happened, we were going to stop, no matter where we were or how late we were running or what the weather was like outside. We were going to stop and do time-outs at the nearest safe location. In fact, we were going to do one right this very second. "But mama," one of the kids told me, "it's pouring." Yes, it was. That was one of the reasons I chose this particular moment. We all did our time-out in the grassy island in a random parking lot in the pouring rain, where we got wet and cold and sloppy because this constant bickering in the car was going to stop. And it did. It was a moment they remembered. After that, I simply had to ask, "Do I need to stop?" and whatever they were bickering about was resolved very quickly or dropped.

Meetings are another arena where I become overly efficient. I know the value of human connection. I know that taking ten extra minutes on every topic can reap longer-term rewards. But time is precious, and we need to get through this agenda because I don't want to reconvene tomorrow. We are all here. Allow me to use my torch to light our asses on fire so we can get this shit done.

I am not proud of these things; I know they are problematic. When I stubbornly slam into brick walls, there is collateral damage. When I burn bridges, I alienate people. My focus on efficiency limits connection. We are all sopping wet on a muddy island in a half-empty parking lot, for heaven's sake. We look crazy!

But we are not arguing. We are not offtrack. We are not getting sucked back into more drama. It's done.

~

To balance all of that a bit, I will add that there is also a piece of me that simply appreciates the connective and narrative nature of the dramatic moment. I do not mind being the dramatic villain in the story when the story is fun. As my kids aged, they loved telling the story of that rainy time-out, along with tales of other drama-filled family moments. I guess I am saying that I don't seek the drama, but I'm not afraid of it and sometimes appreciate it, so long as it doesn't hurt anyone.

~

I have read many memoirs and learned a lot from each of them. I have mentioned that Glennon Doyle's *Untamed* had a huge impact on me, encouraging me to reject selflessness as an ideal. Becoming "full of myself" finally allowed me to celebrate the woman I was created to be (enhancing my relationship with God). It also allowed me to grow parts of myself to the point that they are strong and overflowing (which means I have something authentic to offer people around me, including the chance for a true connection, which could enhance my personal relationships).

That doesn't mean my "full of self" offering or outlook will always be accepted, much less celebrated. I have to remember that this is not how I was raised to think, and that it runs counter to much of what I still hear.

For example, just last year my mom texted an extended group of family members a picture of her Christmas tree and challenged us to find photos of ourselves on the ornaments. I sent back the same image, having found and circled my photo. I captioned it, "I found myself! (A statement the family has been waiting to hear me say for decades. ☺)"

Among the many responses I received (including some positives), one mentioned that my next step, after finding myself, was "dying to self"—a reference to a perhaps misunderstood Biblical idea. This message was not a surprise, but it was jarring enough that I texted a snippy reply: "Time elapsed from when Kristi finds herself and must die to self = three minutes. But what a glorious three minutes it was!" This elicited a reminder that I shouldn't worry because once I had died to self, I could be "born again!"

I am not bashing beliefs here. I am a Christian. But I am absolutely bashing the notion that I must reject myself on any level. God created me. Denying myself is disrespectful. Growing my authentic self is a testament to, and a means of honoring, the God who made me. And growing my self to the point that it overflows and touches the world is an act of service—actually, an act of *connection*. A positive engagement where I recognize the divine in you and you recognize the divine in me, and we both learn more about the divine by learning more about—instead of trying to change—each other.

〜

I also appreciate another idea Doyle presents in *Untamed*: that we should break structures instead of people. So many of us are trying to break ourselves to fit into families and institutions and political parties and all other sorts of affiliations. Doyle points out that we can "break and rebreak our structure instead of allowing any of us to live broken."[2] As a person—and as a parent—I love this idea. It has helped me better embrace myself, and it has helped me treasure each of my children for exactly who they are.

It is a vital question for any parent to consider: Given the choice, will you break your child or a structure that will not accommodate them? If you are currently applying pressure to a kid (while hoping to see a bend instead of hearing a snap), I would encourage you to stop for a bit and check in with your child—and to consider celebrating their tallest self instead. Like Doyle, I have been through this process with a child. Both of our cases happen to involve celebrating a child who is extraordinarily sensitive. For me, it is a wonderfully caring, lovely, and much-loved daughter named Sienna.

Sienna is an intensely empathic child in a world that is hurting—and it is hard on her. She often needs to stop and feel, which doesn't always mesh with the pace of the world. This might frustrate the world on occasion, but I believe we should see her hesitation as a gift. It is not something to overcome; it is something to pay attention to. To cherish. Many books advised me on how to get Sienna moving, but Doyle reminded me to appreciate that she stops, and to honor her nature as the gift it is.

Once, when my kids were all little, I was getting them ready for bath time. Everyone was running around my bedroom as the tub filled. Somehow, the Bible I kept on my nightstand—my forty-year-old Bible with margins full of thoughts I had recorded over decades of discovery—ended up in the water. I cannot imagine the look on my face when I realized what was sitting at the bottom of the tub. I knew I could get another Bible, but those notes in the margins were irreplaceable. All those scribbles that revealed who I was and what I thought about spirituality as a child, then as a teenager, then as a young adult—they were *gone*. The Bible had thousands of thin pages that would clump together as they dried, and tear as I tried to reopen them. Decades of development would be unreadable. I was shocked and heartbroken and my whole body stilled.

My kids saw my face and they scattered—except for this very young child. Sienna said, "Oh, mama." And then she sat with me for over an hour, tearing our only roll of paper towels into tiny pieces that we could use to separate the wet pages. She felt with me and stayed with me and patted my back. We moved on when we were ready.

All of my kids have their own natures and their own gifts. I could write pages about each of them. But this particular gift is so often misunderstood by the world.

~

Sienna's name is a color. My aunt, an artist, celebrated it in an email just after she was born, writing, "Her name is going to be perfect . . . a warming sunset, a fiery evening sky, a toasty glow."

Sienna is warm. She is fiery. She glows.

She feels deeply and sees things differently.

Once, Sienna was in a group that was trying to list as many types of balls as possible. Everyone chimed in. We heard "basketball" and "soccer ball" and "football." When it was Sienna's turn, she shocked us all by saying, "Eyeball." It was different. Often, different is how Sienna prefers to think.

Another time, I was trying to keep a very young Sienna occupied during a church service. I handed her the bulletin and asked her to circle every S on the page. She circled one S, then another. Then she hesitated. After that brief pause, she drew a huge circle around the entire text and handed me the bulletin. "Here you go, Mama. Every S on this page is circled."

She was right. One big circle, around every S on the page.

This gift of seeing things differently—from every perspective, including the rarely noticed ones—is wonderful. But it comes with several price tags.

One price is external. Not every teacher will appreciate how Sienna approaches assignments. So far, we have been lucky, but I know the day is coming when someone will tell Sienna she is doing something the wrong way. Throughout her life, Sienna will have to choose when to maintain her unique approach and when to acclimate.

This constant choosing could tire her—an internal price to pay. But there is another internal cost to consider also, because Sienna not only sees things from others' perspectives; she also *feels* what others are feeling, in a deep and often overwhelming way.

Sienna's teacher once called us to ask if it was OK to have Sienna skip the socio-emotional learning videos they were showing elementary school students. The point of the videos was to elicit empathy, but the teacher told us Sienna was already so empathetic that the videos were just too upsetting. While the teacher was encouraging most kids not to laugh at the actor who had dropped his tray of food in the cafeteria—to instead imagine how he was feeling—Sienna would visibly shrink and then ruminate about this poor kid for days. Weeks. Every time she walked into the cafeteria. This poor kid was alone in the video. But not in the world! Because Sienna carried his pain.

No pain escapes Sienna. When her school did a Jump Rope for Heart fundraiser, she learned how her own grandfather's life had been extended by the insertion of a pig valve between his heart's chambers.

"That is amazing!" everyone exclaimed.

"What happened to the pig?" asked Sienna.

Sienna! Oh, how I love her heart.

We have taken steps to protect that heart—to make sure her bright, beautiful spirit will not be crushed under the weight of the world's pain.

One of those steps is celebrating all the other aspects of this wonderful girl: her quick smile. Her fun sense of humor. Her connection with animals. Her creative expressions.

Sienna loves to sew, recently making lavender-scented hand warmers for her always-cold mama. She loves photography—a gift that allows her to share her unique angle with the rest of the world. She has the ability to find joy and peace in things others skim over or complain about: cooking a warm meal, setting a beautiful table, hanging Christmas lights during the season—and twinkle lights during every other part of the year.

Another step we have taken is giving Sienna something to *do* with the world's pain, beyond simply feeling it.

Our family's nonprofit, briefly mentioned earlier, is called Kids Coloring For a Cause. The tagline is "Drawing In; Reaching Out." We started it in 2014, the year my oldest child Ella turned eight.

Ella is a voracious reader. She always has been, and she will read anything. When Ella was eight, my mom visited us. She was cleaning out her house and brought with her a stack of *Childcraft* encyclopedias from the 1970s, thinking a former teacher might find them useful. Ella grabbed the set and went through them all—as a third grader—page by page.

One of the books was about endangered animals. Ella became obsessed with endangered animals in general and with this book in particular. Every night for weeks, she brought this book to dinner and told us about a new species that was dying. She placed Post-its on almost every page. We did not have the heart to tell her that the book was over thirty years old and some of the species were already gone.

 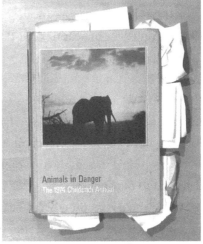

One night during Ella's evening report, Sienna, age six at the time, covered her ears. She could not listen to one more story about these animals; she was in too much pain.

How had I not seen it? I had one daughter trying to focus our attention on a problem, and I had another daughter being crushed by its weight. And I had two boys who spent every day dressed as superheroes, intent on saving the planet.

Perhaps, as the mother of these children, and as an environmentalist, an activist, a teacher, and as someone who is married to a professional fundraiser, I should *do* something.

Perhaps *we* should do something, as a family.

After a month of brainstorming and research, Kids Coloring For a Cause (KIDSFOR) was born.

~

KIDSFOR has a small financial impact. Our primary sponsor typically donates $120 per year. We have a few anonymous sponsors that contribute, and we add in our own funds. One hundred percent of these donations go to good causes. So far, all of those causes have been environmental.

KIDSFOR has a large educational and interpersonal impact. Our mission is to nurture the caring, can-do spirit in kids by supporting them as they support a cause.

Our first year we raised money for a group called Kids Saving the Rainforest. We taught hundreds of students about how this organization needs new rope bridges to save endangered titi monkeys, who are dying as roads and power lines encroach on their jungle home. Lots of KIDSFOR students worked incredibly hard on their amazing artwork, which we then delivered to our sponsors.

Our primary sponsor is the health center of a local retirement community. Each year our family visits the health center and delivers smiles, treats, and KIDSFOR artwork to its members. And each year, that health center thanks us for brightening their day—and their hallways—by making a donation to the cause. That first year, they donated $120 to Kids Saving the Rainforest—the exact price of a lifesaving blue rope bridge in the Costa Rican rainforest.

SAMPLE ARTWORK KIDS CREATED TO FUNDRAISE FOR ENDANGERED & AT-RISK SPECIES	SUPPORTED GROUP
 Helping Titi Monkeys (Black-Crowned Central American Squirrel Monkeys)	**Kids Saving the Rainforest** kidssavingtherainforest.org
 Helping Cape Parrots	**World Parrot Trust** **(Cape Parrot Project)** parrots.org/projects/cape-parrot
 Helping North Atlantic Right Whales	**Center for Coastal Studies** **(MAER Team)** coastalstudies.org/rescue

continued

Helping Sea Turtles

**Local Ocean Conservation
Watamu Turtle Watch
(via the African
Conservation Centre US)**

localocean.co/watamu-turtle-watch

Helping Elephants

**Save the Elephants
(via the Wildlife
Conservation Network)**

wildnet.org/wildlife-programs/
elephant

Helping Monarch Butterflies

Save Our Monarchs

saveourmonarchs.org

Helping Gouldian Finches

World Wildlife Fund-Australia

wwf.org.au/what-we-do/
species/gouldian-finch/

Our goal is to have these young world-changers experience how it feels to see a cause, care about it, and do something to help. In addition, our process allows us to connect the youngest members of our community to our most senior, in a way that brightens both of their spheres. Finally, it funds efforts we truly believe in. Over the years, we have supported the groups noted in the chart. (Also, since we don't want to leave anyone out, I will mention that current kids, sponsors, and environmental partners are always being celebrated at www.kidscoloringforacause.org.)

The nonprofit has provided me with a way to express my environmentalist, activist, and teacher identities. I design the lessons and teach the kids. It also provides my children with an opportunity to engage, which has helped them in a variety of ways.

Sometimes it serves as a blueprint. You care about something? Now you know how to make a plan to invest in it.

At other times, it serves as a focal point. This was particularly valuable for Sienna when she was small. We told her we could not tackle every issue she was going to hear about (natural disasters, violent acts, etc.), and we didn't have to. We were part of a team of global helpers. We just had to do our part. On many days, our part was working for the nonprofit. We would hear about a disaster abroad, and then later find Sienna in her room coloring more animal artwork. She was part of a team. She knew other team members were working on the disaster we had just heard about. She was going to work alongside them in the way that she could.

Always, it reminds me how powerful children are. And how much we need to listen to them and celebrate their unique and beautiful gifts.

~

Doyle explains that being "untamed" is becoming who we actually are instead of who the world tells us to be.[3]

Am I untamed?

I don't know. I want to be.

I want to say proudly: "This is me."

I want to say, "Wow, that was a tough process, but it was worth it and now that I know, and have announced, who I am—I can live *free*."

But it has not worked that way for me. I have to keep going through the process of becoming untamed over and over again. I had to become untamed within different arenas: professional, then spiritual, then personal. I had to repeat the process during different eras: fighting to find the real me in my twenties, then trying to find her again in my forties. I have to keep discovering and rediscovering myself and then keep reminding myself what I actually believe.

And those traps born of the world's expectations—they don't feel like cages I can escape and leave behind. Instead, they feel like camouflaged choking vines, some of which have been grafted onto the center of me. I keep discovering them and cutting them out and trying to weed. Some of them require precision cuts to separate them from parts of my nature. Some require full-on assaults with a tiller at the root. Others are like the Devil's Snare vine in *Harry Potter*: They feed on my angst. They are fueled by my fight. And the only way to get rid of them is to relax. And to hope that if I can relax—and be gentle with myself—they will wither or recede.

Regardless, all of these vines keep coming back. As much as I would like to become untamed and stay that way, expectations keep encroaching. And so I go through the process (outlined by Doyle) again: *Feel* it all. *Know* what the true me wants to do next. *Imagine* what my most beautiful life could look like. And let the rest of it *burn*.

When I go through this process, good things happen. I become an increasingly true version of myself, which allows for more authentic connections.

But undesirable things happen, too. The process burns and hurts people—at least in the short term—and that is so incredibly hard to see.

~

Following my heart hurts the people I love.

I first wrote that as a teenager. And I have felt it again and again. Leaving medicine hurt my parents. Traveling off the grid scared loved ones who worried about me. Ending and transforming romantic relationships upset significant others. Writing this has meant less time with my husband and risks hurting people who have shared segments of their lives with me.

I have burned bridges and missed moments. I hate it.

But the part I struggle with most is trying to keep the fires controlled. Not burning more than is necessary. How do I let burn what needs to be ashes, while still maintaining what is truly important to me?

I think there are two keys.

The first is fireproofing what's valuable. Trying to coat the relationships I care about in positive protective elements including time and communication, even as I protect myself with the space and privacy the discovery process requires of me. That balancing act is tricky, but important.

The second is recognizing that life is not about extremes. It's about connection. I do not have to stand alone and scream, "I am unfettered!" Sometimes being true to myself means honoring the part of myself that loves you and is willing to sacrifice for your needs.

~

Earlier I wondered what it meant for a marriage when you realize you and your spouse don't share identical visions.

What I know now is that our visions don't have to be identical for us to journey together, but they do need to be compatible. If something seems to render us incompatible, we need to remember that we love each other (and in my case, made a vow)—and we have to each examine that issue and ourselves very closely. Is it a complete nonnegotiable, or is there a common path forward? And then if we do find a path forward together, we need to figure out if we can walk it with grace, without judging each other or ourselves so harshly.

I am pretty good at remembering the first part. In general, accepting differences and finding common ground is doable for me.

The second part is trickier. How much do you change yourself (or your path) for someone you love? I spent years figuring out who I am. I don't want to sacrifice any part of that. But I also spent years looking for someone who inspired love on incredible levels, and I don't want to sacrifice that, either. I have been advised to never let *me* go once I find her. I'm sure my husband has heard the same thing about himself. But if we choose to negotiate on something that really matters to both of us—and seems to have become an incompatibility—it might not be as simple as deciding that I must choose myself or this other person. Perhaps adjusting something a few degrees is not dishonoring myself. Perhaps it is honoring the part of me that loves him. And yes, that honors him also. Can't that be a good thing? Hopefully he honors me as well. I need to remember that love is a divine gift—not something to be taken for granted or minimized. An authentic self is a gift to be honored, but so is an authentic love.

That brings us to the last big question. We've found a path forward together. Can we walk it with grace, without judging each other or ourselves harshly?

This is the hardest part for me. Partnering with someone means compromising. I will not be everything I can be in every arena because of those compromises. Neither will my husband. We will say no to requests and opportunities and possibilities if they aren't good for the relationship and family. We will have to do that without regret (the individual angst-maker) or resentment (the couple-killer). It doesn't seem I am going to live the vagabond life with my husband, even though I may feel called to it. I have to forgive myself for missing that call. My husband is not actively seeking the position of athletic director, even though it was his original dream. He has decided his current role is a better fit for our family, and he is trying to show himself grace for not pursuing that passion. We have both missed those marks, but we have found other things.

I struggle with these emotional elements. I blame missed marks on him instead of taking responsibility for choices I made. I hold grudges. I accuse him of not prioritizing my needs. I stop trusting in our ability to protect one another's most important dreams, and that leads me to build thick walls around parts of me I should consider sharing with my spouse. I make mistakes and throw barbs and retreat.

But I am trying. I am working with my husband to figure out how we can forgive ourselves and each other. How we can trust ourselves and each other. How we can protect our individuality and our marriage. How we can work through all of that while also actively setting that work aside to simply be happy—to celebrate each other and these precious moments with our children. There is so much to celebrate! I have to remind myself to take the advice friends gave us at our wedding to not only work at our marriage, but to *play* at our marriage, too.

Work. Warmth. Play. Laughter. Mistakes. Frustration. Grace. Consideration. Appreciation.

Rinse and repeat.

~

So this writing has turned into a memoir, and this section explores identity expressed as a garden. Maybe it is time to unearth a few things.

I have already revealed, in an earlier segment, that I shrugged as my childhood teachers asked members of the LGBTQIA+ community to deny themselves. Since we were all being asked to fight various parts of our own nature, I just viewed the directive to war with yourself as the norm. Same battle, different fronts. So I shrugged.

Here I will confess that I was no better in college.

As an undergrad, I deluded myself into thinking I was more loving because—for the first time—I had friends and teammates who embraced their LGBTQIA+ identities. I felt loving because I said, "OK!" in a spirit of *acceptance*. We were friends!

I now realize that acceptance is an insultingly low bar. I also realize that I am not an actual friend unless I am also an ally.

~

Back in my undergraduate era, my college basketball coaches gave every player on our team a gift—a gift everyone learned about when they were being recruited and then experienced when they were a player. The gift was that, at some point during each player's four years, a game would be scheduled near their hometown. I loved that idea. When I left home for Princeton, I enjoyed knowing I would eventually get to come back and play—one last time—for a big hometown crowd.

My junior year, I asked one of my coaches (who happened to be a lesbian) when we would play in Alabama. She looked at me and said, "I went to Alabama *one* time, to recruit you. I brought you here, and no one from our staff is ever going back there again."

Yikes. What happened in Alabama?

I don't know. Maybe nothing. I wasn't a great college player—frequently injured and not always clear on my role. Maybe she just didn't want to invest in a trip to my area of the country. But I got the sense it was more than that. I knew my hometown was not known for embracing members of the LGBTQIA+ community, and I wondered if she had seen or heard something that made her feel uncomfortable during her trip. Still, I didn't ask. And I thought I was being so helpful by not pushing for information or checking in—for not pushing her to keep her word that, at some point during college, I would play close enough to home to invite extended family and old friends. I thought I was being incredibly gracious when, instead of getting upset about the broken promise, I just nodded and shrugged.

"No problem," I told her.

But there was a problem—not with the game, but with me. With my focus, which was incredibly narcissistic. I suspected something about her trip to my home state had been hurtful, and I didn't look outside myself enough to find out what it was. I didn't ask if she was OK. I didn't offer my help.

I regret that. I regret disregarding what LGBTQIA+ members of my community experienced. I am sorry for not showing up when they were struggling, and for not showing up in a more enthusiastic way when they were celebrating. I shrugged in so many situations when people needed my support or encouragement or enthusiasm. I did not show up as an ally, which calls into question my identification as a friend.

~

Recently, I listened to a podcast discussion between Brené Brown and Austin Channing Brown. They were talking about proximity. Specifically, they were discussing those who claim they cannot be racist because they have a Black friend. There are parallels to those who claim they cannot be homophobic because they have a gay friend. In both situations, there are people who use their Black or gay friend as evidence of their status as an ally to an entire community.[4]

They posed the question: Are these people implying that their work for that community is spending time with their friend?

During the discussion that followed, Brené talked about how dehumanizing this concept is—this (perhaps unwitting) implication that *having this friend* is your *work*. Austin stated directly, "I am not the work." She also emphasized that the "White people in my life who I could call 'friend' are doing the work." That work, Austin revealed, is this: teaching our kids to be anti-racist, diversifying our bookshelves, working to make sure our schools have diverse staff and inclusive curricula, protesting when there are threats to immigration or Pride, and—in short—attempting to "right a million other broken systems."

That is the work. Having a Black or gay friend is not the work.

Until recently, I was allowing various friendships to be my work for various communities. But not anymore. From now on, I am going to start as an ally, and work my way up to friend.

~

I have one more set of roots to explore, in the realm of religion.

I have turned away from many aspects of my childhood faith—including the exclusivity and the judgment—but I still consider myself a Christian. Why?

Because to me, being a Christian means one thing: It does not mean accepting the Bible as a literal set of directives. It does not mean dividing the world or eternity into "us" and "them."

It means following Christ. And not the Christ I met as a kid. Not the one who wears pristine white robes and sits behind pearly gates vouching for people on Judgment Day.

I am talking about the Christ I know now. The one who upended everything. The one who chose love over law. Who focused on the poor and outcast instead of the powerful. Who paid attention to people's hearts instead of their associations. Who fought—nonviolently *and* by flipping over tables—for all of us, especially the downtrodden.

And the one who encourages me to do the same. To focus on love, to alleviate suffering, to concern myself with hearts instead of affiliations, and to fight—nonviolently *and* by flipping over tables—for everyone, especially the downtrodden.

It makes sense to me that a loving Creator would want to connect. That a divine presence would walk on the earth, teach us how to love, insist that we extend that love to everyone, and then offer us hope. Hope for this life, if we can love indiscriminately. Hope for something beyond this life—a reconnection with lost loved ones and with our Creator. Hope that comes when a divine presence lives and loves here—among us—and then conquers the grave.

It makes sense to me. And I sense the truth in it. Not an exclusive truth. Not a scary truth. Just a loving assurance that we can make things better here if we will fight for it—or can at the very least comfort one another through hardship. And a loving assurance that the best for everyone is yet to come.

~

Who am I?

I am an introverted lover of words and stories.

I am someone who wrestles with my own issues and wants to fight for justice out in the world.

I care about people on a very deep level. I am sensitive, reflective, well-meaning, and kind. I want to connect, but a full calendar makes me anxious. I like my independence, my space, and some degree of control.

I am spiritual, creative, passionate, and orderly. I am a workhorse. I have to remind myself that it's OK to be happy. To relax. To enjoy the world while working to improve it. And then I have to remind myself that others don't always have that privilege.

I am privileged. I am part of a systemic problem that harms people of other races, backgrounds, and identities. I am a White, heterosexual, Christian, American, cisgender female who has moved to the left side of the political spectrum and needs to be a better global citizen of the world.

I am a student. I love learning from everyone, especially those who don't expect someone to listen. I am a teacher. I love sharing what I've learned.

I am someone who naturally questions and reflects. I try to reflect the light—and to reflect on and think about both the light and the shadows—and to then act thoughtfully.

I might seem like a mediocre friend because I don't stay in touch, which means I don't always know when you need me, and I'm often unaware when there is something to celebrate. But there are so many people out there who mean more to me than they will ever know, who I think about more than they will ever realize. I hate the telephone (and most forms of technology). I get anxious about social events. But I love my friends, my family, and people in general.

I love traveling. I love discovering old homesteads on a hike and new places on an adventure, and I love walking down a wooded path to the ocean wondering if the waves will be calm or chaotic, and if it will be high or low tide. I will be heartbroken, and then get really angry, if I see that someone has insulted a culture—or damaged a dune. I will be especially heartbroken and self-loathing if I realize *I* have been the inadvertent perpetrator.

I hate confronting people, but I will do it. I don't sleep well if I avoid an important conflict. I don't sleep well if I engage in an important conflict, because I worry about what and how things came across. I am often tired.

I am someone who is always going to struggle on some level. The pull toward the atypical (even as I battle against the whole privileged notion of anything being typical) and the pull of crafting a dramatic plot for myself (even though I sense plot needs to take a back seat to character) creates tension within me. Journeying through different spheres and trying to decide whether they should be respectfully left alone or challenged or connected also makes me tense.

Still, I am increasingly at peace. The world is full of injustice. But there is an army of good out there, and I've met a lot of the soldiers, and I've seen the next generation, and there is *hope*.

I love my husband and our family. I am a wife and a mother and a daughter and a sister. I am someone who derives so much joy from those roles. I want my children in particular to hear me say that I love being their mother. After my own father died, the only condolence that brought me any comfort was a note penned by one of his friends that read, "He enjoyed his life so much more because you were in it." I enjoy my life so much more because my kids are in it. I am so grateful to each of them for sharing their days with me.

I am also *me*, outside any relational contexts. Someone who is finally examining and accepting her own nature, while seeking to improve how it finds expression among others. My goal is to be a better version of my authentic self tomorrow than I am today—and learn how to share the best parts of that self with the world.

WHAT HAVE I LEARNED?

n Robert Fulghum's book *All I Really Need to Know I Learned in Kindergarten*, there is a well-known list of elemental truths that can be applied at every stage of life: "Share everything. Play fair. Don't hit people. And the list goes on."[1]

Like Fulghum, I was taught a lot of things during my kindergarten year. And yes, some of them were valuable lessons I keep having to revisit and relearn.

But others were lies that I keep having to excavate from my own psyche.

I want to remember the truths: Pay attention. Look and listen. Be kind. Be respectful. Work hard, but don't forget time for play and rest. There are people who care about me and about the world.

But I have to excavate the lies. I have to fight to get them out of my mind and to replace them with truths I learned later.

> *Lie*: You cannot trust your own nature.
> *Truth*: I can trust myself.

> *Lie*: The best road map to a good life is right *there* (said as others point to their own trails or sources).
> *Truth*: The concept of a good life is subjective. We can learn a lot from one another's ideas. External input is useful as a resource and out of place as a dictator.

Lie: The playing field is level. People get what they deserve.
Truth: The world is not just. Privilege is real. Awareness and activism are important. So is hope.

Lie: The teacher is the one at the front of the room—or at the front of the congregation.
Truth: There is something to learn from everyone. Anyone you pay attention to can be a teacher.

Lie: There are lots of *yes* or *no* questions that matter. You should raise your hand to indicate your position, without talking to your neighbor.
Truth: Life is not a *yes* or *no* quiz, where you cover your one-time answers until they are collected and graded. Instead, it is an action project. Working with your neighbor is encouraged, and you are allowed to change your answers.

Lie: Repeatedly asking *why* is obnoxious.
Truth: Asking *why* is important. Asking *why not* is important, too.

~

This book began as an exorcism. There were words inside me I had to get out. When those words emerged in the form of a book—specifically a memoir—I sought advice and was told two things: First, make sure the book has arc; then, decide whether to offer it to an audience or a therapist.

If there is a big arc to my character-not-plot-driven story, it is this: I have gone from someone who was at risk of disappearing under the waves to someone who has several flotation devices. I no longer feel like the real me is going to drown under someone else's expectations or within my own angst. I no longer worry that I will not have enough strength to keep myself afloat after meeting everyone else's needs. I am no longer at risk of letting myself go under in some warped attempt to live and die nobly. Instead, I am buoyed by several new things.

I am buoyed by a new understanding of the role of self in spirituality. My nature is a friend, not an enemy. Dying to self is not a noble thing.

I am buoyed by a new acceptance of myself, with all of my odd external and internal juxtapositions. The world is not a puzzle that I need to find my place within. My own psyche is not a puzzle that I will eventually sort and snap into some cohesive, serene scene. It's all messy, and that's OK. It's me.

I am buoyed by faith in a Creator who wants me to be me—and you to be you—and all of us to be good to each other.

I am buoyed by moments of happiness and relaxation, both of which have to be a priority.

I am buoyed by authentic connections, where we all give and receive—and by the willingness to cut ties when something is pulling me under.

I am buoyed by authenticity—mine, yours, and everyone's. I want to make sure there is space for all of us at the water's surface to be ourselves and to breathe.

I am buoyed by a new sense of scale and purpose. Big strokes aren't always needed. There is not a Treasure Island out there I am trying to reach.

And finally, I am buoyed by the realization that I don't have to be in deep or rough seas all the time. I can rest— touch bottom, tread water, or relax on the beach.

~

My second buoy mentioned accepting my own messy form.

I spent so many years trying to figure out where I truly fit (seeking external adhesion). The world seemed like it was full of puzzles that needed pieces, but none felt like exactly the right space for me.

I spent more years trying to force my inner components to fit comfortably together (seeking internal cohesion), but I could never snap my own oddly paired pieces into an organized grid.

So the question became: Could I transform from someone who sought adhesion (asking "Where do I fit?"), then cohesion (asking "How do these parts of me fit together?") to someone who is OK without either? Someone who is OK with the parts of herself that don't seem to fit. Someone who can live with the tension her mix of elements and experiences create—and then learn from the dissonance.

This question is a big deal for me because there are so many juxtapositions and odd pairings in both my psyche and my experience that create tension. In fact, sometimes I feel like my whole life has been a series of elements that are oddly paired.

I am a left-leaning Independent in a family of Republicans. A Southerner at the Northern school. An affluent with ascetic impulses. A Christian who embraces pluralism. A girl raised to be both a tenacious tiger (on the court) and a charming, self-sacrificing, people-pleasing gazelle (everywhere else). I am someone who fits everywhere—and nowhere. Someone who does not know whether to declare a side and burn bridges or see if she can become a bridge. Someone who wants to connect while sitting in a room by herself.

I am an odd fit within many communities.

For so many years, I fought the tension this created. Eventually, I developed decision fatigue. I became tired of trying to choose among different things. I became weary of seeking external adhesion, and I became frustrated trying to develop internal cohesion.

Recently I've begun to wonder if there is a way to celebrate all these elements within myself and my communities without feeling like the tension always has to be ugly.

~

While thinking about all of this, I googled the words "adhesive," "cohesive," and "tension" and found only one nonscientific source that contained them all: a pottery magazine.

It turned out the words were not contained within one article. (Darn it! I was hoping someone would connect the dots for me.) Instead, the words were scattered randomly throughout the magazine, mainly in advertisements.

But as I was abandoning my quest, the magazine's[2] photo of this "Mockingjay Vase" caught my attention.

The blue (left) side of this vase abuts the yellow (right) side of this vase. Just above the open space in the base, there is a seam. Along that seam, blue and yellow tones collide—but they also connect within green tendrils that remind me of gardens and growth. Photo credit to the creator of the vase: Shana Salaff, *Mockingjay Vase*, ceramic, 2013.

I like this Mockingjay Vase because it looks the way I feel—full of elements that are oddly paired—and because it looks the way I *want* to feel—unique and beautiful. The yellows and blues offer something in their own right but also combine to form a green that looks like growth.

I also like this vase because the artist who created it, Shana Salaff, described the process as one involving both refinement and something she calls "playfulness or flow." For her, flow happens when "the critical part of my mind is able to slow down and allow a flexible, responsive energy to overtake precedence or habit." This receptive energy allowed her to engage new ideas. In addition to improving her form on the project at hand, these fresh ideas offered her "incentive to return to the studio for the next round."[3]

Refinement. Playfulness. Flow. Prioritizing flexibility and responsiveness over precedence and habit. Fresh ideas. And incentive to return for another round.

I'll take it.

~

Along with my big arc—from a woman submerged to one buoyed—there are sub-arcs. These character arcs track the way my thinking has changed in several arenas, including:

Thoughts about my own human nature:

Before, I thought: My core is bad.

Then I thought: My core is good, but I need to remove the external baggage that has settled on it.

Currently I think: My nature is a garden. There are native and imported seeds. I can choose what to grow and what to weed.

Thoughts about God:

> *Before, I thought*: I trust what other people and books tell me about God.

> *Then I thought*: I trust what the nudges (of my created self) tell me about God (who created me).

> *Currently I think*: God is revealed in lots of places, including within my nature and within yours. Let's talk.

Thoughts about happiness:

> *Before, I thought*: I have to choose between improving the world and enjoying the world.

> *Then I thought*: I can do good *and* be happy.

> *Currently I think*: I do the most good in the times and spaces when I am happy.

Thoughts about service:

> *Before, I thought*: If I am charitable and of service, it helps them (with resources).

> *Then I thought*: If I am charitable and of service, it helps them (with resources) and me (alleviating guilt and making me feel "good" in both senses of the word).

> *Currently I think*: It is not about being charitable or serving. It is about connecting with people—including

those in different circumstances—and appreciating what everyone in the room has to offer. It is about enjoying time together, respecting each other, and recognizing that we all have something to offer and something we need to receive.

Thoughts about my "self":

> *Before, I thought*: I must deny myself—for you and for God.

> *Then I thought*: I must find myself—for you, for me, and for God.

> *Currently I think*: Growing my authentic self—to the point that the real me is strong enough to survive exposure and large enough to overflow into the world—is the only way I can have authentic connections with you and with my Creator.

Or said in a different way:

> *Before, I thought*: Selflessness is ideal. I will sacrifice myself for others.

> *Then I thought*: This is suicide. I am actually killing my psychological self and the physical me is beginning to suffer also.

> *Currently I think*: The only way to have a true connection with anyone is to know and grow my authentic self to the point it can sustain exposure and interaction.

Thoughts about quitting:

> *Before, I thought*: Finish what you start. Never quit.
>
> *Then I thought*: Don't stick with something you know is a mistake. You will know it's a mistake because it almost kills you.
>
> *Currently I think*: Don't stick with something you know is a mistake. You will know it's a mistake if you listen to and trust your inner voice.

Thoughts about the opinion of an acquaintance:

> *Before, I thought*: It matters what other people think of me.
>
> *Then I thought*: It doesn't matter what other people think of me.
>
> *Currently I think*: Other people aren't thinking about me that much.

Thoughts about the opinions of those close to me:

> *Before, I thought*: I am supposed to be what they tell me.
>
> *Then I thought*: No. And to make the point that I am free of their expectations, I'll be exactly the *opposite* of what they tell me.
>
> *And then I thought*: No, again. There are a lot of external sources (people, expectations, etc.), and defining myself in opposition to them *still* gives them control.

Currently I think: Currently, I *think*. For myself. What a concept. And here is one thing I learned while doing that thinking: External input is useful as a resource and out of place as a dictator.

Thoughts about pace:

Before, I thought: I'm moving at the right pace if my life is full, and my tank is empty.

Then I thought: I'm not moving at all. That's me, collapsed in the passing lane.

Currently I think: I am moving at the right pace if my heart is full, and there is space in my calendar for rejuvenation and connection.

Thoughts about diversity:

Before, I thought: Treat everyone the same. Don't let their race, religion, ethnicity, gender, sexual orientation, etc. influence your association. Be blind to difference.

Then I thought: Acknowledge differences. Celebrate diversity. Fight with those who are marginalized against those who are prejudiced.

Currently I think: Acknowledge prejudice that exists in systems and institutions as well as in individuals, *including myself*. Learn. Educate. Dismantle. Rebuild together.

Thoughts about womanhood:

Before, I thought: Being a female means I must submit, charm, and nurture in some realms, while breaking the glass ceiling in others.

Then I thought: Being a female means whatever the hell I want it to mean.

Currently I think: Being a female means what I want it to mean, for the most part. It also means I belong to a group that has been subjugated in the past and still fights against that. The only way to protect my body, my professional interests, my psyche, and my sisters is to have a heightened awareness of how we are perceived and how we are at risk. I want to be conscious of our increased risk of being stereotyped or harassed or restricted, while also recognizing our tremendous feminine power.

Thoughts about life and its meaning:

Before, I thought: I will figure out life.

Then I thought: Here's what I think. No, here's what I think. No, scratch that, too. Here's what I think.

Currently I think: I will learn forever. Tomorrow I may be embarrassed by what I think today. I have to show myself grace when I look back at my journey (and my journals, including this one). I have to show others grace also.

Thoughts about fit:

> *Before, I thought*: My goal is adhesion. The world is a puzzle, and I need to figure out what space I can fit in and stick with.

> *Then I thought*: I give up on adhesion. I don't fully fit anywhere. Now my goal is cohesion. I am a puzzle. I want the pieces inside me to fit together to create an internal serene scene.

> *Currently I think*: I give up on cohesion, too. I am OK with the parts of myself that don't seem to fit. Now I just want to be someone who can live with—and learn from—the tension her mix of elements and experiences create. I want to appreciate diversity everywhere, including within myself.

~

These are all character arcs, tracking how my thoughts changed over the years. Writing them down allows me to mark the direction of my growth.

While I like being able to trace the trajectory, admitting I had to learn something can be embarrassing. Apologizing for misperceptions, and actions based on those misperceptions, is hard. Still, I have to do it. I didn't know everything. I still don't know everything. I am going to make errors and missteps. I will try to tread lightly to mitigate damage. I will try to repair things I break. I will apologize for my mistakes. And I will try desperately to learn something from all of it.

I do worry sometimes that this practice (and the growth mentality that inspires it) is squashed by modern society. We are making it harder for people to evolve. Opinions are now recorded much more frequently (and more publicly and at a much younger age), and they become defining. Even if folks stand up later and say, "I'm sorry. I've changed my mind," we tend to shame them instead of acknowledging the growth. Yes, we have to hold them accountable. Yes, they need to apologize and make amends. Yes, our priority remains the folks they have harmed—the victims. But it might do all of us some good if we also made time to ask, "What changed your mind?" and then tried to learn something from it.

I am so grateful to the people who could have written me off but instead allowed me to apologize and kept encouraging me to grow.

~

With that growth-goal in mind, I have a few more arcs to consider. These arcs will include more introduction and explanation because they are more complicated. Changing our thinking often is.

I was very young when I first thought: *Following my heart hurts the people I love.* That statement still frequently rings true for me, and I hate it. I have followed my heart into lots of places that have made my loved ones worry, cringe, and ache. I have followed it into this book, and I fear these pages will hurt someone. I'm not sure what to do with that, other than be sensitive and careful and recognize that being true to myself will ultimately allow me to make more authentic connections with people I care about.

Unfortunately, the hurt I have caused is more of a constant than an arc. But my awareness of it and the way I deal with it has shifted a bit.

Thoughts about being true to myself (and worrying it will hurt other people):

Before, I thought: Being true to myself scares and hurts the people I love. I'll find another way.

Then I thought: Not being true to myself is hurting me— first psychologically, then physically. I'll find *my* way.

Currently I think: I'll be true to myself and careful with others. I will communicate my goal of authentic connection.

Thoughts about expanding my narrow vision:

A thought that has consistently resurfaced during my journey is that
my field of vision is too narrow, and I need to expand it. For a while, I
saw medicine as *the* way to serve. I saw Christianity as *the* way to God.
And I was told that *the* way to be a Christian was to be a heterosexual,
Republican, submissive-if-you're-female evangelical who stays on a very
narrow path.

Many times—as a result of both external influence and internal
angst—I thought that I had to live *there* or do *that*; that I had to structure
my family *this* way or raise my children *that* way, only to later realize how
limiting it all was. How prescriptive.

Now I look at the world with all its variety—places with different landscapes and landscapes with different colors and colors with different shades;
seasons of the year, of our lives, or even the variety of seasonings we can
apply to and then ingest from our plates; people with different interests
and instincts and expressions and appearances and feelings and ideas—and
I think, *How did I ever believe that whoever created this wanted us to all be
the same?*

Becoming the person you were made to be—and celebrating as loved
ones become who they were made to be—feels spiritual and important.
And it is impossible to do if the only path allowed is prescribed and narrow. What if we all expanded our individual visions? What if we all worked
together to expand opportunities across the board instead of limiting them
to the privileged? What if we encouraged people to survey the field, find
what personally resonates—and have everyone share what we discover with
each other? What a world *that* could be.

If I could wrestle it into an arc, the development in my thinking might
look like this:

Before, I thought: Your way is right.

Then I thought: My way is right.

Currently I think: There is more than one way.

Thoughts about dichotomies and spectrums:

There have been many moments when I thought, *I have to choose.* Yes or no. In or out. This or that. So many things appear to be dichotomies, but over time I have learned there are very few true dichotomies and a whole lot of spectrums.

There are also phases and seasons (times when you choose *this* and then shift to *that*), but for now I want to focus on spectrums—ideological spectrums in particular.

One spectrum I think about a lot is:

Objective Ideals (External Truth) <---------> Subjective Ideals (Internal Truth)

I no longer accept this as a dichotomy. I do not have to choose between a prescribed theology and my own inner compass. I believe in objective ideals (love, compassion), and I believe in my subjective experience and expression of them. (It does occur to me that this is as much a symbiosis as a spectrum.)

Another spectrum is:

Community Investment <---------> Individual Expression

This one gets complicated. Those who are more conservative prioritize the community in the personal arena ("we are a faith unit, a family unit, here is our creed") and the individual in the political arena (individual rights trump community need, in terms of opposing gun control, mask mandates, and socialism).

Those who are more liberal tend to do the opposite, seeing spirituality as very individualized and personal, while viewing government as one arena where we should gather to address community needs. (This is me.)

My point is that it is not as simple as saying, "I prioritize the community or the individual." Most people do different things in different arenas.

~

Let's take it out of the realm of religion and politics and move into day-to-day family dynamics for a moment. Consider the following question: How do you create a family ethos while encouraging each individual to independently explore?

It is not a theoretical question. It actually manifests in real-time choices. If there is a family event scheduled, what justifies an individual's absence? An invitation from a friend? An unanticipated practice or rehearsal? A pressing need at work? How many of our individual moments do we sacrifice to exist as a family? How much family togetherness do we sacrifice to celebrate individual pursuits? And how do we make sure it's not the same members sacrificing all the time?

As parents, my brother Todd and I seem to be on opposite ends of this spectrum. On a given day, his eight children are more likely to function as a unit, while mine tend to be doing something individually. But we can still learn from each other, and we can slide along that spectrum. My brother and I both exist in one space but value and travel to the opposite frequently.

My unit-oriented brother still wants his children to find individual expression. As an individually oriented parent, I still want my kids to know they are on a team. My brother and I appreciate and learn from each other as we parent.

A few years ago, we were talking while on vacation together. My girls (ages twelve and ten) had invited his eleven-year-old daughter and a few other tween cousins out for ice cream. My brother hesitated; if anyone was going, shouldn't all seventeen cousins (including the littles) go? I wasn't convinced—these were tween-aged girls in a safe town where they could bike independently; what a great opportunity to spread their adolescent wings. After we sorted out the immediate plan, my brother and I debriefed. It turned into a larger conversation about fairness, equality, family identity, and individuality. We didn't try to change each other, but we both learned something. (This is one of many things I love about my younger brother—he really is a thoughtful and respectful, not to mention fun-loving guy.)

During that (pre-COVID) conversation, I heard myself say how rare it was to have dinner with all my children because someone was always at an individual practice or lesson. I resolved to make connecting over family meals more of a priority. My brother heard himself say one of his children had requested a private space in a crowded home to think on occasion and had been denied it—just logistically and spatially impossible. He began thinking more about how he could make that work.

We were learning from someone who tended to think differently, and we were applying the lessons. It *is* possible to value more than one thing.

Both of these are examples of things I have been encouraged to see as dichotomies. I should pick a side. Declare a position.

I personally find the idea of dichotomies very stressful. But to many, they offer comfort. Categorization. Community. Ease. It is so convenient to choose a side and never again have to think. (This infuriates me, particularly when folks present a refusal to revisit or consider nuance a sign of their honorable steadfastness.) So many times I have heard: "I am X, so I believe A, B, and C" (without giving A, B, and C individual consideration) or "Our community is this. Are you in or out?"

Dichotomies simplify things. But that level of simplicity is overrated. And exclusive. And narrow. And harmful. Dichotomies come at an incredibly high price—one I am almost never comfortable paying.

I will attempt to capture that in a thought arc:

Before, I thought: Should I choose this or that?

Then I thought: Maybe I can create a third option . . .

Currently I think: I don't want to be in a box. I don't even want to be stuck in a spot on a spectrum. I'll forfeit categorization (and the appearance of steadfastness) in order to consider things as they come.

Thoughts about parenting:

A section on parenting could turn into its own book; I am not going to write that book here. I am simply going to say that parenting is not easy. It involves nurturing individuality while also instilling values. It involves figuring out when to encourage and when to step back. My arc as a parent has trended from uptight to more relaxed about almost everything.

For me, this parental arc involves increasing levels of self-awareness, relaxation, and grace.

Before, I thought: I won't pile expectations on my family.

Then I thought: Yikes. I avoided some land mines and stepped on others.

Currently I think: It's OK. These amazing kids know I love them and that I will try to correct my mistakes. And we are going to *enjoy* getting to know ourselves and each other within a safe, fun, shared, grace-laden space.

Thoughts about marriage:

Marriage could be another book also. Instead of writing that book, I am going to tell you about something my husband said to me back in 2021, when we were talking about the COVID vaccine.

He qualified for a shot and received it. I was in a later group, so I was eagerly waiting for my turn to be vaccinated. As I waited, my husband remained careful, not wanting to bring the virus home.

There were times, as he declined to attend or engage in certain things, that people from those circles offered me access to a shot before I was eligible. It was well intentioned, but none of the opportunities felt right to me. They were probably on the up-and-up (doses that would go to waste otherwise), but I always wondered: *Why is this shot available to* me—*was it really available to anyone or was this born of privilege?* So my answer was always to please redirect it, and that I would wait my turn. When everyone had access, I would most enthusiastically take the vaccine.

As my decision to wait in line impacted my husband's life and work and peace of mind, he said one of the nicest things anyone has ever said to me. He said, "I want you to know that I really love and admire and *like* the part of you that wants to do things in the way that feels right to you, even when it makes things harder for our family."

That moment will go down as one of my favorites within our marriage. Within my life.

There is so much about me that makes things harder. I know I am not easy to live with.

He loves me anyway. He knows I am really trying.

I finally have the answer to the question I asked earlier: my husband likes *me*.

This amazing man has forgiven me for lashing out during my personal struggles. I have forgiven him for his verbal missteps also. We still have things to work through, but we love each other, respect each other, enjoy each other, and we make a good team. He is my husband: a caring, honorable, fun, hardworking guy who has my respect and admiration. In an arc, that looks like this:

Before, I thought: I found him!

Then I thought: I've lost myself.

Currently I think: Here we both are. Let's follow the first two pieces of advice from that wedding reading. We'll "work at our marriage." We'll "play at our marriage." We will make the effort. Enjoy the laughter. Acknowledge the mistakes. Work through the frustration. We will show grace, consideration, and appreciation. We will rinse and repeat.

~

I have four thoughts about life's "big" moments:

1. *Big moments are often disguised as very small moments.*

As an adult, I have to remind myself that small moments can be a very big deal. But as children, we all knew it. Most of us can recall—even decades later—a small act of kindness (or malice) that mattered. And it's nice to think we could embody that small act of kindness for almost anyone, in an easy outreach, on any given day.

To illustrate, consider the random Tuesday when a young child farted at the bus stop near my school. Unfortunately, it was loud and immediately drew the attention of the entire group. I knew this child well. This was not a child who would think this was funny. This was a not a child who would wear whatever fart-associated-nickname that was coming with pride. This was a child who would never want to ride the bus again and was currently thinking, *I would like to crawl into that nearby snake hole* and die. Nearby, there was an adult who had devoted countless hours to this child—had given this child time, energy, support, outreach, and love. But later, the child would say to that adult, "I think the nicest thing you ever did for me was claiming that fart at the bus stop."

A fart no one there that day really cared about—except for this young individual and a grown-up who loved them. An adult who became a hero because they took a small action that indicated big love for a child.

~

2. *Big moments are not always actions. They are not always plot points. Sometimes the biggest moments are seemingly subtle shifts in character or perception.*

This realization has been life altering for me.

I have always been a storyteller—and I have wanted my own actual life story to be interesting. This desire for plot points has served me well so far. It has made me brave. I have been willing to try things I genuinely wanted to do because whatever didn't work out would still make a good story.

But recently, this line of thinking has become problematic. It has made me dissatisfied with what is actually a very good life. I have been asking "what's next?" while thinking about plot points. I want to *do* something. When combined with midlife angst and the desire to enact some "significant" good, this plot-seeking becomes dangerous. It puts everything at risk. I do not mind risk. But risk for the sake of a narrative or risk born of angst or risk due to a warped idea of "big = significant" is unnecessary—maybe even dumb.

For that reason, it is life altering, perhaps lifesaving, for me to realize that "big" happens in a lot of ways.

Some of the biggest moments in my life occurred while I was in quiet conversation and heard something that made me think differently. Some of the biggest shifts in my life were not shifts in circumstance or location or plans. They were shifts in perception. For example:

> It was big when I read that Henry James quote during high school and thought: *I don't have to please everyone— and there are some people I shouldn't please.*

> It was big when my mother pointed out that while I considered myself a free-thinking independent, I was actually oppositional—which meant that external forces were still charting my course.

It was big when Jim helped me get comfortable with discomfort, enabling me to welcome a female minister in a
place I had been taught to reserve for men. That moment
taught me that psychological comfort is not as important
as deconstructing privileged and discriminatory systems.
Since growth is often uncomfortable, being uncomfortable could mean you are on the right course.

It was big when I heard Laura say, "Why is it that in all
these movies the ultimate symbol of a Southern woman's
strength is to *endure*? Preferably in *silence*? I'm *sick* of it.
Why can't it be strength to buck it all and break free?"

It was big when I heard that exterminator in Kensington
vow, in such animated fashion, to battle our bugs. When
I saw chins, eyes, and hopes lift. When I felt my own bur-
dens lift as I watched him and realized, *I don't have to be
a doctor to serve.*

It was big when I realized, in that North Carolina classroom, that my attempts to be color-blind were harming
my students.

It was big when I realized, in that Brookline classroom,
that discrimination is not just individual but institutionalized. When I discovered we must fight it on a systemic
level, and—because we have been socialized into a racist
system—also fight it within ourselves.

It was big when I realized that after a lifetime of running
from expectations, I was pouring them onto my husband
and children. Not in the same way, and not in as many

arenas, but still. It was big when I realized the people I love are not me, and that is a good thing. We can support and celebrate each other.

It was big when Denise said, "Your children are strong. They can handle this. Let them exercise those caregiving muscles." It was big when I realized shielding my kids might do more damage than good.

It was big when I read Glennon Doyle's words in *Untamed* and recognized that selflessness is not an ideal. It was big when I finally understood that being devoid of self means I cannot offer myself generously or forge authentic connections.

It was big when I began celebrating my kids for the amazing individuals they are and began respecting their processes as well as their persons. It was big when I realized this was relationship altering—and perhaps relationship saving.

It was big when I heard my own inner voice say, *It is OK to relax.*

These are big moments. They are seismic shifts that occurred under the surface during days when I had nothing out of the ordinary on the agenda—days when I was in class, or at work, or walking out of a movie, or reading a book, or standing in my own home. These are moments that illustrate how character development does not require chucking it all in a dramatic plot twist. These are moments that are fairly equally divided between me being on the go and sitting completely still.

I need to remember these moments—how they subtly altered so much—and realize that their power delivers this message: To have a big impact, I don't need to make a big plot-centered move. I just need to have an open mind and keep an open dialogue with people who think differently. I need to share how I think and perceive—and listen to how other people think and perceive—and hope we all grow.

I don't have to upend my whole existence in order to have a life-altering, even world-altering, revolution.

~

Thinking about all of this reminds me of the essay that Princeton recruit wrote—the one my college coach told me about as we drove to the airport. The assignment was to describe the most important decision she would ever make. The writer argued that while it was tempting to detail big decisions about college, career, and spouse (things she described as significant but reversible), she saw more power in the small choices we make during regular days.

Everyday choices.

When I am walking down the street and I encounter someone who looks different from me, and I must choose whether to allow my socialized reflexes to kick in, or to instead acknowledge and fight any prejudice I have internalized.

Or when I am working my way through a list of tasks or errands, and I experience a small nudge that tells me to abandon my agenda and instead "go do this" or "stop and pay attention."

It is in those moments that I need to remember the next lesson—lesson number 3—about big things.

~

3. *I have learned that small nudges can be a big deal.*

I don't always pay attention to—or allow myself to be moved by—the small nudge. But when I remember to listen and respond, it matters.

One day I was out for a walk when I saw a group of eight people strolling together: five adults and three young children. I had never met any of them, and they were all clearly in motion. Still, I had the strangest feeling that I should interrupt their activity and ask if they wanted me to take their picture with my phone. I approached them, offered, and they agreed. One of them gave me her email address so I could send her the photo.

A few days after I sent the photo, I received her emailed reply. The very first line said,

> Hello Kristi,
> You had no way of knowing how much your photo means to us.

She then proceeded to tell me about the group I had captured in the snapshot. The walk had occurred during a few days the family was gathered to grieve two major events: a recent death of one family member and a frightening new diagnosis for another. She told me the photo captured a moment when they were all contemplating how "precarious life can be," confronting the idea that there might not be many walks with this group in the future, and recognizing that it was "just so good to be all together." She then wrote that, in the midst of that, "you came along and captured the moment for us." She ended her email with a quote and an expression of gratitude, writing:

> "Sometimes someone says (does) something really small, and it just fits right into this empty place in your heart."
> —from the television show *My So-Called Life*.
> I just wanted to say thank you from the bottom of my heart for taking the time to snap that picture.

Nudges. Small acts. You just never know.

~

There are other times when I ignore nudges. For twenty years, I have ignored the nudge to send Wendy Kopp an email. For *two decades* this email has been in the back of my mind. Wendy is the founder of Teach For America. While working with TFA, I had an idea about something the organization could offer its schools. The idea was simple enough to summarize in one line, but its inspiration and implications were complex enough that I seriously considered it as a dissertation topic. During that stretch I thought, *I should email Wendy and see how she would feel about me studying the why and how of this idea.* After deciding to focus on a different topic for my dissertation I thought, *I should still email Wendy, just to toss the idea out there in case someone else wants to consider it.*

I have never sent that email, even though I think about it several times each year and every time someone asks me about Teach For America.

I have a long list of excuses for not sending that note. I have not sent it because I am busy. Because someone else probably already had the idea. Because the email would probably go to her spam anyway. Because it is a bit risky—the idea is just edgy enough that it could offend this brilliant person who has helped so many. Because who am I to email Wendy Kopp? Because it's a bit embarrassing to admit that I have now waited twenty years to say something.

Also, it's just an email. What difference could it possibly make?

I don't know. But here's the thing: that part is not up to me. My part is sending the email. Listening to the nudge. Performing a small action.

Performing an action because it feels right. Without worrying about whether it is big enough to matter. Without worrying about if someone will think it's silly or small. Because when I pay attention to that inner voice—when I honor that inner voice—that voice grows stronger. And that's a big thing, no matter what else happens.

Darn it! I have to go send a really awkward email.

~

These three arcs have helped me reframe what constitutes a "big" moment.

I have learned that I need to stop looking for ways to have a big impact. I have to stop worrying about scale. Moments that seem small—quick interactions at the grocery store, tiny nudges to ask a question or send a note—really do matter. Sometimes they matter because they allow me to honor or grow my inner voice. Sometimes they matter because they help someone else. Sometimes they matter because once our tiny loaves and fish are out there, they multiply in ways we never anticipate. Regardless, they matter. No true or kind act is too small.

I have learned I need to stop striving for a big adventure. Mine can be a character-driven life—with some adventure thrown in because I enjoy it, not because I want plot points to define me.

Big shifts are not always alterations of course. Sometimes they are shifts in perception, opening your mind to a new point of view right where you are.

I have learned that some of my biggest moments occurred when I paid attention to voices that would have been easy to overlook. Voices that called from marginalized communities. Voices that bounced off my closed mind. My own inner voice that took me decades to trust.

Mother Teresa once said, "Not all of us can do great things. But we can do small things with great love." With all due respect to that amazing lady, I think we *can* all do great things. And sometimes doing a small thing with great love is exactly the way to make it happen.

～

4. *It only takes twenty seconds to make a Big Move, and there are two ways to do it.*

In the movie *We Bought a Zoo* (based on a true story), the character Benjamin Mee says, "Sometimes all you need is twenty seconds of insane

courage, just literally twenty seconds of embarrassing bravery, and I promise you something great will come of it."[4]

I loved the idea: Twenty seconds of insane courage. To say yes to something. To say no to something. To start something.

But as I am typing this, it occurs to me that—yet again—I am exclusively focused on plot. I want to know what we are going to *do* during
those twenty seconds. Benjamin Mee bought a zoo! I want to match that
energy. I am ready to *move*.

But—if I am invested in not just my plot, but my character—it might
be important to take twenty seconds while *stopped*. What if instead of
opening our throttles (twenty seconds of going for something new), we sat
still and opened our minds (twenty seconds with a new thought)?

I remember vividly certain points in my life when I was afraid to open
my mind, for so many reasons.

In the realm of religion, I was afraid of actual hellfire.

In several romantic relationships, I was afraid to contemplate ending
it because I could lose the good along with the maybe-not-good-enough.

In many arenas, I was, and am, afraid of admitting I have wasted energy,
resources, and time.

In too many spaces, I have been afraid of admitting that I had a closed
mind.

But what if, in each of those arenas, I faced those fears? What if I took
twenty seconds to sit with my most scary thought? What if—in religious,
relationship, and all other arenas—I simply sat with the following ideas:

"There are things about this belief system that don't ring true for me."

"This relationship is not right."

"This career or path or space is not working anymore."

"I could be *wrong*."

Brandon Steiner, author of the book *You Gotta Have Balls* (a play on
words, since his career was in sports marketing—I still see you, ladies),
talked about the movie's courage quote in an article. He wrote that the idea
of twenty seconds is valuable because "starting these things is the tough

part; once you're *in them*, they might still prove difficult, but the *fear* melts away. And that makes all the difference."[5]

I tend to think fear comes in waves rather than meltable icebergs, but I do think he is correct about the first twenty seconds being the hardest. Admitting there is another way to think about something is difficult. There is security in your belief system, your relationships, your path, and your confidence. They are psychological support structures, and when you crack them open to consider their validity, you risk a lot of things crashing down. There is shame to be overcome when you realize you might have been wrong.

But there are rewards. Maybe you will end up reinforcing something. Or maybe you'll end up replacing it with something stronger. Maybe you'll realize those support structures were actually bars and that being surrounded by the rubble of a prison is better than living within it.

Either way, the twenty seconds are well spent.

~

I want to give an example of what twenty seconds of thought might look like.

In 2020, just after the death of George Floyd, we took the kids to a Black Lives Matter rally. We put a sign in our yard. We attended a BLM march. I wanted to be a part of the *action*.

Meanwhile, my friend Melanie opened her eyes and her mind. She paid attention. She started thinking, and reflecting, and looking at her own life.

And she noticed something. Specifically, she noticed that a group we both belong to—a group that discusses different books, podcasts, ideas, and service opportunities; a group that is technically open to everyone but is currently 100 percent comprised of White middle-aged females—was spending the vast majority of our time focusing on media authored by White women. There was the occasional male author (Rob Bell) or Black voice (an Oprah podcast), but we were tuned into White female authors for the absolute bulk of our time.

Melanie sat with this thought for a bit and asked herself what it meant. And she made the decision to open her mind to the possibility that we—a group of self-proclaimed progressive women—were not as progressive as we thought. And maybe there was a reason our group looked the way it did.

The night Melanie brought it up to the group, we were all embarrassed. But not a single person defended it. No one. It might be the only time our chatty crew was completely silent. For about twenty seconds. Until some-one said, "You are absolutely right."

In that twenty seconds of silence, our minds cracked open.

There was, and is still, a lot to be done. But that first twenty seconds of sitting with it—of not becoming defensive, of staying open even though the idea felt awful, of believing "this feeling can teach us something if we don't fight it"—those twenty seconds *mattered*. Opening the throttle matters, too. It's not either-or. But sometimes we have to start with opening our *minds*.

~

I can attempt to capture those four thoughts about life's big moments in an arc:

> *Before, I thought*: I want to have a big impact, go on big adventures, and seize the big moments. To make a big dif-ference, I need to live a big life.

> *Then I thought*: I am running out of time to have this big life. I need to get some plot points happening now.

> *Currently I think*: Scale is deceptive. Moments that seem small (quick encounters), adjustments that seem small (seeking a new perspective), and muted voices that are hard to hear (from marginalized communities or from within yourself) are so incredibly important. Character

development doesn't require big plot points as much as it requires paying attention and keeping an open mind.

Thoughts about Me Too, conversations, and cancellations:

A man in my own life—a man for whom I have great respect and who has proven himself an ally to women in the workplace and beyond (let's call him Bill)—brought up actor Matt Damon's comments about the Me Too movement specifically to share with me how much he agreed with them.

Damon—who later apologized for the 2017 remarks—had said that while it was "wonderful that women are feeling empowered to tell their stories," it was also important to recognize there is a "spectrum of behavior." He specifically stated that "there's a difference between, you know, patting someone on the butt, and rape or child molestation."[6] His point was that while we should eradicate them both, we should not conflate them.

When Bill said this to me in a tone of celebration and relief—someone had finally said what Bill was thinking—I was triggered, but calm. The eerie kind of calm. The kind of calm that occurs when you know there's a shark in the water, but it has not yet broken the surface.

Where does Bill think my Me Too moments fall on the spectrum?

If you don't count all the times I have changed my running paths or travel plans because my gender puts me at greater risk, or all the times I have had to work harder for respect (on a basketball court or at a professional table), or all the expectations I have to navigate and roles I am assumed to occupy because I have breasts and a vagina, then we can just focus on two Me Too moments I detailed earlier.

Both occurred at times in my life when I was absolutely at my most hopeful—when I was thrilled to be thinking, *I am standing on a launching pad testing my wings, and I am going to fly*—and instead of flying, in both of those moments I was brought crashing down and made to stop thinking about my aspirations and start thinking about my body. Because that is where the nearest man's attention was focused.

It happened at my very first precollege gathering, when I was poised to fly from my hometown. When a male pinned me down, laughed at my struggle, and tainted my hopes for college with fear.

It happened during my very first solo international experience, when I was poised to leave the peer pod and engage the world as an independent agent. Until a professor stepped in, began rubbing my arms while discussing his red-blooded maleness, and sent me fleeing back to the pod.

I was not raped. Whether I was molested or not depends on which definition of the word you use. But in each moment, I was reduced to what my body could offer. And each time, a bit more light faded from my eyes.

What did I say to Bill in that moment?

Well, I asked him about his daughter. I asked him if he would rather her spirit and light die because of a thousand paper cuts or because of one traumatic event. And I pointed out that in either instance, her spirit and light could absolutely die.

I asked Bill to imagine his daughter working for years in a career she was passionate about. Learning from mentors. Overcoming hurdles. Generating ideas. Working incredibly hard to earn respect and advance. And then having a moment in a professional setting where a colleague (to use Damon's example) puts his hand on her butt.

I asked him to imagine what would go through her mind in that moment. And I told him what would go through mine. That hand-on-the-butt moment would call my entire experience into question. Did I actually spend all those years being heard and appreciated and respected and valued for the ideas and effort I brought to the table—or was I being "enjoyed" on a level I never wanted or realized? Was I being mentored or was I being *groomed*? That positive feedback I valued—was it authentic, or part of something ugly? I thought I was one thing in this setting. Now I am not sure.

Those moments on the so-called less traumatic end of the spectrum shake a lot of foundations, stop a lot of momentum, and snuff out a lot of very vibrant lights. A seemingly small moment can have a large impact on the trajectory of a life. And when you are dealing with dozens of those moments every month, it is very hard to fly.

Bill was stunned. In his mind, that hand-on-the-butt moment would have been an isolated incident. Just a "moment of weakness on the man's part," he called it. Not something that should call everything else into question within a woman's mind.

But the idea of that light in his daughter's eyes fading? It upset him. The idea that she would wonder about everything prior? It upset him. The idea that she might be continually distracted from her flight plan? It upset him.

Bill thanked me for talking with him and said it had opened his eyes.

The conversation opened my eyes also. To the possibility that while those moments do call everything into question for me, maybe some of those questions have different answers than I thought. Maybe—am I still allowed to hope this?—just maybe some of what I thought were inspirational interactions actually were. Maybe I wasn't being groomed the entire time.

I think Bill and I helped each other. And when he told me, weeks later, that he really appreciated being able to talk to someone who would engage instead of writing him off, I told him I valued the conversation also.

There have been so many of those conversations on other topics where I am in Bill's position: a position of power that I only begin to recognize through dialogue. A position of gratitude when someone is willing to allow me some missteps while I learn as we talk.

There are two arcs here to consider.

First, with regard to my wings:

> *Before, I thought*: Here are my wings.

> *Then I thought*: Wait. I was focused on my wings. Why is someone talking about other parts of my body?

Currently I think: My launching pad is going to have some ground rules. People allowed near it are going to respect them. My flights are delayed, not canceled.

And then, with regard to conversations and cancel culture:

Before, I thought: It is not my job to educate privileged people who have distracted and harmed me.

Then I thought: Sometimes it's me in a position of privilege. Sometimes it's me who distracts and harms. I am so sorry.

Currently I think: Whether to cancel or converse is a complicated choice. I appreciate those who have allowed me to learn and grow after I commit offenses. I try to extend the same grace to those who offend out of ignorance and show a genuine interest in growth. I also appreciate those who have been distracted and harmed and simply cannot engage with ignorance anymore. When I can, I will work on your behalf. When I cannot, I will appreciate those who work on mine.

∼

Thoughts about how to make a difference:

I have learned there are lots of ways to make a difference.

Sometimes you have to blow things up. Sometimes you have to make one simple statement. Sometimes you have to stop talking and open your mind.

I still struggle with which method different situations require.

I mentioned that I dated a mixed-race man with brown skin—Malcolm—for several years in college and that he sometimes dealt with prejudice. On one such occasion, a store owner trailed him, afraid he would steal something. I was not there, but I heard the story. Here is how my boyfriend handled it: He approached the store owner, said he knew he was being profiled, and extended an invitation. He said something like: "The fact that you are keeping a close eye on me makes me think you must have had some trouble in your past with young, Black males. I am sorry about that. I would like to change your impression of us. Can I treat you to lunch?"

The stunned shop owner accepted. Over that first lunch, they swapped stories: problems the man had experienced in his store, problems my boyfriend had experienced being profiled. And then other stories—the disconnect between townies and students; the connection when they discovered a mutual love of jazz.

When I met Malcolm, over a year later, he had another lunch scheduled with this guy.

Would that happen today? A private, extended conversation with someone who had demonstrated such prejudice? I don't know. I think if it were now, and with different individuals, we would be more likely to hear about it on social media. Maybe accompanied by a call to boycott the business and a hope that the video would go viral. And I want to emphasize that there are absolutely times for that, especially when someone doesn't feel safe during an individual encounter or when they become overwhelmed with the pervasive and institutional nature of the problem.

But there are also times to talk.

Many years ago, I was visiting an elementary school PE class. I was there as a guest during "Bring someone to PE!" week. I was focused on the child who had invited me, smiling at the teacher who had opened his door to me, and appreciative of the experience as a whole.

Until we began playing a game called Captain's Deck.

It was a fun game at first, kind of like Simon Says. The teacher was the captain, and we modeled different motions as he called out orders. We "swabbed the deck" and "walked the plank," and when he yelled "Captain is coming!" we saluted—frozen in that sign of respect and (this was an important part of the game) intentionally ignoring all other orders until he specifically let us know we were "at ease."

This captain demanded *respect*. Anytime someone did the wrong motion (or any motion at all while they were supposed to be saluting the captain), they were out.

I had the best time. I swabbed the deck, walked the plank, and saluted that captain with all my might.

And then the teacher yelled out, "Captain's wife!"

This was a new order. The elementary school kids had to show their adult guests the motions, and those kids were happy to comply.

When the teacher yelled, "Captain's wife," that same group of eight-year-olds who had saluted the captain (and maintained that salute at all costs) modeled a woman by doing an en-masse, high-pitched, mock-air-heady-giggle while pretending to shimmy long hair back over each shoulder.

Hee-hee-hee. Hair flip. *Giggle.* Shimmy.

And after the children modeled it for us, the adults joined in.

I have an iPhone, and I know how to use it, and I am confident that if I had videoed the class and captioned it in a charged way, I could have created enough fuss that the teacher resigned or got fired. But why?

My goal is not to shame someone. My goal is to improve the situation and improve the culture for the next generation. And I genuinely believed it had never occurred to this teacher that these representations were sending the dangerous message that an assumed-to-be male captain was worthy of respect and that his female wife was an airhead to be mocked. And that it was awful to reinforce these ideas in a class specifically designed to promote healthy practices surrounding our bodies.

It took one email to point out the perspective, and one conversation to have it monitored by a trusted administrator in the building—someone I believed could evaluate and track things better than I could, and better than an outraged community would. Do I worry that I didn't do enough?

That this particular element of the game is still being played in gyms across the country? Yes, I do.

So, I will address it here: If this is an element of the game in your own PE class, please stop incorporating it. And tell your students why you have stopped incorporating it. Designate a different child each time to be the captain—and actually have the kids turn and salute that classmate when you yell, "Captain is coming!" And make sure that captain is a female student at least 50 percent of the time.

Here is my arc for this section:

> *Before, I thought*: I have to blow things up to make a difference.

> *Then I thought*: Not necessarily . . .

> *Currently I think*: Different approaches are called for at different times.

~

Thoughts about my insular world:

When Melanie challenged our group to take stock of its own psyche and spaces, we all realized that voices were missing from our group, our communities, and our minds. She suggested we begin listening to a more diverse array of voices—everywhere, including in that very space, right then—as we selected the book to read for our next session. "Any ideas?" she asked. "Yes," our friend Jen responded. "Have you heard of Austin Channing Brown?"

At the time, I hadn't. I had been living in a predominantly White suburban neighborhood (but it's ok because there are BLM signs on every street!) and avoiding social media (but it's good! I am present instead of on my phone!), while never fully realizing that being *physically insulated* and *digitally absent* meant I would only encounter folks who shared my vantage point.

Enter Austin Channing Brown.

In her book, *I'm Still Here: Black Dignity in a World Made for Whiteness*, she asks us to prioritize justice over comfort. She points out we are "more worried about being called racist" than about whether our actions are racist or harmful. And she pointedly asks, "What are you going to do differently?"[7]

I encourage you to read her book, and if you look like me, please let it be a gateway instead of a token representation on an otherwise White shelf. Let her introduce you to the world of authors who do not look like you and do not experience the world the way you do.

Also, let her words inspire some authentic self-exploration. After reading her book, I continued my self-exploration by reading *White Fragility* and was finally able to admit (in general, as well as on my illustrated identity garden) that I am "problematic." We are socialized into a racist system, which means we have racist tendencies. I have to acknowledge mine in order to fight them, and I am making a commitment to doing both. (Also, to illustrate how my own wheels still spin as I navigate this road, I will confess here that it was only while editing this text that I realized I went straight from a line about diversifying our bookshelves into recommending a book by a White author. I do think it is an important and powerful read—thank you, Ms. DiAngelo—and I am leaving the text here intact because it accurately records what books I read when. Still, I need to expand both my self-awareness and my reading list. I need to hear directly from—and I want to support—Black authors. To that end, *Me and White Supremacy* by Layla F. Saad is the next book on my list.)

Finally, with all that in mind, I do know the last thing the world needs is me centering myself—a White woman—in a discussion of race. But Brown suggests I take responsibility. So I am trying to do that here: I know I am prejudiced. I know I am part of a systemic problem. I know

I need to open my mind and listen. It's a start for me—for all of us—to acknowledge it, even if we don't always know what to do with that knowledge right away. Even if our wheels sometimes spin. Recognizing our own complicity matters. We need to learn more now, so we can do better going forward.

To summarize all of that in an arc:

> *Before, I thought*: To be present and mindful, I must focus on those around me and limit my consumption of social media.

> *Then I thought*: There is a problem. I am physically insulated and digitally absent, so I tend to encounter people who look like me. It is limiting my perspectives in harmful ways.

> *Currently I think*: I have to connect. Exploring NAACP-recognized resources is a good place to start. Buying these and other resources from Black-owned businesses is a good place to start. Becoming someone who recognizes her own complicity and sees the pain it inflicts is a hard, but important, place to start. I trust what I learn to guide me from there.

~

Thoughts about vantage points and the blinders of privilege:

Melanie's challenge to our women's group came during a global pandemic, when we were meeting on a Zoom call due to concerns about COVID. As the pandemic threatened not only the health of our members, but also their jobs, their children, and their melting ice floes of discretionary time, attendance in the group declined. We had been challenged to throw open our doors right at the moment when the world was most hesitant to enter into physical spaces. We wanted to grow. Instead, our membership shrank.

Still, our self-awareness has grown. Our minds have opened. We are working on ourselves and attempting to engage outside ourselves.

I am taking the same steps as an individual, while also acknowledging that they are baby steps.

One of my first baby steps toward expanding my circle was the intentional expansion of my reading list—learning from a diverse array of authors. During my pandemic isolation and 5 a.m. to 7 a.m. writing sessions, these are the folks who spoke to me. They became part of my COVID pod (even if they didn't know it), as I met them each day in their memoirs.

For example, it was Elaine Welteroth who visited me, in the form of her NAACP-award-winning book *More than Enough* and forced me to admit something embarrassing. Here it is: When the Black Lives Matter movement began gaining more momentum in 2020, there was part of me that thought, *Finally! Everyone* else *is waking up. At last,* their *eyes will be open.*

I didn't say it out loud. But I thought it. In my mind, I had already switched vantage points. What a relief! At least *that* part, expanding my vision, was done.

So I was shocked when Melanie pointed out things I was not seeing in my own "awakened" sphere and when Jen reminded me there was more to learn. I was humbled when Austin Channing Brown taught me through her book and her interview. And I was reminded to stay humble when Elaine Welteroth explained that the work of seeing things from a new vantage point is *never* done, writing that,

> "wokeness" doesn't work like a light switch. You don't just turn it on and *boom*, "You're woke!" Instead, it is a process of learning, listening, stripping away the blinders that privilege puts on.[8]

It's not a dichotomy! We are not awake or asleep. Our brand of impaired vision requires peeling away layer upon layer of blinders—not turning on light bulbs. Thank you, Ms. Welteroth. And thank you for crediting DeRay McKesson for also teaching that lesson, because it has inspired me to add his book to my reading list as well. I am sure he has another vantage point from which I can learn.

My arc for this idea reveals an ongoing exploration.

> *Before, I thought*: Everything looks good from here.

> *Then I thought*: Oh. Wait. *Now* my eyes are open. I see it. I wish everyone else could, too.

> *Currently I think*: I don't see everything—and pretending I do is obnoxious. The truth is, I will *never* see everything. But I can keep trying. I can keep working to peel away the blinders of privilege. I can keep making an effort to look harder, listen more, and—with deeper humility—*learn*.

~

Thoughts about activism and age:

The hope is that this learning will eventually guide me toward informed action, which means I need to think about activists.

The empathic and do-something parts of my nature steer me toward being an activist. My aversion to conflict hinders this ambition. And my upbringing directed me away from it completely. As a child, I was given a long list of what "ladies" were supposed to do. "Smooth over social situations" was near the top. "Attend rallies" was nowhere on it.

In high school I was inspired by environmental activists. The impact was immediate (when I cofounded several environmental programs as an eleventh grader), consistent (continuing in college), and remains today (through our family nonprofit).

In Kensington, a requirement of my Catholic Worker program was attending a weekly demonstration with activists. This meant every seventh day, I was holding up a social justice sign at a tiny gathering in the inner city. I admired the two women who were often the only other people there—showing up consistently for their community in every possible way.

In Boston, my students' end-of-year projects took me into all sorts of activist settings as an educator. I chaperoned them during Walk for Hunger parades, edited their letters to congressmen, and escorted them as they photographed things in their community that needed attention. Teenagers are incredibly powerful activists.

My husband appreciates activists also; we have this in common. Still, there was a funny family moment when he wondered if I had perhaps overextended my approval. We were in the kitchen, where our three-year-old was throwing a bona fide tantrum about something that was meaningful to her. Perhaps she was horrified that she was being forced to nap; I don't remember. But whatever it was, she was absolutely and expressively enraged. As she stomped and flopped and wailed, I turned to my husband and said, "Well, she's passionate. Can't you just picture her as an adult? I mean, if she's an environmentalist, she's going to be the one who chains herself to a tree and explains why she's done it with a bullhorn."

"Yes," my husband agreed. "And part of our current problem is that you admire that."

I grinned. He was right. I like activists.

~

I have now spent two days searching for a quote I should have filed more carefully. I cannot find it, and the internet is not helping, so I am hoping my memory can do it justice.

It was written by an older woman who was responding to an article. She talked about how she was becoming an activist as she aged. Her words struck me because I have spent so much of my life working with youth activists. In a world full of adult back-and-forth, these young voices stand out. I hope our youth will keep talking. They will certainly get my attention.

This woman's voice got my attention, too. She was older than me. Her kids were grown. Her career had ended. She talked about how much of a juggle it had all been. How consuming it all was for people of my working and child-rearing age.

But she was past that. She was retired from her job. While her daughters mothered, she grandmothered. And while she was still busy, for the first time in a long time she had spare time. She said something like, "I'm old. I look old. I go to the doctor for increasingly intimidating ailments. But I've decided that I'm going to use my remaining time to *fight*."

I got the impression she would not be fighting in any loud, long marches; her voice and body were not up for that. But she talked about how effective she felt hobbling up to rallies and planting herself, with the mentality of "I need to sit, so I'm going to sit here where I can be counted." She said she felt very powerful when the opposition looked at her, and she knew they were thinking, *What do we have to promise to get her out of here?* She said that she imagined them being afraid of the hell it would raise if she died mid-rally: No one wanted her dying on their stoop, and the police certainly didn't want her to die in custody.

I so want to be this woman when I grow up.

And I appreciate her now. She makes me feel like my power might grow—even as glossy magazines tell me it will fade. She gives me something to look forward to. Maybe *I* will be the one to chain myself to a tree and yell through the bullhorn. And someone will say, "Look at that big voice coming out of that little old lady using that tree branch as a chair."

So, in the realm of activism:

Before, I thought: Adults have the power.

Then I thought: Wow. Those kids' voices are so powerful.

Currently I think: We can wield power at every age.

~

I have spent decades thinking about how I will measure my life.

Here's my current answer: I will *not* measure my life by how depleted I am. Sacrifices, angst, poverty, exhaustion, and illness are not badges of honor. And I will *not* measure my life by how full I am. Achievement, accolades, and accumulation (of money, experience, or anything else) are not the goal.

I have considered carefully whether I want to measure my life at all. My measuring stick has done a lot of damage over the years. I am weary of measures. I have been hurt by measures. I have hurt others with measures. And I believe in giving and receiving grace, which makes measures fairly meaningless anyway.

But—after all this time and all these pages—I know myself. And I know that near the end of my life, I am going to have a moment where I really wonder—and it really matters—whether I've led a good life and been a good person. That means I feel a personal need to figure out what my version of "good" looks like and how to move toward it.

~

I have decided that, for me, "good" will mean "attentive." Attentive means to notice, to care for, and (according to the *OED*) to "stretch toward." If I can spend my life noticing, caring, and stretching—if I can be consistently attentive through a thoughtful process that nurtures positive growth— then I'll consider it a good life.

Here are my two final arcs to help me monitor if I am leading a "good" life: if I am actually paying attention to my true self and to others.

I will know I am paying attention (noticing, caring, and stretching toward) my authentic self if I can:

Reject the idea that my nature is bad.

Embrace who I am.

Grow as a person (nurturing my self, my interests, my ideas, and my character).

If I do these well, I will live an authentic and good life. I will be able to understand, care for, and enjoy my true self. This will honor me. It will honor my Creator. And it will enable me to *attend* to others.

I will know I am paying attention (noticing, caring, and stretching toward) others if I can:

Reject the idea that difference is threatening.

Embrace other people and communities for who they truly are.

Grow as an ally and friend (nurturing individuals, relationships, and causes).

If I do these well, I will live a connective and good life—able to understand, care for, and enjoy relationships with people and entities outside myself.

~

Finally, when there are competing demands for my attention—when there are times I cannot give myself and others the attention I would like—I will do the following things:

I will acknowledge the difficulty. It is hard to feel pulled in different directions.

I will reject the dichotomy. There is not a stark line between me and the world. Focusing on myself for a while prepares me to authentically connect with others. Focusing on others for a while honors the caring, connected part of myself.

I will make the best choice I can in the moment, without relying on— or feeling I am setting—a precedent.

I will set boundaries. Nothing gets all of me.

And most importantly, I will show myself *grace*.

WHAT CAN I OFFER?

I mentioned receiving two pieces of advice about writing a memoir.

The first was to figure out the arc. I have tried to do that.

The second was to decide whether to share it with a therapist or an audience. Well, this is one of those dichotomies I don't understand. If the obstacles of time and money are surmountable, why not both?

Janet Mock once said,

> I believe that telling our stories, first to ourselves and then to one another and the world, is a revolutionary act. It is an act that can be met with hostility, exclusion, and violence. It can also lead to love, understanding, transcendence, and community. I hope that my being real with you will help empower you to step into who you are and encourage you to share yourself with those around you.[1]

My story is different from Janet Mock's. She is a writer and director, as well as a mixed-raced, transgender woman. I do not pretend to have faced even a minuscule portion of the hurdles she has faced—or continues to face. But I really do believe that all of us struggle on some level with authenticity and with connection.

I look back now and think, *How on earth did I buy into the idea that there was only one acceptable path for me, and that someone else should dictate it?*

It took me—a strong, stubborn, independent, affluent citizen in a free society—decades to decide it was OK to do things that are ridiculously acceptable: vote the way I think, write the words I believe, travel where I am nudged, and stand in a classroom and teach.

The effort it required to say, "I will not be an exclusionary, evangelical, submissive, ultraconservative, professional proxy" almost destroyed me.

And then—once I discovered an identity and career I loved—I allowed life to bury it. It took another near-death experience to convince me to create space for myself to *breathe*.

I cannot imagine how those with fewer resources—or greater hurdles to acceptance—do it. If you are one of those individuals, you have the ultimate in respect, admiration, appreciation, and support from me.

How do you do it? And how do you *keep* doing it? I mentioned before that I don't view expectations as cages from which we need to escape; I see them more as choking vines we keep having to weed.

I needed a tool to remove those weeds, so that authenticity and connections could grow. This book has become that weeding tool, for me.

～

In a film called *The Notebook*, a woman forgets who she is, and—spoiler alert—has to hear her own story to remember. Even though she lived it. Even though she wrote it. While fighting a battle, she forgets. It is only when she hears her own words that she comes back to herself and her community.

I needed to write a book I could read. To remember why I am authentically me.

～

In the film *Slumdog Millionaire*, a man knows who he is, and that identity serves him well as he competes on a million-dollar game show. The problem is that other people cannot understand how someone with his background could come up with unexpected answers to hard questions. They accuse him of cheating, and he has to remind himself, through a series of flashbacks, that his responses are legitimate. His life experiences—moments of joy, camaraderie, fear, shame, and shit-covered submersion—reveal that each response is his own. Even though he has to phone a friend on occasion, there is authenticity.

Does he win the game? How about the million? Well, it turns out that was never the point for him. The whole goal of answering the questions—of remembering what he learned from life—was to forge a connection with someone off-screen.

Maybe these words will connect us.

~

So what can I offer?

I give you authenticity.

I hope for connection.

Real connection between the real you—and the real me.

FEAR AND HOPE:
AN EPILOGUE

Hope and fear can coexist. Not everyone believes this; some argue they are opposites. I disagree.

I give you authenticity. I hope for connection.

At the same time, I am terrified that being the real me will end or negatively impact relationships I care about.

The real me feels nudged to share this book. To carefully offer it to my husband and my family, and to use it as a tool to further conversation. To reach out to folks mentioned in these pages and ask their permission to share. To put it out in the world and see what happens.

But the entire process terrifies me.

Will these pages connect us—or break us apart?

It matters—because these are real human beings who deserve a say in how they are represented, and because the most authentic me admires and loves them on many levels and doesn't want them to leave.

~

In the middle of this book-writing process, I began having chest pains. I actually went to the doctor, who recommended an echocardiogram, and I scheduled an appointment. I took my laptop with me in case there was time to write while at the hospital. Here is what I wrote that day (part while at the hospital and the remainder at 5 a.m. the next morning):

> I don't want to write this book. It scares me. So many people I love are in it. What if they hate it? What if reading it makes them hate me? What if I got it all wrong? What if I got a snapshot of someone right, and then they changed, and now they are misrepresented in my pages? What an awful thing to do to people who gifted me their time and their stories. What if I write the wrong thing about God and end up in the hell my old teachers described to me? What if I write the wrong thing about race or injustice and create a hell on earth for someone else?
>
> What if writing about my life and my perspectives is just plain narcissistic?
>
> I want to record here the exact moment of my typing. I am currently in my car. I am parked just outside UNC Hospital. It is December 10, 2020, at 2:27 p.m. I just had an echocardiogram, to discover the source of chest pain that shoots down my left arm. I am sobbing as I type. My tears have *nothing* to do with the health scare. They have everything to do with putting on paper how afraid I am of this tiny piece of me that finally, finally has expression. If my chest pains don't source on the echocardiogram, they are due to anxiety. And I know what I am anxious about: this writing. I cannot stop. I feel like if I don't birth this through my fingers, it will explode out of my chest like that creature in the *Alien* movie. But the finger-birthing is requiring too much. I am going to bed early so I can wake up early to write—a time I thought I could do it without neglecting my family. But the routine is hurting my marriage. I don't go to sleep with my husband. I don't wake

up with him. And for two hours each morning, I live in a world I cannot talk to him about—during any part of the day—because this part of me is still too fragile to share.

My kids need me to do other things during those two hours—this year especially. There is a global pandemic going on. I cannot outsource anything. There is no family nearby. There are no sitters in our "pod." There is no in-person interaction with teachers or ministers or coaches. I am in charge of my children's spiritual development, physical activity, schooling, socialization, meals, dentist appointments, medical prescriptions, and keeping enough soap, hand gel, COVID-filtering masks, reading-leveled library books, and (God help me) toilet paper in the house. I am in charge of traditions. They have lost so much this year. I need time to figure out how to do birthdays and holidays. What can we alter? What do we lose, and how do I teach my children to simultaneously mourn and count their blessings?

I should be home right now. But I know the family will not fault me if an echocardiogram takes twenty minutes longer than expected—it will be me who later feels guilty that my delay meant my eight-year-old had to watch classmates jump rope online because he couldn't find his equipment. He will miss it because I thought, *Today, I could steal twenty minutes to write while the sun is up without bothering anybody.* But I was wrong. There is always a price to pay.

Speaking of cost . . .

Last night, my husband and I took all four children shopping for a Christmas tree. Where are all the Christmas trees in 2020? Nobody knows. It is just another thing this stupid year has taken from us. And from our kids. The silver lining is that—as we head to our third tree farm of the evening in hopes of finding an evergreen—we are all together in the car. The kids are looking at Christmas lights, and my husband and I have a moment to talk.

I am reminded during this conversation about why my husband and I get along. This week, both of us had separate Zoom calls that asked us to describe our current mental or physical space in only two words. Both of us were in groups where everyone shared thoughtful responses. Unbeknownst to each other, both of us went weird on our groups. My two words were "hamster wheel"—indicating my sense that I am in constant motion but going nowhere. My husband told his group he was having trouble deciding between "over it" and "f- this."

Both of us are overwhelmed. Both of us realize we are lucky. Despite a COVID pay cut, he makes enough that I can focus on the kids this year. I do not currently need to work outside the home. I tell him I feel like I'm working—that my journaling feels demanding—and he jokes that it is missing an important job element, since it does not pay at all. He winks at me—a supportive charmer, this one—and I ask him what price tag he would put on having a sane wife during quarantine. He replies, "Just so I understand fully, is this 'sane wife' something you are offering me if you continue this process? Or is the wife I am looking at right now what we are considering sane?"

It is a sweet moment that energizes us as we head to farm number four. But it is also somewhat telling. To nurture this part of myself, I am going to have to let everything around me get a little bit crazy. Crazier than it already is, actually. There will be no discovery or revelation without sacrifice.

And—here's the hard part—it's not going to be just me who's sacrificing. It's going to cost the people I love most something also. Maybe they are going to have to sacrifice time with me, or expectations of me, or their own peace of mind as something I do scares them.

~

I am scared, but also hopeful.

I am scared sharing this book with my family will negatively impact our relationships. But there is also hope that it could be a tool for dialogue and connective growth.

I am scared sharing this book with a larger audience will make me a target. I have written about charged topics, and I expect to receive criticism from all sides. But there is also hope that, if I can stay open, I will learn something from those voices. To that end, I am giving myself two reminders: My growth is more important than my comfort, and that growth tends to happen when I let hope push me past fear into vulnerability.

You can talk to me. I will be uncomfortable, but I will do my best to listen and reflect and learn and do better. Sometimes insights born of these conversations hit me instantly—lightning bolts of illumination. More often, it takes me years to quietly process. If I am quiet, I am thinking. If I speak, I may say the wrong thing and retreat and recharge and rejoin, but I am not going to quit.

Finally, if I could ask only one thing, it would be that you remember this about the individuals who allowed me to share stories in these pages: They are pushing past fear into vulnerability also, in hopes something good will grow from this; their stories are both incomplete and told from my perspective; and they did not put themselves out there. I put them out there—and the versions that are on the page have evolved since. I am grateful to all of them for their willingness to share and for the ways they shaped and strengthened and supported me.

～

I am scared, but also hopeful.

Before, while trying to determine my "word," I considered "hopeful." At the time, I decided "reflect" was a more authentic representation of me.

But I am a writer now. I claim words. And I can claim more than one if I want to.

So I will conclude by saying this: I am hopeful about my ability to reflect, going forward.

And I am hopeful that—after all of this—I will know better which situations call for me to reflect the light in my surroundings, and which require me to contemplate dark corners and reflect, as in think.

I am hopeful. And scared. But still, hopeful.

Hopeful enough to disrupt the peace and the equilibrium for the chance to have more authentic connections with those around me.

～

With that hope in mind, I have spent the last many months offering pieces of this book to those mentioned on its pages. My sister, my husband, and my mother have read it in its entirety. I gave it to my sister, Ashley, first—partly because she is Ashley, and partly because I need her to tell me if sharing it with my husband or my mom will blow up a family.

When Ashley finished reading it, I asked her several questions. She responded to some by speculating that relationships would survive—and reminding me that even if they didn't, she would still be with me. After expressing my gratitude for that powerful moment of sisterhood, I asked if anything in the book had surprised her.

"No," she said. "I feel like I saw you in the black-and-white version of this movie. And now I've seen you in color."

～

This book has revealed my backstory, thought bubbles, and hues—so much color. But Ashley's comment—along with months of reconnecting with many folks mentioned here—reminds me that everyone has backstories and thought bubbles and hues. Everyone has shades we don't see.

My mom went through things I spent a lifetime not knowing. *How much of her do I really understand?* My husband sacrificed parts of his identity to fatherhood. *I hadn't thought.* As we share, both relationships deepen.

When I talk to Malcolm, we discuss more about race than we ever did while a couple. Luke and I wonder if our service was an attempt to save others—or ourselves. Denise and I commiserate on our midlife quests for identity. I remember how lucky I am to have these friends. These teachers.

Liz A. and I have a long conversation. We have different religious backgrounds and different sexual orientations. I ask if I can read her the sections on identity. I am not asking because I think she can speak for a group, and I am not asking because I think she can absolve me. I am asking because I am afraid reading what the younger me was in these pages will hurt her. And the older me wants to be there to apologize in person, and to personally tell her I want to be an ally as well as a friend.

She is gracious, calling our conversation a gift that will deepen our friendship.

More importantly, she is *Liz*: Insightful. Inquisitive. Inspired. And willing to say what I need to hear.

After a lot of nice words, Liz issues a gentle reprimand. I have just told her that I want to publish this book, but I am not sure I should. My hope is that someone with my background will read it and learn from my teachers. My fear is that I will take up space on a not-diverse-enough shelf.

Liz leans forward, and she says, "Kristi, everyone has to do what they can. The world is in crisis. Look at how some people are struggling. And at how others are voting. We have to say something. All of us."

I listened intently as Liz continued.

"You started this conversation by telling me about how much shame you had to overcome to go on this spiritual journey. But now we are at the end of our conversation, and you are acting ashamed.

"The first segment you read me expressed your belief that all stories are valuable. But now we are at the end of our talk, and you are expressing hesitation at sharing your story.

"Let go of the shame. Overcome the hesitation. Because in our fight for beauty amid hardship, we need soldiers who are going to show up and stand tall."

My hope for everyone in the world is that they someday have friends and teachers like mine. Friends and teachers like Liz. Her encouragement reminded me that I do have something to say, and I am going to say it.

~

Earlier in this book, I posed two questions. I asked, if the world (or someone safe in your world) was *really* listening, what would you say? Also, is there anything your inner voice is trying to say to *you*?

My inner voice is telling me to write. So I am writing.

And if anyone in the world is really listening, I want to say this: Be you. The best version of the real you. Dig deeper. Dig past any prejudice you have internalized and any expectations you have ingested. And once you have the real you in your sights, be kind to her. Fight for her. Celebrate her. And then be kind to and fight for and celebrate everyone else, too.

~

Also, to those readers with my background—White, Southern, conservatively-primed women—please hear me: Folks in this country have been speaking with us and about us, but I want to say something from a different vantage point. I am not a neighbor; I am one of you. I have sat at your tables for decades listening and learning. I am part of the family. (Maybe I am on that weird branch of the ancestral tree you don't often reference, but still . . .)

We are hearing from others that we should be ashamed of our region's history. And that, at the very least, we can make amends by voting differently. I want to take a scalpel to that argument: not a sledgehammer, but a scalpel—a very fine, precision-point blade. There *are* things we should apologize for. Racism, Discrimination. Using religion as a weapon. Using litmus tests to tune people out.

But there is much to take pride in also.

My grandmother taught me the peace of a rocking chair: no yoga or mindfulness classes required. My neighbors taught me the wisdom of farmers: You have to both work hard and know that growth comes from God. My mother taught me tradition: It means something when you pull out that old handwritten recipe or fragile lace ornament. Some good ol' country folk taught me how to fight, and I needed to know how to do it. I am scrappy. I am sentimental. I am *Southern*, with pride.

Like everyone else in the world, I can embrace parts of my heritage while acknowledging that other parts are flawed. And then I can begin to make amends for those flaws by seeing, and acting, and voting differently.

We are Mockingjay Vases—a mix of many elements. We are also Katniss "Mockingjay" Everdeen, and the resistance is telling us our assistance is required.

So please listen. I am not asking you to reject your history. I am asking you to study it—and to reflect on your own personal story through this series of *if* statements:

If you ever felt corralled as a child or adolescent . . .

If you ever felt like you had to look or live (or not look, or not live) a certain way . . .

If you still feel that and want to be *seen* . . .

I see you. I am cheering for you—the *real* you. The you that is trying to break free without hurting your family. The you that is trying to find yourself under everyone else's piles.

And I am hoping for you—and for the world—that you *will* break free of those corrals and unearth yourself from those piles. And that once you do, you will look up.

And that when you look up, you will realize that the constraints you experienced (while *real* and *large*) are only a fraction of what others are dealing with.

And that you will take your tremendous strength and grace and endurance and influence and empathy—as well as any energy you can muster—and use it to celebrate your children and your neighbors for whoever they are, and to fight against the ongoing, corralling, oppression of *all* individuals and groups.

~

I have hopes for all of us.

I hope we will keep the dialogue going, never losing sight of the humanity of those who think differently.

I hope we will get to know the real people impacted by our ideologies—and let them influence the evolution of our thoughts.

I hope we will notice who is missing from our spaces and work on our welcomes.

And mostly, I hope that *all of us* will recognize our authentic selves and use our unique voices and wield our tremendous power to work alongside *all of the rest of us.*

Because *all of the rest of us* have authentic selves and unique voices and powerful personhoods that also deserve recognition and rights and respect from everyone.

Everyone. Including the real me, and the authentic, kind, and powerful *you.*

ACKNOWLEDGMENTS AND AUTHOR'S NOTE

When I gave an early draft of this book to my husband, and then to my mother, I told each of them (separately) that—after they read it—I was hoping we could talk about two things.

First, most importantly, could we talk about us?

Second, less importantly, could we talk about what I should do with this massive document?

Both of them said yes to the first question. I cannot thank them enough for reading and talking and listening and sharing such important space with me.

When we got to the second question, both of them asked what I wanted to do. Having them turn the question back to me was—on its own—a tremendous gift. And then they each gave me another gift. As I worked to figure out what I wanted to do, they offered support. They turned toward me, instead of away. They encouraged my writing, instead of writing me off. They honored my recollections and interpretations, even when theirs were different. They worked with me to fix objective errors (though I am sure there are still some, for which I alone am responsible), while also giving me the freedom to share my subjective experiences.

I am so grateful to—and for—each of them.

Mom, thank you for being the strong, brilliant, independent woman you are. I am stronger because of your example and our journey. I am happy our roads intersected naturally when I became your daughter, and that even when they don't, we still choose to travel together. The following photo of us (with a tiny Ashley peeking over your shoulder) is a gift and a reminder of the joy.

Tim, thank you for choosing me and for being the man I would choose again and again. I admire the person, husband, and father you are, while also celebrating your adjectives, which include (by my observation, as you are too humble to list them) magnificent, patient, wonderful, and fun.

Ella, Sienna, Tyler, and Hudson—there are not enough words to convey how much I love being your mother. My perfect day is a day with you. Each of you will always have my support and my heart. My greatest joy is seeing your stories unfold.

Ashley, you are both my rock and my soft space to land. Thank you.

Lloyd & Holly, Todd & Betsy, Brian & Ashley (yes, Ashley again, because this book needs MORE SISTER!), as well as all of my nieces, nephews, aunts, uncles, cousins, in-laws, and more—thank you for showing me, my children, and the world how families can love each other.

Amy, Ana, Betsy B. Chris, Darlene, Denise, George, Gina, Jen, Jenny, Jim, Kathleen, Katie, Kevin, Laura, Liz A., Liz M., Melanie, Priya, Rachel, Sarah, Susan, Susannah, my "BB circle" ladies, all the masked and pseudonymised folks I won't list here out of respect, and so many others—thank you for the friendship (and the extraordinary wisdom, but mostly the friendship). It means the world. Also, extra shout-outs to friends who hosted playdates that freed me to edit, and to Denise who read and responded to every word and believed the words were "worth it," even as I shared my deepest fears. Thank you.

I am also grateful to everyone at Greenleaf Book Group: Editors extraordinaire: Anne Sanow (who helped both the book, and this new author, develop), Hayden Seder (who fixed all the tenses and offered reassurance when I was tense about letting this text out into the world), and Lee Reed Zarnikau (our team captain, who created space for me—and for lots of last-minute photos); cover designer Mimi Bark (whose vision made me feel seen); Madelyn Myers (for going above-and-beyond, for the book and for me); and so many other members of the team including Adrianna Hernandez, Chase Quarterman, David Endris, Kayleigh Lovvorn, and Tiffany Barrientos.

Thank you to the artists who contributed photos to this book. To Shana Salaff, I am grateful for your artistry, your words, and for sharing your photo of the Mockingjay Vase. Many of the other objects were photographed by Sienna Smith, my daughter. Sienna, thank you. I love seeing these objects—and the world—through your eyes.

Also, this book celebrates many individuals, students, teachers, and authors I admire. Thank you to all of them for sharing their stories with me. Pseudonyms include Addy, Alice, Bill, Cora, Mr. Davis, Evangeline, Ms. Gunderson, Ida, James, Jeremiah, Joe, Logan, Luke, Mabel, Malcolm, Naomi, Nick, and all student names (Antonio, Curtis, Darnell, Eliza, Jamal, Kashay, Kiara, Larissa, and Melinda).

~

A few quick author's notes:

First, I referenced the words of Reverend Molly Shivers—the ones posted on my kitchen wall for many years—by including an excerpt. The full text of her quote, which she originally emailed me on May 23, 2014, is included here. While I am technically including it here in case any mothers battling my old version of angst find it encouraging, it is worth noting that it fits with one larger trend of this book: expanding our definition of the sacred. Back then, I needed to hear that helping a sleepy child pick up legos could be a sacred act. But I now understand that any act can be sacred, if it comes from the heart. We don't have to be ministers or parents (or any other nouns) to be part of something divine. With that said, here is Molly's unabridged quote, in case it helps lighten a load (of dishes, laundry, or something even heavier):

> Mothering is sacred work and counts as ministry. I have often wrestled with valuing the work of mothering as equivalent to the work of ministry. It has taken me a long time to reconcile that extending love and care to our children counts as much as extending love and care to the stranger. In fact, for many months—if not years—who is as vulnerable and dependent as young children? When children are born, they would not be able to eat, to be clothed, to be clean, to be warm, or even to survive without our care. Surely God honors the mother who is up in the night with her sick child(ren) as much as God honors the person who travels to Panama or Jamaica or Haiti to build schools and clinics. I'll go even farther and say that the God that I know in Christ is a Mother every bit as much as God is a Father or a Lover or a Rock or a Counselor or a Friend. Mothering flows from the heart of God and is sacred work.

As a second note, while referencing people, activities, and institutions throughout this book, I tried to acknowledge the limits of my vision. Here, I can provide a concrete example of something I missed.

In the book, I described my very first (and very limited) exposure to Ella's UUMC class in order to reveal how it sparked a conversation. During that talk, Ella and I steered away from the question of confirmation into the question: Who am I?

Since then, I have discovered the UUMC course actually devotes time to asking the exact "Who am I?" question that I thought we had to swerve to see. While I am still glad Ella explored the question independently, I feel compelled to highlight the course's parallel inquiry, as it provides an example of something *right there* that I did not see at the time. In addition to thanking the UUMC teachers (Chadd, Charlie, Jenny, and Mary—who truly mean it when they encourage the kids to be exactly who they are), I also want to express my gratitude to all the other people and institutions that have welcomed me over the years—and I want to celebrate any positive parts of them that I failed to see or acknowledge. I also want to acknowledge the sources I referenced but could not identify including the essay writing recruit, the mommy blogging "naked laundress" and the older-than-me-activist who has become my role model. I greatly appreciate all of their words.

Finally, two concluding thoughts:

I want to honor the creative and comforting spirit (that felt like God to me) during this journey. Every morning at 5 a.m., when my alarm went off and I fought fatigue to get up and attempt to write another page, I said the same prayer while trudging down the hallway to my laptop: "If you keep showing up, I'll keep showing up." It wasn't well thought out, and it certainly wasn't fancy. Most mornings it was actually kind of grumpy. But the truth is, this presence (that feels like God to me) keeps showing up in my life, and I am grateful. And it inspires me to keep showing up, too.

And here at the very end, I want to thank my husband for offering what has to be the last word of this book. When he read my thoughts of hoping for connection, he said, "We can't just hope for connection; we have to make it happen." He is right. And that goes for all the other hopes expressed in this book, too. We can't just hope. We have to make it happen. I am grateful to all of you out in the world working to do exactly that: to transform our hopes into our happenings—into our new reality. I am with you.

ENDNOTES

EIGHT YEARS, SEVEN LESSONS

1. Peter Maurin, "Catholic Worker Movement," accessed 2020, https://www
   .catholicworker.org/petermaurin/.

2. David Anspaugh, dir, *Rudy* (TriStar Pictures, 1993). This rendition, forty-four
   minutes into the film, varies slightly from Rockne's original speech which was
   transcribed and stored as "Knute Rockne's Recreation of a Pep Speech." University of
   Notre Dame Archives.

3. Huston Smith, *The World's Religions* (New York: HarperOne, 2009), 2.

4. Glennon Doyle, *Untamed* (New York: The Dial Press, 2020).

5. Smith, *The World's Religions*, 73.

6. Craig Greenfield, "Yes. Jesus Was Subversive. Here Are 10 Overlooked Examples,"
   Craig Greenfield (blog), April 18, 2016, https://www.craiggreenfield.com/
   blog/2016/4/18/yes-jesus-was-subversive.

7. Jen Hatmaker, "Hi. I'm Jen." *Jen Hatmaker*. Retrieved 2020 from http://
   jenhatmaker.snappages.com/about (website has since been updated and changed).
   Original can be found at https://web.archive.org/web/20200927194720/http://
   jenhatmaker.snappages.com:80/about.htm.

8. Kate Holbrook et al., *Global Values 101: A Short Course* (Boston: Beacon Press,
   2006), viii.

9. Holbrook et al., *Global Values 101*, x.

RELATIONSHIPS

1. *Spanglish*, directed by James L. Brooks, Columbia Pictures, 2004.

2. *Spanglish*, Brooks.

MARRIAGE AND MOTHERHOOD

1. Rosalind C. Barnett and Caryl Rivers, *She Works/He Works: How Two-Income Families Are Happier, Healthier, and Better-Off* (San Francisco: Harper San Francisco, 1996), 179.
2. Barnett and Rivers, *She Works/He Works*.
3. Barnett and Rivers, *She Works/He Works*, 185.

CANCER

1. Anna Whiston-Donaldson, "To Jack's Friends on Graduation," An Inch of Gray, June 16, 2017, https://aninchofgray.blogspot.com/2017/06/to-jacks-friends-on-graduation.html.

OXYGEN

1. Becky Zuckweiler, "Stages of Grief After Losing a Breast," *Amoena4Life* (blog), Amoena, https://www.amoena.com/us-en/amoena-life/stages-grief-losing-breast/. Originally published on The Breast Care Site, 2012, and retrieved from original source September 2017.

NOT WAVING BUT DROWNING

1. Lizzie O'Leary, "Elizabeth Gilbert Is Owning Her Past Mistakes," *The Atlantic*, June 15, 2019, https://www.theatlantic.com/entertainment/archive/2019/06/elizabeth-gilberts-new-novel-mistakes-and-adventures/591781/.

LITMUS TESTS

1. Doyle, *Untamed*, 75.
2. Elizabeth Gilbert, *Eat, Pray, Love* (New York: Penguin Books, 2006).

REFLECTIONS

1. Gilbert, *Eat, Pray, Love*, 103.
2. Gilbert, *Eat, Pray, Love*, 104.

WHO AM I?

1. Robin DiAngelo, *White Fragility* (Boston: Beacon Press, 2018).
2. Doyle, *Untamed*, 76.

3. Doyle, *Untamed*, 6.
4. Austin Channing Brown and Brené Brown, "I'm Still Here: Black Dignity in a World Made for Whiteness," *Unlocking Us*, podcast audio, June 10, 2020, https://brenebrown.com/podcast/brene-with-austin-channing-brown-on-im-still-here-black-dignity-in-a-world-made-for-whiteness/.

WHAT HAVE I LEARNED?

1. Robert Fulghum, *All I Really Need to Know I Learned in Kindergarten: Uncommon Thoughts on Common Things* (New York: Random House, 2003).
2. Shana Angela Salaff, "A Mockingjay Vase," *Pottery Making Illustrated*, May/June 2013, 35–38, http://media.icompendium.com/shanasal_SalaffMockinjayFinalHiRes1.pdf.
3. Salaff, "A Mockingjay Vase," 38.
4. Cameron Crowe, dir, *We Bought a Zoo*, 20th Century Studios, 2011.
5. Brandon Steiner, *You Gotta Have Balls* (Hoboken, NJ: Wiley, 2012).
6. "Matt Damon opens up about Harvey Weinstein, sexual harassment and confidentiality agreements," *ABC News*, December 14, 2017, https://abcnews.go.com/Entertainment/matt-damon-opens-harvey-weinstein-sexual-harassment-confidentiality/story?id=51792548.
7. Austin Channing Brown, *I'm Still Here: Black Dignity in a World Made for Whiteness* (New York: Convergent Books, 2018).
8. Elaine Welteroth, *More Than Enough: Claiming Space for Who You Are (No Matter What They Say)* (New York: Viking, 2019), 262.

WHAT CAN I OFFER?

1. Janet Mock. *Janet Mock Quotes*. Retrieved 2021, https://www.azquotes.com/author/30783-Janet_Mock. Original Source: Janet Mock, *Redefining Realness: My Path to Womanhood, Identity, Love & So Much More* (New York: Atria Books, 2014), xviii.

ABOUT THE AUTHOR

KRISTI J. SMITH grew up listening to southern stories before taking her ears on the road (and then off-road). Her eclectic mix of teachers include a Nigerian rainmaker, homeless men, rebellious students, haunted veterans, cheeky children, lively street vendors, and the exterminator who changed her life. She is indebted to all of them. She has degrees from Princeton, Harvard, and UNC-Chapel Hill, has learned while teaching in underserved urban and rural (Teach For America) schools, and currently serves as the adult advisor to "Kids Coloring For a Cause," a non-profit she cofounded with her family. She likes to write, wonder, and wander with her husband and four children. Their gateway to the world is a happy home in North Carolina.